CHAOS, COMPLEXITY, AND NONLINEAR ECONOMIC THEORY

Series on Advances in Mathematics for Applied Sciences – Vol. 92

CHAOS, COMPLEXITY, AND NONLINEAR ECONOMIC THEORY

Wei-Bin Zhang
Ritsumeikan Asia Pacific University, Japan

World Scientific

NEW JERSEY • LONDON • SINGAPORE • BEIJING • SHANGHAI • HONG KONG • TAIPEI • CHENNAI • TOKYO

Published by

World Scientific Publishing Co. Pte. Ltd.
5 Toh Tuck Link, Singapore 596224
USA office: 27 Warren Street, Suite 401-402, Hackensack, NJ 07601
UK office: 57 Shelton Street, Covent Garden, London WC2H 9HE

Library of Congress Cataloging-in-Publication Data

Names: Zhang, Wei-Bin, 1961- author.
Title: Chaos, complexity, and nonlinear economic theory / Wei-Bin Zhang, Ritsumeikan Asia Pacific University, Japan.
Description: New Jersey : World Scientific, [2023] | Series: Series on advances in mathematics for applied sciences, 1793-0901 ; vol. 92 | Includes bibliographical references and index.
Identifiers: LCCN 2022048783 | ISBN 9789811267413 (hardcover) | ISBN 9789811267420 (ebook) | ISBN 9789811267437 (ebook other)
Subjects: LCSH: Economics, Mathematical. | Nonlinear theories. | Chaotic behavior in systems.
Classification: LCC HB135 .Z535 2023 | DDC 330.01/51--dc23/eng/20221021
LC record available at https://lccn.loc.gov/2022048783

British Library Cataloguing-in-Publication Data
A catalogue record for this book is available from the British Library.

For any available supplementary material, please visit
https://www.worldscientific.com/worldscibooks/10.1142/13173#t=suppl

Desk Editors: Logeshwaran Arumugam/Lai Fun

Typeset by Stallion Press
Email: enquiries@stallionpress.com

Preface

I first met with modern economics in 1984 when I was sent by China, as one of the second group of made-in-China undergraduates since 1949, to Japan in 1983 as a graduate student in civil engineering at Kyoto University. The library on campus was a wonderful world filled with freely available classical books for the poor student from the poverty-stricken country (when a mainland Chinese worker earned 7 USD per month in Beijing and Shanghai with the exchange rate in the early 1980s). The library was a pleasant and comfortable place for me to "kill" leisure time with philosophy, histories of sciences and mathematics, mathematics, mathematical biology, nonlinear sciences (typically, Prigogin's and Haken's works), as well as economics. I happened to read the works of some great modern economists like Samuelson and Arrow, luckily being introduced to mathematical economics with that the rigor, simplicity, creativity, beauty, passionate faith, and flexibility of mathematical economics of that generation.

I passionately digested many modern and classical works in economic theory and had soon mathematically organized these theories. I was naturally attracted to classical economists, such as Adam Smith, Mill, and Marshall, because they explained economic principles with socioeconomic phenomena illustrative for me. The phenomena in their works were somehow like what took place in China in the 1970s and 1980s. It had taken me only few years to recognize the necessity and possibility of generalizing economic theory. Samuelson's milestone achievements are reflected in two directions: one is summarized in his celebrated *Foundation* and the other is in his most celebrated textbook and numerical articles which mathematically formulate or generalize traditional economic ideas and theories. Before Samuelson (more accurately his generations), mathematics was not yet applied so extensively and so systematically to economics. The *Foundation* basically contains what could be done mathematically with linear sciences by the time of its publication. I — equipped with modern nonlinear science and mathematical biology — soon extended Samuelson's *Foundation* to nonlinear world with my first book *Synergetic Economics* (Zhang, 1991). The book was published in Professor Haken's influential series *Synergetics.* My second goal, inspirited by Samuelson and some other economists, was to integrate all the main economic ideas from Adam Smith to contemporary Nobel Prizes in a single set of equations. The mission seemingly impossible was — at least as a somehow primary but integrative attempt — achieved with my recent *The General Economic Theory* (Zhang, 2020a) and other over one hundred articles published in journals. The construction of the general economic theory took me long time because I had needed even some years to digest and re-formulate each subfield of modern economics. Samuelson accounted his choice of economics at exactly the right time: "To a person of analytical ability, perceptive enough to realize that mathematical equipment was a powerful sword in economics, the world of economics was his or her oyster in 1935. The terrain was strewn with beautiful theorems begging to be picked up and arranged in unified order." After I published my first two books, *Synergetic Economics* and my dissertation *Economic Growth Theory* (Zhang, 1990) simultaneously in 1989 (as research reports), I started to construct the general economic theory. In the *Foreword* to the Japanese translation of *Synergetic Economics* (Zhang, 1994), I outlined my aspiration to build the general economic theory in the following way: "Indeed, it is only after laborious work in many fields of theoretical economics that I began to be conscious of the fact that it is time to build a logically compact theory which includes the main economic ideas of Smith, Malthus, von Thunen, Ricardo, Marx, Mills, Walras, Marshall, Schumpeter, and Keynes. It should also include, as special cases, the well-established mathematical models, such as the Arrow–Debreu general equilibrium model, the Tobin model, the Solow–Swan–Uzawa growth model, the Oniki–Uzawa trade model, the Kaldor–Pasinetti two-class model, the Ricardian Models by Morishima, Samuelson and Pasinetti, the Keynesian theory, and Alonso location model, to explain certain economic phenomena which cannot be explained by the traditional works. I have concentrated on this single task, since ... the spring of 1989." This book is a continuation of my endeavor in complexity theory in economics. It is a continuation and "updating" of three of my previous books:

Synergetic Economics. Heidelberg: Springer-Verlag, 1991.

Differential Equations, Bifurcations, and Chaos in Economics. Singapore: World Scientific, 2005.

Discrete Dynamical Systems, Bifurcations and Chaos in Economics. Elsevier: Amsterdam, 2006.

Synergetic Economics was, perhaps, the first comprehensive book on applying modern nonlinear theory and ideas from natural sciences to economics. It is a further development of Samuelson's *Foundation.* Since 1990, there are numerical publications on nonlinear economics. My other two books, as the titles suggest, introduce new results in the field from 1990 till the early 2000s. They provide systematical introductions to nonlinear differential and difference equations theories which are fundamental to complexity theory in economics. This book gives a range of examples in recent advances in nonlinear economics. Most of these models are constructed by introducing some nonlinear elements to the traditional economic models which are mentioned in microeconomic or macroeconomic courses in undergraduate or graduate levels. To study complexity theory requires some years on advanced mathematics to digest technical details. Moreover, economics is composed of a great range of models/theories — each with its assumptions, refined structures, and complicated techniques. This book introduces some of recent developments in nonlinear economics with minimum mathematics and a plenty of simulation results with illustrative plots.

I am very grateful to Editor Lai Fun Kwong for effective co-operation. I would like to thank the two anonymous referees for the valuable comments and suggestions. I thank for my wife, Gao Xiao, for caring. Daily digital-connected chats always warm my heart since March 2020 after the COVID-19 started. The pandemic has kept many family members far away from each other. It is the stability and order that conquer external chaos and comfort the heart. There are some quotes which I don't provide sources as almost all of them are from https://www.brainyquote.com, with a few exceptions by googling. I completed this book at the Ritsumeikan Asia Pacific University. From February 2020, I have been missing the beautiful campus and its lively international life.

I am grateful to Editor Logesh for the efficient editorial work.

Wei-Bin Zhang
Beppu
Summer 2023

About the Author

Wei-Bin Zhang, Ph.D. (Umeå, Sweden), is Professor at Ritsumeikan Asia Pacific University since 2000. He graduated in 1982 from Beijing University. He obtained his Master's Degree and completed his Ph.D. at the Department of Civil Engineering, Kyoto University in 1987. He completed his dissertation on economic growth theory in Sweden, 1989. Since then, he researched at the Swedish Institute for Futures Studies in Stockholm for 10 years. His main research fields are complexity theory in economics (nonlinear economic dynamics, chaos theory, and synergetic economics), history of ancient Chinese thought, Confucianism, American civilization, and economic development and modernization of Chinese societies. He single-authored 360 academic articles (180 in peer-reviewed international journals, https://ideas.repec.org/e/pzh151.html) and 29 academic books in English by well-known international academic publishing houses (https://www.amazon.com/Wei-Bin-Zhang/e/B09LLS593T?ref=sr_ntt_srch_lnk_1\&qid=1648007965\&sr=1-1). He is in the editorial board of 12 peer-reviewed international journals. He had published a book of poetry in Chinese by a well-known publisher in the field. Professor Zhang is the editor of *Encyclopedia of Mathematical Models in Economics* (in two volumes) as a part of the unprecedented global effort and *The Encyclopedias of Life Support Systems*, organized by the UNESCO.

Contents

List of Figures

Chapter 1

Complexity Theory in Economics

The Nobel Prize in Physics 2021 was awarded "for groundbreaking contributions to our understanding of complex systems" according to the prize committee. Half of the prize money was jointly awarded to Syukuro Manabe and Klaus Hasselmann "for the physical modeling of Earth's climate, quantifying variability, and reliably predicting global warming" and the other half to Giorgio Parisi "for the discovery of the interplay of disorder and fluctuations in physical systems from atomic to planetary scales." The prize reflects the importance of complexity theory for the development of sciences and understanding nature and humanities. Complexity theory, which is almost exchangeable with chaos theory, synergetics, bifurcation theory, or catastrophe theory in this study — in economics (with formal mathematical modeling and computer simulation) — has been developed as an academic field since a few decades ago as soon as formal modeling of chaos was conducted in natural sciences and mathematics. Diffusion of ideas, methods, and techniques in natural sciences and mathematics to economics is nowadays quick. Complexity theory is theoretically and practically valid for dealing with interactions between politics, economics, cultures, and environment.

1.1 Traditional Economics with Newtonian World View

Newtonian world view had been the dominant vision of economic science since Adam Smith created his theory of economic equilibrium with perfect competition and division of labor. Both his great books, *Wealth of Nations* and *Theory of Moral Sentiments*, are constructed with Newtonian approach to complicated problems. The analytical approach is characterized by dividing a complex system into various individual parts and treating each unit as a whole system. His approach explains why he did not integrate his moral theory and economic theory — each theory creates a beautiful long-term stable equilibrium point, just like a pendulum of the clock of his time. There are oscillations — but they are created owing to exogenous or temporary forces. The system always either self-destroys (unstable) or finally achieves at a stationary state (moving smoothly at a constant speed) or static equilibrium point. In Newtonian vision, time-dependent phenomena, such as aperiodic motion, chaos, and bifurcation, — well observed — are considered negligible or exogenous.

Economic systems are characterized by complex systems with close interdependence of multiple forces. Traditional science fails to systematically explain well-observed economic phenomena. Faith is necessary for constructiveness and satisfaction. Over centuries, scientists shared a set of intuitive beliefs about changes. One of these beliefs is that simple systems would behave in simple ways. A pendulum follows a deterministic law, and its motion is stable and predictable in the long term. It also implies that well-observed complex behavior should be owing to complex causes. Visibly irregular behavior in stock markets must be governed by a multitude of independent components under the influences of random external forces.

Human society is a collection of heterogeneous people. Man is collectively conformal with the group identity for co-survival. Personal behavior appears random and unpredictable. A social system made of many parts may behave with some regular pattern or predictable phenomena. In physics, an example is a gas in a container with the gas molecules as the parts. In a macro world, Newton's law of motion can predict the regular motion of planetary orbits under certain conditions. Predictability in Newton physics is well applied to economics, especially by economists who had faith in nothing but free market, such as Hayek. His influential books are mostly constructed with the vision of traditional physics. In traditional scientific theory, if the present state of the system is known, it is possible to foretell how it will move in the future and to describe how it has moved in the past. When applying the determinism and irreversibility to human history, it implies that if we know the dynamic mechanisms of societies and sufficient information at any single point in time, it is possible to know its states one hundred years ago and one hundred years late. This vision of physical world is often referred to as Newtonian. It came from classical mechanics. Newton made a revolutionary contribution to the earlier development of classical mechanics. There are many mathematical methods invented by, for instance, Leibniz, Lagrange, and Euler in the 17th century, to describe the motion of bodies of a system under the influences of forces. In the 18th and 19th centuries, more advances were made, leading to new fields, such as Lagrangian mechanics, Hamiltonian mechanics, and analytical mechanics. Classical mechanics are very successful when describing the motion of large objects that are not extremely massive. It is not effective when objects move at speeds approaching the speed of light. When objects are too small, quantum mechanics, a subfield of mechanics, is needed. Special relativity theory is necessary to study objects with speeds approaching the speed of light. General relativity theory is applied to study extremely massive objects.

Classical economics since Adam Smith until modern times has been influenced strongly by natural sciences. Scientific thought and experiments have had a strong influence on economic thought. Toffler (1984) reasoned about the efficiency of modern economics: "One of the most highly developed skills in contemporary Western civilization is dissection: the split-up of problems into their smallest possible components. We are good at it. So good, we often forget to put the pieces together again." The Indian parable of the blind men and an elephant, dated at least c. 500 BC, illustrates the point as well. The story tells that a group of blind men, who have never had any idea about elephant before, come across an elephant. They describe the elephant through touching, imaging, and thinking. Each blind man touches a different part of the elephant, and no two or more men touch the same part. Each blind man describes the elephant differently from the others. One described the elephant as being like a thick snake as his hand landed on the trunk. Another claimed the elephant as a kind of fan as he touched its ear. Others portrayed the elephant like a tree trunk, a rope, or a wall. Each blind man believes in himself and blames all the others as dishonest, cheating, and narrow-minded. They finally began to fight against each other. The globally well-known story has various versions and diffuses for different reasons. In some versions, the elephant is perceived as God. In Japan, for instance, it informs that common people tend to fail to appreciate properly a great man or his great work. The parable hints that humans tend to get addicted to the thought based on their limited and subjective experience and to ignore and even deny others' experiences and ideas.

Modern world is characterized by a refined division of labor and complicated social, economic, cultural, and political structures. Professionalism is conducted for the sake of professionalism and is historically applicable mainly to soldiers. But the attitude and spirit are applicable to almost every profession in post-industrial or knowledge-based or information-based societies. Max Weber characterized modern societies as specialists without spirit and sensualists without heart. Modern people cannot find identity, consistency, trustfulness, and often not even social justice in social and economic life. For instance, during the current pandemic, different people see the tragedy with varied perspectives. A medical doctor may only suggest some probabilities of different consequences. One political party may neglect possible health consequences for people with low income and low social status but insist on economic benefits (of the rich) in the name of national benefits. The other party in rival may be concerned only with the importance of medical care for the poor. An economist believing in Adam Smith may suggest freedom and no government intervention. Another one believing in socialism may suggest government control. The list can be continued. No one knows what can occur with certainty, but many have great self-confidence in selling their own opinions.

Economics evolves as analytical and illustrative tools are advanced. Classical economics is like painting, neoclassical economics is like photo, and modern economics is like movie. Adam Smith's *Wealth of Nations* is full of sentences without mathematics and illustrations based on mathematical principles. His work makes modern reader feel inaccurate. His works are intuitively rich, like a poem, but have less law-like and empirically testable theory. Neoclassical theory is mostly like photo. Neoclassical economics was not widely tested with extensive data. Contemporary economics, treating the previous economics as special cases, are like movies owing to modern mathematics and computer.

The reductionist approach to economics had been dominant in analytical economics. It fosters the detailed study of each school of economics. However, over the last 40 years or so, an alternative approach has emerged for the study of complex economic systems in association with recent advances in nonlinear science, mathematics, and computer. Keywords such as self-organization, complexity, nonlinear interdependence, emergence of new structures, path dependence, the whole being greater than the sum of parts, and chaos characterize this approach. Linearity means that the rule that determines what a piece of a system is going to do next is not influenced by what it is doing now. More precisely, this is referred to in a differential or incremental sense: for a linear growth economy, the increase in GNP is proportional to the value which the economy is producing, with the growth rate exactly independent of how much the economy has already produced. Linear models enjoy an identical, simple geometry. The simplicity of this geometry allows a relatively easy mental image to apprehend the essence of a problem. For nonlinear problems, there is usually no simple and universal geometry. Investigation was case by case.

Samuelson (1970) described the attitude of neoclassical economists as "naturally tended to think of models in which things settle down to a unique position independently of initial conditions. Technically speaking, we theories hoped not to introduce hysteresis phenomena into our model, as the Bible does when it says. 'We pass this way only once' and, in so saying, takes the subject out of the realm of science and into the realm of genuine history." Nonlinear science treats "hysteresis phenomena" as a normal and regular part of organic systems during its processes. Chaos is useful and beneficial in some situations, like gaming machines and stock markets, and is harmful and should be avoided like natural disasters and wars. This attitude is explained by Mirowski (1990): "Neoclassical economics was blocked from following physics into the realm of a serious formal dynamics, including the formal structure of Hamiltonians, and instead into the spurious pseudo-dynamics of ceteris paribus conditions. This inability to emulate the core of the ideal of deterministic explanation tarnished the entire program of imitating physics. ... [T]he absence of a legitimate dynamics also compromised the ideal of a scientific empiricism.... What could it mean to attempt to fit neoclassical equilibrium displayed no necessary stability from one moment to the next? Instead, most prominent first- and second-generation neoclassicals were hostile to attempts to import techniques such as least-squares estimation into economics; and the earliest efforts in this area were pioneered by individuals skeptical of neoclassical theory.... Such disputes over the meaning of scientific activity also compromised claims of neoclassical theory to have attained 'scientific status."

1.2 Chaos Theory or Complexity Theory as Revolution in Sciences

There are great changes in sciences in association with nonlinear mathematics and computer. Modern technology enables contemporary scientists to see and simulate the complexity of the world unimaginable by humans even a few decades ago. Modern nonlinear sciences create theories that would have been treated as trivial or practically useless. Many theories and assumptions in traditional sciences which had been accepted as being general are considered limited and partial. Among these progresses in sciences, complexity theory, as far as economics is concerned, is the most important change. It is the first time in human history that economists can empirically test and simulate complex economic systems composed of interactions of multiple agents.

Chaos theory makes scientific communities to re-examine classical sciences. It goes beyond the principles of uncertainty and relativity discovered by Werner Heisenberg and Albert Einstein. It "discovers" another side of nature and society which is characterized by instability, spontaneity, and unpredictability which have been treated as trivial in Newtonian sciences. Chaos theory demonstrates that simple systems give rise to complex and unpredictable behavior. A nonlinear system described by a single variable with some simple nonlinear interactions with fixed time-environment environment can lead to chaos. This is beyond anyone's imagination before computer was applicable, even though this is almost common knowledge in contemporary sciences. The law of complexity has been identified in vast areas of physics, chemistry, biology, economics, politics, and human as well as animal group behavior. It has supplied science with a new vision that theories and ideas are created in separate scientific disciplines like physics and economics that treat classical Newtonian scientific explanations often as special cases. A typical example is Adam Smith's economics. His theory is still valid under certain circumstances, but not as a general, not to say a universal, valid doctrine even for capitalism. He failed to recognize self-destructiveness and chaos in capitalism systems without government intervention. Keynes, smartly claiming that we are all dead in the long term when being asked about the survival of capitalist systems, proposed that the government can save capitalism by making proper interventions. Under his advocates, capitalist governments have been expanded to such a degree that the so-called capitalist economies are making far more intervention than some former socialist economies. Centralized planning economies, as properly advised by Hayek, was correct in pointing out unsustainability, inefficiency, and chaos of planned economies.

Chaos on modern computer was first identified when American meteorologist Edward Lorenz was playing weather games. He discovered that simple systems of just three variables can give rise to indeterministic phenomena. Seemingly random or negligible exogenous changes, which would not affect the trend significantly as Newtonian science tells, are rapidly multiplied, soon resulting in totally chaotic behavioral patterns. This is the pioneering discovery in chaos theory in association with the development of computer. Without computer, scientists had little chance to establish chaos theory as a mainstream because even a simple question involves a huge amount of calculation. Chaos theory was serendipitously discovered when fractal theory was developed. Fractal geometry describes and measures the nonlinear forms of nature. It is important for the development of chaos theory. Together with relativity and quantum mechanics, chaos and fractals are claimed as the four greatest discoveries of the 20th century. Order versus chaos, deterministic versus stochastic, linear versus nonlinear, stable versus unstable, and predicable versus unpredictable are no more separate but the feature of complex systems.

Mankind is now simultaneously experiencing profound ruptures in many fields: academics, human relations, national relations, family structures, gender relations, inequality in income and wealth, global environment, pandemics, wars, and the like. Chaos is a proper word to describe the epoch in which we are living. Chaos is around us all time, but chaos which is causing so many structural and unpredictable — often dramatically harmful — consequences in global scales and scopes is not recorded in human history. If one wants to interpret these with traditional thinking or ways of explanations, it is interpreted as caused by human evils and punishments from God (in the West) or the Heaven (in Chinese cultures). Nevertheless, modern sciences equipped with increasingly enhanced capacity of computing, available big data, theories, and ideas from complexity theory try to explore these phenomena as endogenous processes of interdependence between man and nature.

Complex systems with new structures from instabilities can hardly be analytically and accurately described in traditional sciences both owing to lack of analytical methods and computing capacities. Complexity theory implies that laws or rules have no causal efficacy. They do not lead to ordered results or expected consequences. They merely maintain forced orders and consistent relationships in the system. This property can be illustrated by the game of chess. One cannot apply the rules to predict the history of a chess game. People cannot even predict, with certainty, the next move in a chess game. In this system, it is not only the rules of the game. It is also composed of the players and their situation-dependent decisions among a huge number of possible options at each movement. A theory, called synergetics, was developed by Hermann Haken (1977, 1983). This theory inspirited me to apply complexity theory to economics in the late 1980s. Synergetics explains the formation and self-organization of patterns and structures in open systems far from equilibrium. Self-organization occurs in a macroscopic system, consisting of multiple nonlinearly interdependent subsystems. The system self-organizes, depending on external conditions. Haken developed the enslaving principle which implies that the dynamics of fast-relaxing (stable) modes is determined by the slow dynamics of, often, only a few "order-parameters" (unstable) modes. The macroscopic pattern is characterized by the unstable modes. Mathematically, self-organization means an enormous reduction of degrees of freedom. The reduction macroscopically leads to an increase in order. This macroscopic order is independent of the details of the microscopic interactions of the subsystems. Haken's synergetics is applied to self-organization systems in physics, biology, chemistry, sociology, and economics. Haken (1981: Chapter 13) exemplified the principle as follows: "The statistical properties of laser light change qualitatively at the laser threshold. Below laser threshold, noise increases more and more while above threshold, it decreases again.... Below laser threshold, light consists of individual wave tracks which are emitted from the individual atoms independently of each other. Above laser threshold, a practically infinitely long wave track is produced. In order to make contact with other processes of self-organization let us interpret the processes in a lamp or in a laser by means of Bohr's model of the atom. A lamp produces its light in such a way that the excited electrons of the atoms make their transitions from the outer orbit to the inner entirely independently of each other. On the other hand, the properties of laser light can be understood only if we assume that the transitions of the individual electrons occur in a correlated fashion.... Above laser threshold, the coherent field grows more and more, and it can save the degrees of freedom of the dipole movements and the inversion. Within synergetics, it has turned out that is a quite typical equation describing effects of self-organization.... This equation tells us that the amplitude of the dipoles, which is proportional to A, is instantaneously given by the field amplitude $B(t)$ (and by the fluctuating force). This is probably the simplest example which has turned out to be of fundamental importance in synergetics and which is called slaving principle." In recent researches, the phenomenon is identified in different fields.

1.3 Synergetic Economics and Complexity Theory in Economics

Different from natural sciences and biology in which novel things are constantly discovered or created, there are rarely anything novel in complexity theory in economics as far as basic economic assumptions are concerned; every new basic idea or basic mechanism has some sort of precedent or echo from the past. For instance, human motivations and personal behavioral patterns in modern times can be found in records of ancient Greek, Chinese, and other civilizations. There is nothing new under the sun that is applicable, roughly, to economics as far as personal behavior is concerned. Adam Smith argued: "Masters are always and everywhere in a sort of tacit, but constant and uniform combination, not to raise the wages of labor." Nevertheless, economic phenomena are novel and varied greatly across nations. Like an infinite variety of music which is created by combinations of a few musical notes and an infinite number of paintings which result from synthesizing a few colors, economic phenomena come from a few motivations. These basic motivations and mechanisms had perhaps already been "discovered" by classical economists. Nevertheless, theoretical economics has advanced from grave to grave, as Paul Samuelson described. There are already many thousands of journals in economics and the growth of article publications is still in the stage of acceleration. But fast growth in the literature does not provide any "essential" novel insights into economic mechanisms (which have been verbally described by classical economists, conveniently assumed from Adam Smith). Advances in economics reveal new collective phenomena and economic structures which could not be dealt with by classical economists.

Economic systems' components, such as agriculture and industry, man and woman, family and society in large, and the like, interact in complicated relations in various environments. Complexity theory in economics refers to the study of complex economic systems. Nonlinear systems are also characterized by scale-dependent emergence: some properties are observable only when the system is large enough. Even if microscopic components are fully deterministic, macroeconomic behavioral patterns may be chaotic and unpredictable. In economics, many sectors, many households, and many countries interact in multiple interactions, culminating in a higher order of emergence of economic structures greater than the sum of all the parts. The theory studies these complex linkages at various scales. Every day we observe social and economic events which are driven by human crowd behavior. We observe crowd-like phenomena which emerge from interactions between people. Traffic jams emerge from commuters who compete for space on a road in rush hours. Market crashes in financial markets owing to interactions of financial traders. In a financial market, the spontaneous formation of a crowd of people who wish to sell can lead to a market crash characterized by the price falling dramatically in a short time. In recent decades, environment has caused global concerns because global warming is caused by multiple actors across the earth. Environmental problems have always been in human history. But it is only in the recent decades that mankind can collectively destroy not only local environments but also global environments in unpredictable scales and scopes. Mankind is suffering in one way or another from disasters caused by environmental changes.

Nonlinear science tells that traditional Newtonian theory cannot generally predict planetary orbits. When applying this to economics, even if we understand the behavior of all individuals, we cannot be sure about the corresponding emergent phenomena from the people. Organized complexity, like planned economy in China in the late 1950s and early 1960s, is composed of non-random interactions between the parts. These organized relationships can create a structure which leads to phenomena unpredictable or unplanned. In China, many million people lost their lives owing to famines and misplanning in the chaos during the late 1950s and early 1960s. Aggregated or collective behavior manifests properties not carried by individuals. The phenomena "emerged" with an "invisible hand." Such an unexpected phenomenon often occurs in complex systems such as politics, economics, and religions. What Werner Herzog said obviously includes economic world: "Civilization is like a thin layer of ice upon a deep ocean of chaos and darkness." Size matters, as life tells us. If scale matters, a region with a small population may experience different dynamics from another region with a large population. For instance, Taiwan and mainland China, initially with almost identical population qualities in the late 1940s, have experienced quite different paths of modernization. Strong emergence implies that qualitative behaviors are not irreducible to the system's constituent parts. The whole is not the sum of its parts. This further implies that the whole cannot be explained in terms of the parts. It would be misled to believe that it is possible to explain the dynamics of human affairs and physical world by finding out and applying simple fundamental laws. At each level of complexity, there emerge new properties and new structures which do not exist at other levels.

The whole and individuals evolve together. Through dynamic interactions, new forms of society emerge which are not reducible to its past. History lost the capacity to recognize its paths. This property provides a country or society opportunities to make up its history according to its contemporary needs as there are multiple possibilities of the history. The behavior of a dynamic system is not equal to the sum of the parts — the former can be larger or smaller than the latter, or both equal. Complexity theory deals with social evolution from perspectives of adaption and development for survival in constantly changing environment. Evolution is characterized by nonlinearity and uncertainty, like human history. New political, social, economic, and sexual systems emerge through dynamic interactions of these subsystems within and outside. New structures emerge through self-organization, feedback, learning, creativity, with locking-ins, bifurcations, and chaos. Evolution is associated with exchanges of slaving and enslaving processes in the sense that the master variables become stabilized and predictable, while once non-key variables become activated and suddenly emerge as the leading modes. Simple cause-and-effect relationships assumed in traditional theories turn out as sources of confusions in empirical studies. The atomistic approach in theoretical economics, which had been the dominant mode of thinking, is becoming an obstacle to the evolution of economics.

It is essential for economics to explain macro phenomena from micro levels. Persons make rational as well as irrational decisions. Individuals form households and families. There are multiple possibilities of connections that one person may have with other members of the society. Firms and organizations are in regions and cities. Interactions between regions and nations through different channels at various levels form evolutionary networking systems and new structures emerge through self-organization. Different from natural sciences, basic units or agents are self-organizing systems and cannot be described by purely random processes, like in statistical mechanics. Some nonlinear scientists apply concepts and tools from natural sciences but provide little insights into the complexity of human interactions because humans are treated as "atoms." Another implication of complexity theory is that it enables sciences to integrate various subtheories into a unified theory. There is a necessity of economizing economics for eliminating redundancy between schools. Neurath (1983, 172–3) reasons for unifying the sciences: "... the special sciences themselves exhibit in various ways the need for such a unification. For example, the different psychological theories employ so many different terms and phrases that it becomes difficult to know whether they are dealing with the same subject or not... One of the most important aims of the Unity of Science movement is therefore concerned with the unification of scientific language. Distinct terms occur in different disciplines which nevertheless may have the same function and much fruitless controversy may arise in trying to find a distinction between them.... A large collection of terms has been gathered by the various sciences during the centuries, and it is necessary to examine this collection from time to time, for terms should not be multiplied beyond necessity." I have made efforts to integrate different schools of economics in a united framework. I proposed the general economic theory. Its basic purpose is not to build a set of equations that integrate basic macroeconomic patterns, which have been theoretically or empirically identified in traditional economic theories, with microeconomic foundations. The theory allows us to derive the behavior of identified macroscopic structures at least in principle.

Economy is a complex adaptive system which is characterized by a dynamic network of interactions. It is adaptive in that individual agents and collective behavior mutate and self-organize in association with changes in micro events or collection of events. Agents interact, adapt, learn, and create in the system. We daily live in adaptive systems, such as cities, clubs, companies, regions, nations, traffic flows, political parties, wars, terrorist groups, social networks, climates, markets, governments, and industries. Systems such as animal swarms, social insect colonies, immune systems, and the cell and the developing embryo are all dynamically adaptive.

There are some key terms, such as strategy, artifact, agent, population, system, type, variety, interaction pattern, physical space, conceptual space, selection, and success criteria, which are frequently used in modeling complex systems, identified by Axelrod and Cohen (2001). Strategy, for instance, refers to a conditional action pattern that indicates what to do under what circumstances. Artifact is considered as a material resource that has a definite location and can respond to the action of agents. According to, for instance, Cilliers (1998) and Turner and Baker (2020), a complex adaptive system can be characterized as follows (with US and China's relations as examples by the author):

(i) The number of elements is large, and these elements are dynamically interacting. Conventional models are not only impractical but fail to reveal the properties of the system. There are exchanges of information and physical variables that these relations evolve. The system is adaptive and resilient. It is simultaneously ordered and disordered. These interactions are not predetermined and complicated. Any element or subsystem in the system is affected and affects some other elements or subsystems. The system, which is composed of interdependency and great diversity, is self-organizing. The system operates sometimes orderly and sometimes chaotically. During the Deng period, the relations between USA and China were orderly. Even after the Beijing government conducted the military action against people's demand for transparency and more democratization, the relationship between the two sides self-organized to regular patterns after a short period of the event. As far as international relation with the USA is concerned, China's government was a relatively simple and linear system at least by the early 2000s, even though domestic politics within the party has been always complicated. Its behavioral patterns in international relations were more predictable than today.

(ii) The interactions are nonlinear. Small changes in inputs, physical interactions, or stimuli can cause large effects or very significant changes in outputs. The motion is not predetermined but path-dependent. Hence, the system is very sensitive to its temporary conditions. The same force might affect the system differently. For instance, China's reaction to American policy changed dramatically over the last 40 years, although China was dominated by the same party. America could have hardly "predicted" China's behavior, especially in the last one or two decades. The reason was that even China could not have a solid and principle-based policy towards America. The two sides entered "unstable zones" of interactions so that everything was path-dependent, even though the chaotic interactions have not led to mutually self-destructive consequences. No one knows what will happen with interactions even in near future, but the probability of nuclear wars does not "appear" to be high because such a war will bring benefits neither to USA nor to China but almost certainly to their common future competitors, such as Europe, after their political and economic influences are weakened.

(iii) Interactions are not exclusively with immediate neighbors. In an open system like the relationship between USA and China, it involves almost the entire world in one way or another through political, cultural, social, economic, and even psychological channels. In particular, as digital technologies and advanced transportation systems with low costs have closely connected the world, no country could be effectively closed. It is nowadays even difficult to define system boundaries. National relations themselves are switched rapidly. No principle or value system could provide an effective foundation for nations to work as a team.

(iv) Any interaction can feed back onto itself directly or after several interactions with other parts of the system or the environment. It may take some time to feed back. In human societies, collective memory can last over hundred years. One reaction can also recall memories and thus make the consequence even more unpredictable. In peasant and almost immobile societies, memories of human relations and actions could last some generations. Complex systems have history. Even if the system has memory, it cannot go back to its past. The system is irreducible in the sense that the process is irreversible, and the current cannot be reduced back to its original state. For instance, owing to his "frankness," President Trump said many negative things that mainland Chinese people could never dream about America's "genuine" attitude towards people and the nation who had only known a little about modern civilization. His impact has made China's image and masses' mindsets on USA irreversible. The general trust on and the idol role of USA by common Chinese people are perhaps lost forever owing to the influence of Trump's government. It is not owing to the difference between the Trump government and the other American governments but the Trump style which simplified America's approach to China that even common Chinese people could perceive some hidden motivations of the political world.

(v) The overall behavior of the system is not predicted by the individual agents. There is no way to sum or aggregate the behavior of individuals to accurately predict the dynamics of the whole. America had the best experts in multiple fields about China in the world. Every year there have been numerous books, articles, and news on China. But none could have predicted the sudden rise of China in an English-speaking world. If that could be done, China might not be able to rise so rapidly because not only the white world but also Japan and overseas Chinese societies would join to present the occurrence. All parts of China were understood, but the performance of the whole was unpredictable.

(vi) Complex systems operate under far from equilibrium conditions. For life in the long term, a truly equilibrium condition is the ending of life. Life needs constant flow of energy to operate the system. Living systems are adaptive and not necessarily always "progressive." The evolution is not characterized by being progressive and moving towards "higher organisms." China from 1840 to 1980 could be characterized by degeneration rather than progressiveness. There were few higher cultural products left during the period. America could hardly be called "progressive" as an organic system in the last two decades, even though it has made many great advances in technologies. The fruits of these technological changes might not benefit American people but further enrich a limited number of rich people and talented immigrants born outside America.

(vii) Agents in the system may be ignorant of the behavior of the entire system. They react only to the information or physical stimuli available to them locally. Democracy, freedom, and transparency play an important role, it is assumed by liberal thinkers, in maintaining a decent society. Thinkers, like Lao Zi or Albert Einstein, might consider differently. For instance, Lao Zi believed that common people cannot properly understand Dao and it would benefit the society if they were not informed "too much." Einstein does seem to prefer some authorial organization to direct the society.

The system includes mechanisms of emergent structures. Its internal dynamics affect its ability to change in a manner that might be quite different from its history or other systems. Appearance of new industries and new types of products is a daily part of modern economy. It is generally true that evolution includes internal mechanisms towards complexity but does not necessarily lead to sustainability and survival. As the system has become too complicated, self-destruction is a solution. No great civilization has enjoyed a long period of desirable states. Traveling ancient traces of great civilizations, one can only see ruins or things hidden in graves which record the glory. Japan and America have become far more complex than their states in the mid-1980s, but their sustainability (with regard to common people's living standards and environment) is difficult to be true. Mankind might create such a complex system based on future technologies that man evolves into a kind of man that modern man would not see the future man as being human. The meaning of evolution is thus meaningless for contemporary people. All enriched economies with highly educated women experienced rapid population declination. In a self-organized system, human life itself becomes meaningless except for being changeable. In Chinese long-recorded history, complexity built by human society would lead to destruction for simplification and re-constructing the meaning of human life. China's Malthus cycles were repeated over thousand years without few significant social progresses. Many countries have remained poor, even though many modern elements have been injected into the systems. Modern economic miracles of Japan, then overseas Chinese societies, and now mainland China have been achieved owing to their inner Confucian cultural stocks and "fortune" initial conditions of poverty and low education (which enabled them to obediently follow the superpower's "master mode").

1.4 The Structure of the Book

The rest of this book is organized into six chapters. Each chapter, except Chapter 7, focuses on the dynamics of some well-known models with a key variable and finally introduces a general model into which main economic mechanisms of the previous models in the chapter are or can be integrated. Hence, the general model shows a possibility of building more general models for exploring the complexity of economic systems. Generalization is challenging but not impossible because mathematical tools are available. This book is mainly concerned with what economic mechanisms and mathematical structures nonlinear phenomena can be identified and illustrated. We explain mathematical models not in detail because most of the basic economic mechanisms are already taught in basic courses in microeconomics and macroeconomic courses for undergraduates. Moreover, the book does not provide analytical results and mathematical proofs. Proofs are often tedious and can be found in the original sources.

Chapter 2 is concerned with price dynamics which are "classical" mechanisms for explaining business cycles. Section 2.1 deals with the nonlinear cobweb model with normal demand and supply, naïve expectations, and adaptive production adjustment proposed by Onozaki *et al.* (2000). It shows how the simple economic mechanism manifests equilibrium, periodic solution, aperiodic oscillations, and chaos. Section 2.2 demonstrates chaos in a simple demand–supply model. This example draws on Hommes (1991). Supply involves a time lag. At low prices, supply increases slowly, partly because of start-up costs and fixed costs of production. Supply might also increase only slowly at high prices, say, because of capacity constraints. This suggests an S-supply curve. Section 2.3 discusses a disequilibrium inventory model by Hommes (1991). Actual labor employed, $L(t)$, is given by the short side of the labor market. Section 2.4 introduces a worker flow model with a nonlinear outflow rate from unemployment by Neugart (2004). Section 2.5 shows that urban dynamics of an open city can be described by the Lorenz equations. It shows urban chaos in population, land rent, and the city's GDP. Section 2.6 explains the dynamic multi-market Cournot model proposed by Zhao *et al.* (2019). It analyzes the behavior of oligopolistic producers, applying an incomplete information approach to generalize the traditional approach in which each producer applies the expectation to suppose that the opponents' output keeps the same level as previous period's and adopts an output strategy to maximize the expected profit. Section 2.7 demonstrates chaotic inflation and unemployment in a model Taylor Rules proposed by Guevara and Escot (2021). Section 2.8 studies the relatively simple model for financial markets with delays examined by Ding *et al.* (2012). Section 2.9 studies the model by Agliari *et al.* (2018) who deal with a stock market entry model in which participation depends on an attractiveness measure related to market activity and the fundamental value of the market. Section 2.9 introduces a housing market model with rent control proposed by Schmitt and Westerhof (2022). In this approach, homebuyers are assumed to be boundedly rational and able to form expectations with learning. They can switch between extrapolative and regressive expectation rules under the influences of their past forecasting accuracy. Policymakers may use rent control to affect the rent level. Section 2.10 considers the generalized neoclassical general equilibrium theory with Tobin's model and the Taylor rule. It shows how period exogenous inputs generate business cycles in economic growth.

Chapter 3 studies the complexity of economies with endogenous capital and wealth. Chaos appears under different mechanisms of capital accumulation. Section 3.1 applies an approach based on Ros (2000) to demonstrate a poverty trap in an extended Solow model. The model has two equilibria: a Solow-type and an unstable steady state at the level of the capital stock comparable with subsistence consumption. Section 3.2 studies the extended IS-LM model by Ma *et al.* (2017) which exhibits Hopf bifurcation. Section 3.3 shows the existence of chaos in the Keynesian dynamic model with capital accumulation and debts recently developed by Asada *et al.* (2019). Section 3.4 shows endogenous oscillations of debts in a model proposed by Matsuyama (2013). In Section 3.5, we deal with the disequilibrium macrodynamic model by Sasaki (2013). The model incorporates the three important economic mechanisms for approaching modern capitalist economies: ideas on interactions between the rate of employment and income by Goodwin, investment function by Kalecki, and the reserve-army and reserve-army-creation effects by Marx. Section 3.6 demonstrates oscillations in the reformed Solow model with two delays by Guerrini *et al.* (2019). Section 3.7 shows nonlinear phenomena in the reformed Kaldor–Kalecki growth model with capital stock's anticipation and investment lag analyzed by Liu *et al.* (2015) to show that can lead to the emergence of business cycles. Section 3.8 represents a generalized neoclassical general equilibrium theory integrated with monopolistic and perfect competition. The system is subject to various exogenous shocks in technologies and preferences.

Population causes complex phenomena in economies. It interacts with wealth, gender relations, education, and other factors. Chapter 4 presents a few nonlinear population dynamics. Section 4.1 introduces a population dynamic model constructed by Haavelmo in continuous form. Its discrete form was examined by Stutzer (1980), by applying modern mathematics for one-dimensional mappings. It is an early model that shows economic chaos from a simple economic model. Section 4.2 represents the nonlinear OLG model with endogenous fertility and old age support proposed by Chakrabarti (1999). Section 4.3 presents period-doubling cascades in a traditional prey–predator modeling framework developed by Gupta *et al.* (2014). Section 4.4 studies the discrete prey–predator model with chaos by Chen and Chen (2012). Section 4.5 represents the existence of nonlinear phenomena in a spatial extension of the classical prey–predator model with time delay in prey by Rao (2018). Section 4.6 represents the ecological model by Ruiz-Herrera (2017) that explores the effects of carryover effects (COEs) — any process that in one season that affects, non-lethally, individuals in the following seasons — on population dynamics. Section 4.6 provides a model of generalized neoclassical general equilibrium theory with generalized Malthusian theory.

Chapter 5 is concerned with models with endogenous changes and human capital accumulation, which exhibit nonlinear phenomena. Section 5.1 represents the model by Zhang (2006a) which explains path-dependent economic growth. The model synthesizes Solow's physical capital accumulation, Arrow's learning-by-doing, and Uzawa's learning-by-education growth models within a comprehensive framework. It is well known that the neoclassical growth theory based on the Solow growth model focuses accumulation of physical capital as an engine of growth, while the neo-Schumpeterian growth theory stresses innovation. Section 5.2 shows oscillations between the Solowian and Schumpeterian economies in the model proposed by Matsuyama (1999). Declining hours of work during one's lifetime is a well-observed phenomenon among developed economies. In recent years, there are many models proposed to explain the economic mechanisms of endogenous labor supply in association with economic development. Section 5.3 represents a new-growth-theory model for cycles of works by Iong and Irmen (2021). Section 5.4 shows homoclinic bifurcation in the modified Romer growth model proposed by Bella (2017). Section 5.5 shows the existence of chaos in the Uzawa–Lucas model identified by Bella *et al.* (2017). Section 5.6 studies the dynamical behavior of the model for a two-stage Cournot duopoly game with R&D spillover effect and product differentiation proposed by Zhou *et al.* (2019). The original paper investigates the behavior of the model, by applying Jury criterion, central manifold theorem, norm form theory, as well as numerical simulation. Section 5.7 introduces the model by Agliari *et al.* (2018), which is based on the cobweb demand–supply framework with costly innovators and free imitators. Section 5.8 introduces the international trade model with product cycles and growth cycles by Iwaisako and Tanaka (2017). Section 5.9 provides the model of generalized neoclassical general equilibrium theory which integrates Uzawa two-sector, Uzawa–Lucas two-sector, and Onik–Uzawa multi-country models within a comprehensive framework.

Chapter 6 studies economic complexity with environment and resources. Section 6.1 represents the economic growth model with endogenous environment by Liuzzi and Venturi (2021). It explains the existence of pollution-induced poverty traps. Section 6.2 studies the model by Antoci *et al.* (2011) who apply global analysis techniques to economic growth development with natural resources within the Ramsey growth modeling framework. Section 6.3 presents the model of economic growth and environmental resources within an overlapping generations framework proposed by Antoci (2016). Section 6.4 introduces the model by Bosi and Desmarchelier (2018), which is built by integrating the Levins model and the Solow–Ramsey model with pollution externality. Section 6.5 studies the Cournot game model built by Fanti (2015). The model deals with the impact of public environmental policies in a Cournot duopoly game with heterogeneous expectations and limited rationality. Section 6.6 introduces the model of environmental dynamics and development in a multi-regional economy. Chapter 7 concludes the study.

Chapter 2

Business Cycles and Chaos with Price Dynamics

What Andrew Carnegie advised for money management seems spiritually effective for faith in God or professionally useful for some discipline: "The Way to become rich is to put all your eggs in one basket and then watch that basket." The question is to be fortunate enough to have a secured basket. If a nation puts the political power to a politically inexperienced man through the masses' elections, the basket is secured but the nation might get globally humiliated or even be broken. With regard to the role of money in economic evolution, Robert Lucas — who received the Nobel Prize in Economics in 1995 "for having developed and applied the hypothesis of rational expectations, and thereby having transformed macroeconomic analysis and deepened our understanding of economic policy" — stated his Newtonian view: "The central predictions of the quantity theory are, in the long run, money growth should be neutral in its effects on the growth rate of production and should affect the inflation rate on a one-for-one basis." He got the Nobel prize because of this Newtonian vision on economic evolution. Another Nobel Prize winner, Paul Krugman, educated in classical economics and being brought up in the golden American epoch, stated his knowledgeable confidence: "We know that advanced economies with stale governments that borrow in their own currency can be capable of running up very high levels of debts without crisis." Anything is rationally possible in theoretical economics as far as the economist enjoys freedom of speech without social (especially international) responsibility. Galbraith argued: "Nothing so weakens a government as inflation." Henry Ford knew what he observed: "It is well enough that people of the nation do not understand our banking and monetary system, for if they did, I believe there would be a revolution before tomorrow morning." Stock markets are a game between millions of blind or ignorant players (with varied faiths or confidences) and a few (relatively) well-informed and experienced players/controllers. Stock markets, like romantic affairs, are typically chaotic if they are playful. We have little idea yet about what robots can know and do in the future. Prices and value of money are determined by emotions, rational calculations, technologies, market structures, and so on. Money, once wrongly issued for solving temporary national problems or political gains, might cause the national economy to slowly but steadily, or suddenly, deviate from its long-term healthy development path through labyrinthine accumulated effects that resulted from interdependence among almost-all important variables in political and economic systems. Benjamin Franklin said: "In this world nothing can be said to be certain, except death and taxes." Chaos theory demonstrates relations between chaos and order through nonlinear relations. This chapter is concerned with price dynamics which are "classical" mechanisms for explaining business cycles. Section 2.1 deals with nonlinear cobweb model with normal demand and supply, naïve expectations, and adaptive production adjustment proposed by Onozaki *et al.* (2000). It shows how the simple economic mechanism manifests equilibrium, periodic solution, aperiodic oscillations, and chaos. Section 2.2 demonstrates chaos in a simple demand–supply model. This example draws on Hommes (1991). At low prices, supply increases slowly, partly because of start-up costs and fixed costs of production. Supply might also increase only slowly at high prices, say, because of capacity constraints. Section 2.3 discusses a disequilibrium inventory model by Hommes (1991). Actual labor employed, $L(t)$, is given by the short side of the labor market. Section 2.4 introduces a worker flow model with a nonlinear outflow rate from unemployment by Neugart (2004). Section 2.5 shows that urban dynamics can be described by the Lorenz equations. It shows urban chaos in population, land rent, and the city's GDP. Section 2.6 explains the dynamic multi-market Cournot model proposed by Zhao *et al.* (2019). It analyzes the behavior of oligopolistic producers, by applying an incomplete information approach to generalize the traditional approach in which each producer applies the expectation to suppose that the opponents' output keeps the same level as previous period's and adopts an output strategy to maximize the expected profit. Section 2.7 demonstrates chaotic inflation and unemployment in a model Taylor Rules proposed by Guevara and Escot (2021). Section 2.8 studies the relatively simple model for financial markets with delays examined by Ding *et al.* (2012). Section 2.9 studies the model by Agliari *et al.* (2018) who deal with a stock market entry model in which participation depends on an attractiveness measure related to market activity and the fundamental value of the market. Section 2.9 introduces a housing market model with rent control proposed by Schmitt and Westerhof (2022). In this approach, homebuyers are assumed to be boundedly rational and able to form expectations with learning. They can switch between extrapolative and regressive expectation rules under the influences of their past forecasting accuracy. Policymakers may use rent control to affect the rent level. Section 2.10 considers the generalized neoclassical general equilibrium theory with Tobin's model and the Taylor rule. It shows how period exogenous inputs generate business cycles in economic growth

The Nobel Prize in Physics 2021 was awarded "for groundbreaking contributions to our understanding of complex systems" according to the prize committee. Half of the prize money was jointly awarded to Syukuro Manabe and Klaus Hasselmann "for the physical modeling of Earth's climate, quantifying variability and reliably predicting global warning" and the other half to Giorgio Parisi "for the discovery of the interplay of disorder and fluctuations in physical systems from atomic to planetary scales." The prize reflects the importance of complexity theory for the development of sciences and understanding nature and humanities. Complexity theory, which is almost exchangeable with chaos theory, synergetics, bifurcation theory, or catastrophe theory in this study — in economics (with formal mathematical modeling and computer simulation) — has been developed as an academic field since a few decades ago as soon as formal modeling of chaos was conducted in natural sciences and mathematics. Diffusion of ideas, methods, and techniques in natural sciences and mathematics to economics is nowadays quick. Complexity theory is theoretically and practically valid for dealing with interactions between politics, economics, cultures, and environment.

2.1 A Cobweb Model with Adaptive Production Adjustment

Adam Smith explained the foundation of price determination: "People in the same trade seldom meet together, even for merriment and diversion, but the conversation ends in some contrivance to raise prices." But his analytical conclusion on price dynamics is valid only in limited situations. A simple nonlinear cobweb model — even without periodic exogenous inputs — illustrates the invalidity of his thought. A nonlinear cobweb model with normal demand and supply, naïve expectations, and adaptive production adjustment was proposed by Onozaki *et al.* (2000; see also Zhang, 2006b, Section 5.2). Let us consider a market of a single commodity. In period t, a supplier decides his production $x(t+1)$, which may not equal the profit maximum $\tilde{x}(t+1)$. The optimal level is calculated and used as a target of adjustment by the supplier. Suppose that the calculation is made under the quadratic cost function $(bx \wedge 2)/2$, $b > 0$ with the naïve price expectation (which means that his price expectation for the next period is equal to the current price $p(t)$). The profit maximum level of output is given by $\tilde{x}(t+1) = p(t)/b$. It is assumed that the producer will adjust his production according to the following hedging rule in the uncertain economy

$$x(t+1) = x(t) + \alpha(\tilde{x}(t+1) - x(t)),$$

where $\alpha \in (1)$ is the speed of adjustment. Suppose that there are n identical suppliers in the market. The aggregate supply is thus given by $X(t) = nx(t)$. Assume a monotonic demand function with constant price elasticity of $1/\beta(\beta > 0) : p(t) = c/(Y \wedge \beta(t))$. Price clears the market in each period, i.e., $X(t) = Y(t)$. It is straightforward to show that under the above specifications, the motion of the aggregate supply is given by

$$X(t+1) = (1-\alpha)X(t) + \frac{\alpha cn}{bX^{\beta}(t)}.$$

Introduce a linear transformation $z(t) \equiv (b/cn)^{1/(1+\beta)}X(t)$. Then, the above equation is transformed into

$$z(t+1) = (1-\alpha)z(t) + \frac{\alpha}{z^{\beta}(t)} \equiv f(z(t), \alpha, \beta),$$

$$(\alpha, \beta) \in (0,1) \times (0, \infty).$$

For this map, it can be demonstrated that for sufficiently large β, the map f exhibits a *horseshoe*. By a horseshoe, it means here a compact invariant set on which some iterate of f is topologically conjugate to the one-sided full-shift on two symbols. The existence of a horseshoe is assured by that of a transverse homoclinic point. A map is said to exhibit topological chaos if it has a horseshoe or, alternatively, if the topological entropy of the map is positive. It should be remarked that a map restricted to horseshoes behaves in a complicated way; the existence of horseshoes itself does not assume complex dynamics in the long run; the system may eventually settle down to a periodic motion even if horseshoes are present. In the following theorem proved by Onozaki *et al.*, an attractor is said to be strange if it

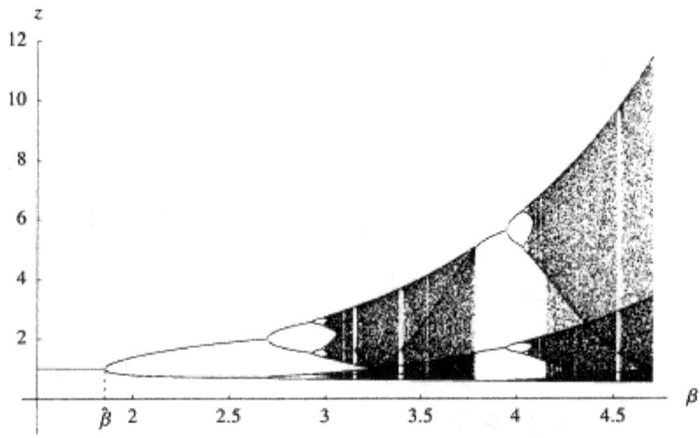

Fig. 2.1. The bifurcation diagram for $15 \leq \beta \leq 4.7$ with $\alpha = 0.7$.

contains a dense orbit with a positive Liapunov exponent. Figure 2.1 depicts the bifurcation diagram of the map with regard to β $(15 \leq \beta \leq 4.7)$ with $\alpha = 0.7$.

2.2 Chaos in a Simplified Demand and Supply Model

We now demonstrate chaos in a simple demand–supply model. This example draws on Hommes (1991: Section 5.1; see also Zhang, 2006b: Section 4.6). We consider that supply involves a time lag. It should be remarked that an analytical framework proposed by Bellomo *et al.* (2020) can be applied to model cases of multiple goods. At low prices, supply increases slowly, partly because of start-up costs and fixed costs of production. Supply might also increase only slowly at high prices, say, because of capacity constraints. This suggests an S-supply curve. The arctan function exhibits such an S-shape. Let us express supply $q^s(t)$ as a function of expected price $p^e(t)$ by such a function: $q^s(t) = \arctan(\mu p^e(t))$. The origin is an inflection point. As shown in Figure 2.2, the parameter μ determines the steepness of the S-shape. The higher the value of μ, the steeper the curve.

It is assumed that demand is a linear function of actual prices, i.e., $q^d(t) = a - bp(t)$, $b > 0$. Price expectation is formed as follows:

$$p^e(t+1) = \lambda p(t) + (1 - \lambda)p^e(t).$$

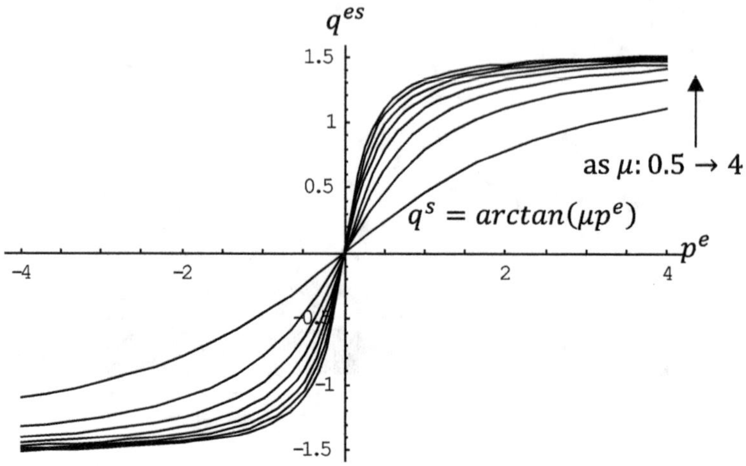

Fig. 2.2. Specified relations between expected price and supply.

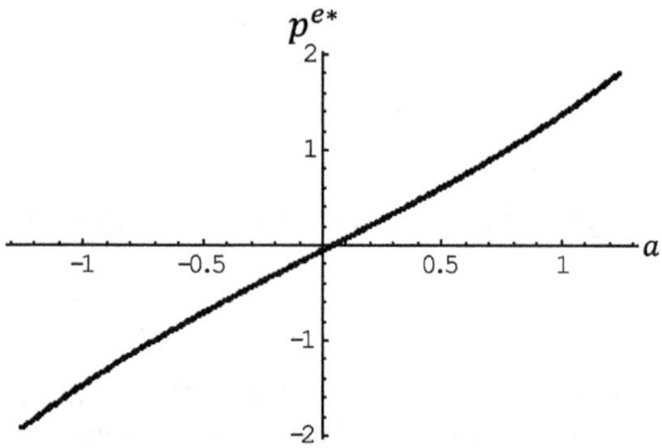

Fig. 2.3. Bifurcation diagram for $\mu = 0.5, a \in [-1.25, 1.25]$.

It can be shown that under these specifications, the market condition that the demand equals supply is expressed by the following difference equation:

$$p^e(t+1) = (1-\lambda)p^e(t) + \frac{a\lambda}{b} - \frac{\lambda \arctan(\mu p^e(t))}{b} \equiv f(p^e(t)).$$

We will demonstrate the dynamic behavior of the model by simulation. In the remainder of this section, we fix $\lambda = 0.3, b = 0.25$ and consider a as a bifurcation parameter for different values of μ. In the case of $\mu = 0.5$, Figure 2.3 depicts the bifurcation diagram for $a \in [-1.25, 1.25]$. We see that there is a unique fixed point for the map f.

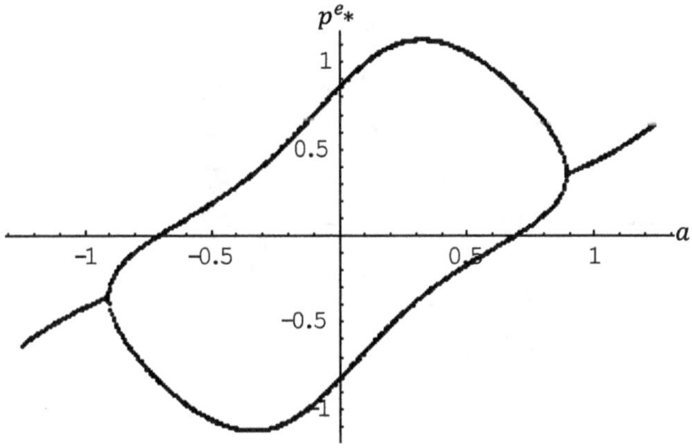

Fig. 2.4. Bifurcation diagram for $\mu = 3, a \in [-1.25, 1.25]$.

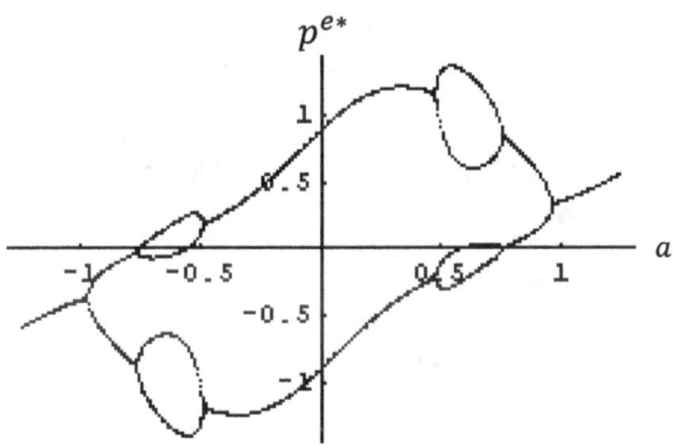

Fig. 2.5. Bifurcation diagram for $\mu = 3.5, a \in [-1.25, 1.25]$.

Let us rise the value of μ to 3 and depict the bifurcation diagram with a as the bifurcation parameter as in Figure 2.4. For low values of a, there is a unique fixed point. Around $a = -0.9$, a period-doubling bifurcation occurs. The stable orbit remains until a reaches 0.9 and then a period-halving occurs. Thereafter, the system settles down again to a unique stable equilibrium. The diagram is symmetrical about the origin because of the characteristic of the arctan function.

Figure 2.5 depicts the bifurcation diagram when $\mu = 3.5$. The figure shows a doubling bifurcation into a period-four orbit, which then turns into a period-two orbit and finally a stable equilibrium.

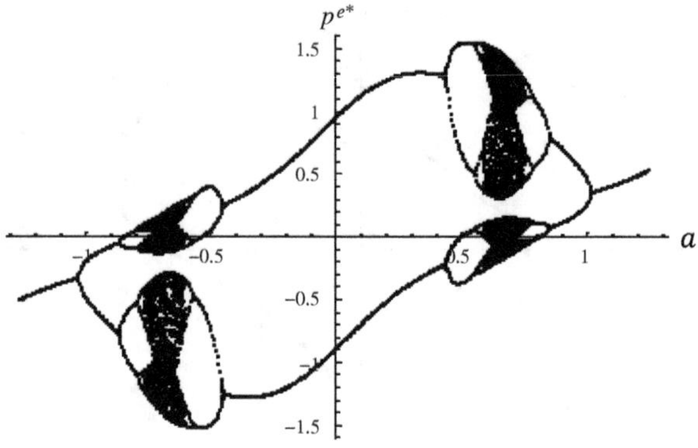

Fig. 2.6. Bifurcation diagram for $\mu = 4, a \in [-1.25, 1.25]$.

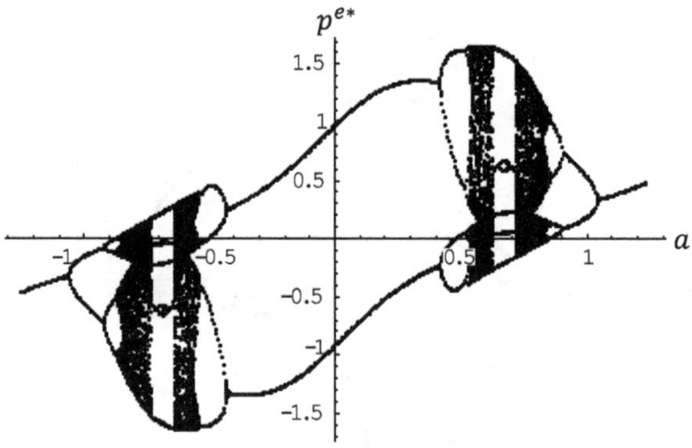

Fig. 2.7. Bifurcation diagram for $\mu = 4.5, a \in [-1.25, 1.25]$.

In Figures 2.6 and 2.7, we depict respectively the bifurcation diagrams when $\mu = 4$ and $\mu = 4.5$. We see that within the period-four orbit, chaos occurs.

2.3 An Inventory Model with Rational Expectations

This example discusses a disequilibrium inventory model. This example draws on Hommes (1991: Chapter 28; see also Zhang, 2006b: Chapter 4). Actual labor employed, $L(t)$, is given by the short side of the labor market, $L(t) = \min\{L^d(t), L^s(t)\}$, where $L^d(t)$ and $L^s(t)$ are respectively demand and supply of labor. Assume $L^s(t) = c$, where c is constant. Let $y^d(t)$

and $y^s(t)$ denote respectively aggregate demand and supply. The level of inventories $I(t)$ is positive when there is excess demand, otherwise it is zero, $I(t) = \max\{0, y^s(t) - y^d(t)\}$. We denote expected aggregate demand by $E(y^d(t))$ and the desired level of inventories by $I^d(t)$. We assume perfect foresight, i.e., $E(y^d(t)) = y^d(t)$. Suppose $I^d(t) = \beta E(y^d(t))$, where β is a parameter. Production is proportional to labor employed, $\delta L(t)$. We thus have

$$y^s(t) = I(t-1) + \delta L(t)$$
$$y^d(t) = E(y^d(t)) + I^d(t) = (1+\beta)E(y^d(t)).$$

Setting the demand and supply equal yields the labor demand function:

$$L^d(t) = \max\left\{0, \frac{(1+\beta)E(y^d(t)) - I(t-1)}{\delta}\right\}.$$

Aggregate demand is assumed to be a linear function of labor employed, $y^d(t) = a + bL(t)$. We assume that labor productivity is greater than the marginal propensity to consume, $\delta > b$. We have thus completed the description of the model. We now show that the evolution of the system can be described by a difference equation for I.

First, we are concerned with $L(t) = L^d(t)$, which implies $L(t) \in (0, c)$. From the above conditions, it is straightforward to check that we have

$$L(t) = \frac{(1+\beta)y^d(t) - I(t-1)}{\delta} = \frac{(1+\beta)(a + bL(t)) - I(t-1)}{\delta}.$$

Solve the above equation for L

$$L(t) = \frac{(1+\beta)a - I(t-1)}{\delta - b(1+\beta)}.$$

Assume $\delta - b(1+\beta) > 0$. As $L(t) \in (0, c)$, then $L(t) < c$ is guaranteed.

Introduce two parameters:

$$\gamma_1 \equiv (1+\beta)a - c(\delta - b(1+\beta)),$$
$$\gamma_2 \equiv a(1+\beta).$$

It can be shown that $I(t) = f(I(t-1))$ is a piecewise function given by

$$I(t) = \begin{cases} I(t-1) + \delta c - a - c, I(t-1) \leq \gamma_1, \\ \dfrac{-b\beta I(t-1)}{\delta - b(1+\beta)} + \dfrac{a\delta\beta}{\delta - b(1+\beta)}, \gamma_2 > I(t-1) > \gamma_1 \\ I(t-1) - a, I(t-1) \geq \gamma_2. \end{cases}$$

First, we specify $a = 0.2$, $b = 0.75$, $c = 1$, $\delta = 1$, and $\beta = 0.2$. The behavior of the map is plotted in Figure 2.8. Although the equilibrium level exists ($I^* = 0.16$), from the figure, it is not clear whether this fixed point will be approached. In fact, as shown in Figure 2.9, the system is chaotic in the present case.

We still assume $a = 0.2$, $b = 0.75$, $c = 1$, and $\delta = 1$ but leave β unspecified. We consider β as a bifurcation parameter. We allow β to range over the interval $(0, 1/3)$, and the value of $1/3$ is determined from the condition $\delta - b(1 + \beta) = 0$. Figure 2.9 depicts the bifurcation diagram. Although the system exhibits chaos over a certain range for β, there is regular alternating behavior.

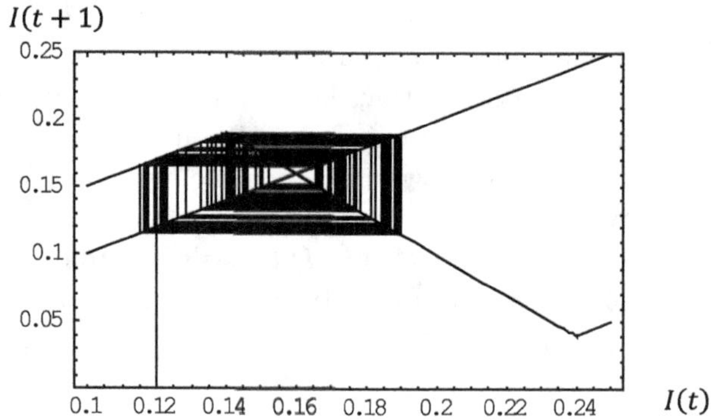

Fig. 2.8. The dynamics with $\beta = 0.2$.

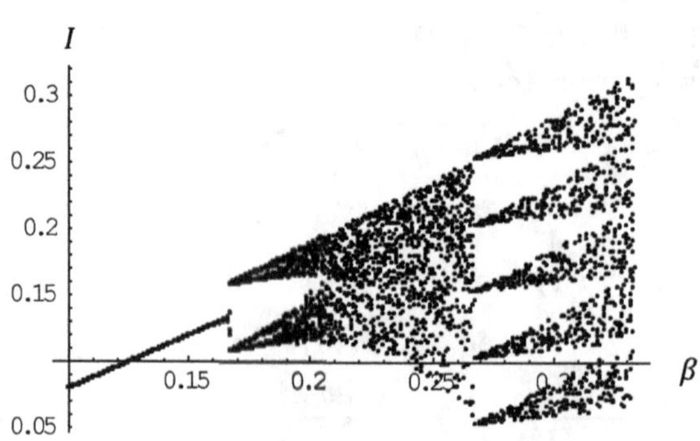

Fig. 2.9. The bifurcation diagram with β as bifurcation parameter.

2.4 Unemployment, Inflation, and Chaos

This section introduces a worker flow model with a nonlinear outflow rate from unemployment. The model is proposed by Neugart (2004; see also Zhang, 2006b: Section 7.6). The unemployment $U(t)$ at period t follows the following identity:

$$U(t+1) - U(t) = i(L - U(t)) - o(t)U(t), \tag{2.4.1}$$

where $i > 0$ denotes the (exogenous) inflow rate, $L(= 1)$ the labor force, and $o(t)$ the outflow rate from unemployment. Here, the outflow rate is defined as the fraction of jobs that come to the market at time t to job searchers, i.e., $o(t) = J(t)/\{U(t) + d(1 - U(t))\}$, where the parameter $d(0 < d < 1)$ gives the on-the-job searchers as a constant fraction of employed workers and $J(t)$ denotes job creations. We specify $J(t) = J_s + \gamma(m - \pi(t))$, where J_s is the job creation due to the structural characteristics of the economy and $\gamma(m - \pi(t))$ describes the cyclical component of job creations, where γ is a positive parameter, m the exogenous money growth rate, and $\pi(t)$ the inflation rate at t. Hence, the outflow rate from the unemployment can be expressed as follows:

$$o(t) = \frac{J_s + \gamma(m - \pi(t))}{U(t) + d(1 - U(t))}$$

Substituting the above equation into Eq. (2.4.1) yields

$$\begin{aligned} U(t+1) &= i - \left[(1 - i) + \frac{J_s + \gamma(m - \pi(t))}{U(t) + d(1 - U(t))}\right] U(t) \\ &\equiv \Lambda(U(t), \pi(t)). \end{aligned} \tag{2.4.2}$$

Assume that firms cannot raise prices to the same extent as nominal wages increase at t. This assumption is reflected in the requirement of $\delta > 1$ in the following formation of inflation rate dynamics:

$$\pi(t) = \frac{1}{\delta}\left(\pi^e(t) + \frac{w_b(t) - w_p}{w_p}\right), \tag{2.4.3}$$

where $\pi^e(t)$ is the expected inflation rate at t, $w_b(t)$ is the bargained wage rate at t, and w_p is the price determined real wage (which equals $(1 - \mu)y$, where $0 < \mu < 1$ is the fixed markup and $y = 1$ is the constant marginal productivity). The bargained real wage $w_b(t)$ is given by $w_b(t) = y - (1 - b)U(t)$, where $0 < b < 1$ is the "reservation wage." The inflation expectation is formed by $\pi^e(t) = a\pi(t-1) + (1-a)\pi^e(t-1)$, where $\leq a \leq 1$

is the weighted average rate. Under these assumptions, we may rewrite Eq. (2.4.3) as

$$\pi(t+1) = \frac{1}{\delta}\left(\pi^e(t+1) + \frac{\mu - (1-b)U(t+1)}{1-\mu}\right). \tag{2.4.4}$$

From this equation and $\pi^e(t+1) = a\pi(t) + (1-a)\pi^e(t)$ we get

$$\delta\pi(t+1) = a\pi(t) + (1-a)\pi^e(t) + \frac{\mu - (1-b)U(t+1)}{1-\mu}$$

Substituting this equation to Eq. (2.4.4) for t, we solve

$$\pi(t+1) = \frac{a\mu}{\mu_0\delta} + \left(\frac{a}{\delta} + (1-a)\right)\pi(t) - \frac{ab_0}{\mu_0\delta}\Lambda(U(t), \pi(t))$$
$$\equiv \Phi(U(t), \pi(t)), \tag{2.4.5}$$

where $b_0 \equiv 1-b$ and $\mu_0 \equiv 1-\mu$. The dynamic system consists of Eqs. (2.4.2) and (2.4.5).

As discussed by Neugart, it is reasonable to choose the following parameters:

$$a = 0.5, \quad \delta = 2, \quad b = 0.5, \quad \gamma = 0.5, \quad d = 0.01, \quad m = 0.03.$$

If $i \approx 0.13199$, then one eigenvalue is equal to -1; a period-doubling bifurcation occurs. It can be shown that the eigenvalue with a positive root never crosses 1. Figure 2.10 depicts the bifurcation diagram of U over i The plot and the following one are from Neugart (2004). Neugart provided more

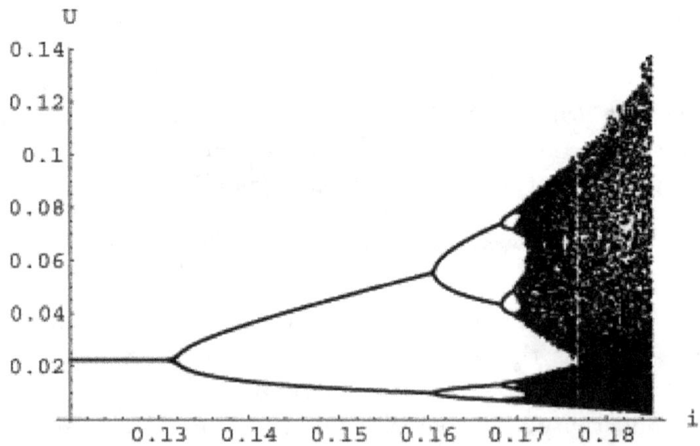

Fig. 2.10. Bifurcation diagram of unemployment over the inflow rate.

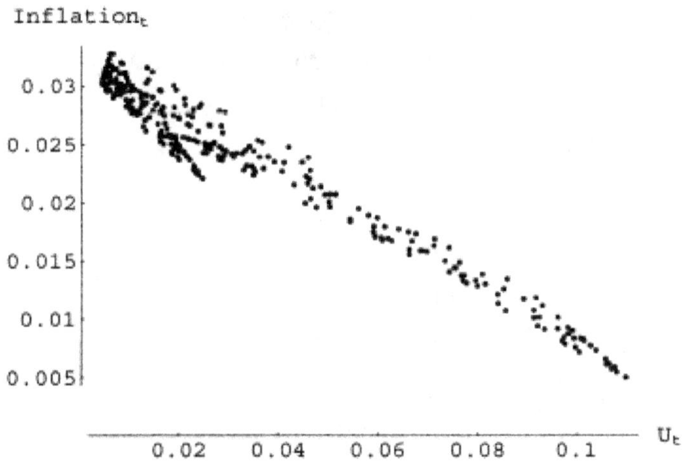

Fig. 2.11. An attractor.

charts for different values of the parameters. Increases from $i \approx 0.13199$ will lead to further bifurcations. Mathematically, the dynamic mechanism is similar to the bifurcations observed for the Hénon map.

Figure 2.11 demonstrates the existence of an attractor with inflation rate over unemployment rate when $i = 0.18$. The attractor looks like a Phillips curve. Nevertheless, in this model, there is no stable trade-off between the inflation rate and unemployment rate. The system shifts up and down a negatively sloped "curve" erratically. A pair of inflation–unemployment rates today cannot tell where the economy will be in the long term.

2.5 Urban Chaos by the Lorenz Equations

It has recently become clear that there are different and very complex phenomena that can occur in systems of third and higher orders that are not present in second-order systems. We now introduce the Lorenz equations to illustrate phenomena of chaos. Zhang (1991: Chapter 6; 2005: Chapter 9) found that some urban systems can also be described by the Lorenz equations. The urban model describes an urban system within a metropolitan area. The system under consideration is small so that its dynamics will have almost no significant impact on the metropolitan area. Businesses and residents are free to choose their location sites either in the urban area or in the outside world. Locational characteristics of the urban system are described by the following three variables:

$$X(t) = \text{the output of the urban system at time } t,$$
$$Y(t) = \text{the number of residents,}$$
$$Z(t) = \text{the land rent.}$$

Zhang proposed the following urban dynamics:

$$\dot{X} = a_1(a_2 Y - a_3 X),$$
$$\dot{Y} = c_1(c_2 X - c_3 Y) - c_4 XZ,$$
$$\dot{Z} = -d_2 Z + d_1 XY,$$

where a_i, c_i, and d_i are positive parameters. The economic interpretations of the model are referred to Zhang (1991, Chapter 6). Under the following transformation:

$$t = \frac{t^*}{c_1 c_3}, \quad \rho = \frac{a_1 a_3}{c_1 c_3}, \quad r = \frac{a_2 c_2}{a_3 c_3}, \quad b = \frac{d_2}{c_1 c_3},$$
$$x = \left(\frac{c_4}{d_1}\right)^{0.5} \frac{d_1 X}{c_1 c_3}, \quad y = \left(\frac{c_4}{d_1}\right)^{0.5} \frac{d_1 a_2 Y}{a_1 c_1 c_3}, \quad z = \frac{c_4 a_2 Z}{a_3 c_1 c_3},$$

the urban dynamics is described by the celebrated system of equations that Edward N. Lorenz (1963) proposed:

$$\dot{x} = \sigma(-x + y),$$
$$\dot{y} = rx - y - xz,$$
$$\dot{z} = -bz + xy,$$

where x, y, and z are time-dependent variables. The Lorenz equations are a quadratic system of autonomous differential equations in three dimensions modeling a three-mode approximation to the motion of a layer of fluid heated from below. A thorough treatment of the Lorenz equations is given by Sparrow (1982). The Lorenz equations are nonlinear as the second and third equations involve quadratic nonlinearities. The system involves three positive, real parameters, σ, r, and b. For illustration, we specify $\sigma = 10$ and $b = 8/3$ in the remainder of this section. It is straightforward to check:

For $1 < r < r_1 \cong 1.3456$, there are three negative real eigenvalues.
For $r_1 < r < r_2 \cong 24.737$, there are one negative real eigenvalue and two complex eigenvalues with the negative real part.
For $r_2 < r$, there are one negative real eigenvalue and two complex eigenvalues with the positive real part.

The following is shown: (1) For $0 < r < 1$, there is only one critical point which is asymptotically stable. (2) For $1 < r < r_1$, there are three equilibrium points: two are asymptotically stable and the other one is unstable. (3) For $r_1 < r < r_2$, there are two asymptotically stable equilibrium points and one unstable equilibrium point. (4) For $r_2 < r$, the three critical points are unstable. We consider solutions for $r_2 < r$. All three critical points are unstable. A trajectory can approach any one of the critical points only on certain highly restricted paths. The slightest deviation from these paths causes the trajectory to depart from the critical point. What is surprising with the system is that no trajectory will approach infinity as $t \to \infty$, even though all critical points are unstable. In fact, it can be shown that all solutions remain bounded as $t \to \infty$. It can be shown that for all positive values of r, all solutions ultimately approach a certain limiting set of points that has zero volume.

We now simulate the model. We compute values of $x(t)$ versus t. Figure 2.12 describes the motion of $x(t)$ with initial condition $(6, 6, 6)$. The solution changes "randomly" from positive values to negative ones. The Lorenz equations are deterministic, and their motion is completely determined by the initial conditions. The attracting set in this case has a complicated structure and is called a *strange attractor*. The term *chaotic* is used to describe solutions such as those shown in Figure 2.12.

A significant feature of the system is that its solutions are extremely sensitive to small changes in the initial conditions. Figure 2.13 shows the solutions $x(t)$ with different initial conditions. The initial conditions of

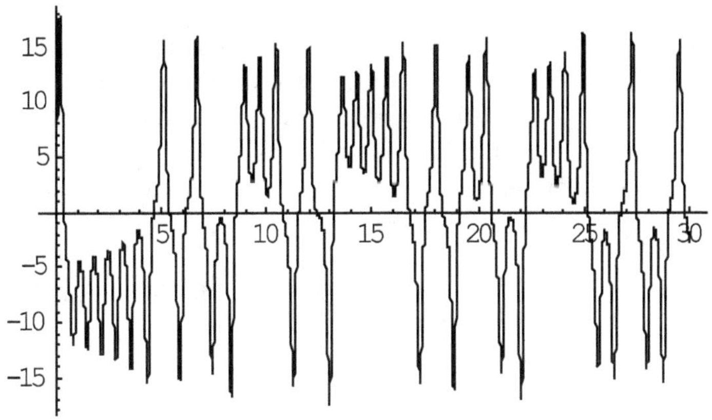

Fig. 2.12. A plot of $x(t)$ for $r = 28$ for initial condition $(6, 6, 6)$.

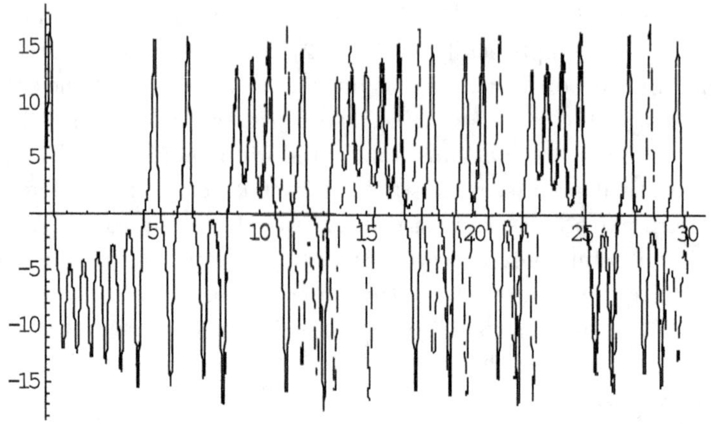

Fig. 2.13. Plot of $x(t)$ for $r = 28$.
Note: $(x_0, y_0, z_0) = (6, 6, 6)$ for solid curve and $(x_0, y_0, z_0) = (6.01, 6, 6)$ for dashed curve.

y and z are the same in the two cases; the only difference is for $x(0)$. The two solutions remain close until t is near 10, after which they diverge rapidly. This property of the Lorenz equations caused him to conclude that detailed long-range weather predictions are probably not possible as any small difference in initial condition may lead to great differences in the future.

Figure 2.14 shows the corresponding Lorenz attractor with $r = 28$ and $(x_0, y_0, z_0) = (6, 6, 6)$. There are two sheets in which trajectories spiral outwards. When the distance from the center of such a spiral becomes larger than some threshold, the motion is ejected from the spiral and is attracted by the other spiral, where it again begins to spiral out, and the process is repeated. The motion is not regular. The number of turns that a trajectory spends in one spiral before it jumps to the other is not specified. It may wind around one spiral twice, and then three times around the other, then ten times around the first, and so on.

The Lorenz attractor is dubbed a strange attractor because there are no asymptotically stable equilibria or period orbits in a global attractor that is a compact, connected invariant set. The geometry of the attractor is exceedingly complicated. We may also visualize projects in xz-plane. Figure 2.15 illustrates the case with $r = 28$ and $(x_0, y_0, z_0) = (6, 6, 6)$. The graphs appear to cross over themselves repeatedly, but this cannot be true for the actual trajectories in three-dimensional space because

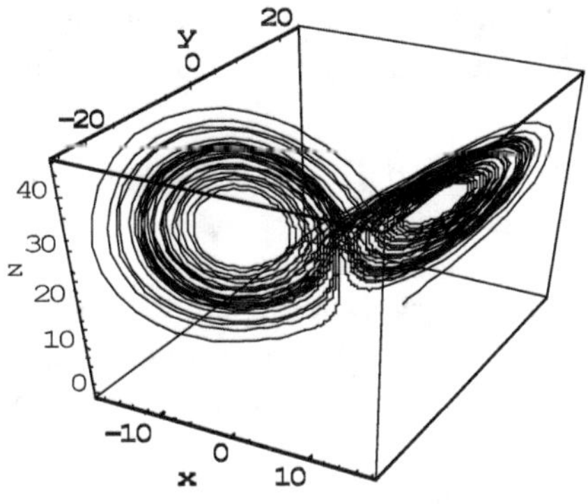

Fig. 2.14. The dynamics of the Lorenz equations.

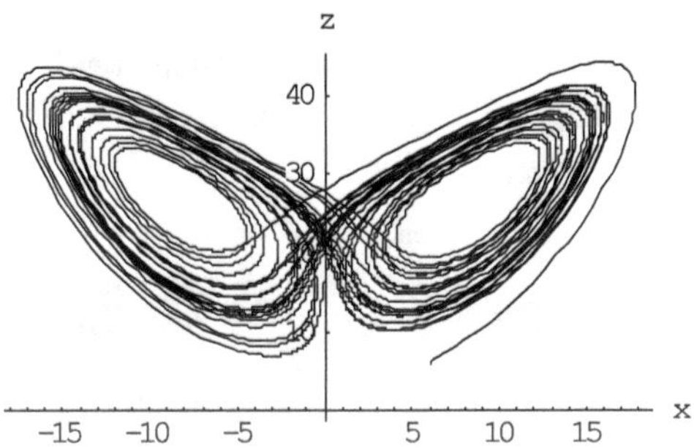

Fig. 2.15. Projections of a trajectory of the Lorenz equations.

of the unique theorem. The apparent crossings are due wholly to the two-dimensional character of the figure.

Since the urban system exhibits the same behavior given by Figure 2.14, the urban system exhibits the following properties: (1) the temporary path of the three urban variables is time-dependent but is not periodic (or "regular"); (2) the motion does not appear to show a transient phenomenon since, regardless of how long the numerical integration is continued, the trajectory is going to continue to wind around and around without settling down to either periodic or stationary behavior; (3) the topology of the figure is not dependent on the choice of initial conditions or integrating route; and (4) it is impossible to predict the details of how the trajectory will develop over any period other than a very short time interval. Considering the above urban interpretation of the Lorenz equations, we see that even if the government is well informed and is composed of well-educated officials and experts, it is impossible for the government to predict the impact of its own actions, such as tax policy, land policy, and infrastructure policy.

2.6 A Cournot Game with Bounded Rationality and Behavioral Chaos

Zhao *et al.* (2019) proposed a dynamic multi-market Cournot model to analyze the behavior of oligopolistic producers, by applying an incomplete information approach to generalize the traditional approach in which each producer applies the expectation to suppose that the opponents' output keeps the same level as previous period's and adopts an output strategy to maximize the expected profit. There are two competing firms ($i = 1, 2$) and two markets ($j = A, B$). It should be remarked that a similar extension to a duopoly Stackelberg game and identification of chaos is conducted by Yang *et al.* (2019). The products are near substitutes but different in their quality levels. Firms can charge different prices for different markets. The demand for firm i in market j is given by

$$p_{Ai}(t) = \psi_i - a_i(q_{Ai}(t) + q_{Ai}(t)),$$

$$p_{Bi}(t) = \beta_i - b_i(q_{Bi}(t) + q_{Bi}(t)),$$

where p_{ji} and q_{ji} are firm $i's$ price and quantity at time t, respectively, in market $j(= A, B)$, and ψ_i, a_i, β_i, and b_i are positive parameters. The total cost function of firm i is

$$C_i(q_{Ai}, q_{Bi}) = \mu_{Ai}q_{Ai}(t) + \mu_{Bi}q_{Bi}(t),$$

where μ_{ji} are positive parameter. The profit of firm i is

$$\pi_i(t) = p_{Ai}(t)q_{Ai}(t) + p_{Bi}(t)q_{Bi}(t) - C_i(t).$$

An approach to generalize static games to dynamic ones is called the bounded rationality approach (Puu, 1996). Zhao *et al.* apply the following dynamic multi-market Cournot model:

$$q_{ji}(t+1) = q_{ji}(t) + \theta_i(q_{ji}(t))\frac{\partial \pi_i(t)}{\partial q_{ji}(t)}, \quad i = 1, 2, \ \ j = A, B,$$

where $\theta_i(q_{ji}(t))$ is the adjustment speed of firm i. It implies that the firms are directly sensitive to demand in markets and their own benefit. Let $\theta_i(q_{ji}(t)) = \theta_i q_{ji}(t)$ and θ_i are treated as positive parameters in the rest of the section. The firms maximize respectively their profits. It is straightforward to get the first-order conditions for maximization.

The dynamics is finally described by

$$q_{Ai}(t+1) = q_{Ai}(t) + \theta_i q_{Ai}(t)(\psi_i - a_i(2q_{Ai}(t) + q_{Aj}(t)) - \mu_{Ai}),$$
$$q_{Bi}(t+1) = q_{Bi}(t) + \theta_i q_{Bi}(t)(\beta_i - b_i(2q_{Bi}(t) + q_{Bj}(t)) - \mu_{Bi}),$$
$$i \neq j, \quad i, j = 1, 2.$$

The above system describes a duopoly game played by boundedly rational players making decision in a process of dynamical investment in the two markets.

The parameters θ_i are chosen as bifurcation parameters. The rest of the parameters are specified as follows:

$$\psi_1 = 4, \quad \psi_2 = 5, \quad \beta_1 = 3, \quad \beta_2 = 5, \quad a_1 = 0.4, \quad a_2 = 0.5,$$
$$b_1 = 0.4, \quad b_2 = 0.6, \quad \mu_{A1} = 0.3, \quad \mu_{B1} = 0.4, \quad \mu_{A2} = 0.4, \quad \mu_{B2} = 0.6.$$

We have Figure 2.16 which plots the bifurcation diagram and the maximum Lyapunov exponents with the adjustment speed θ_1 while the other

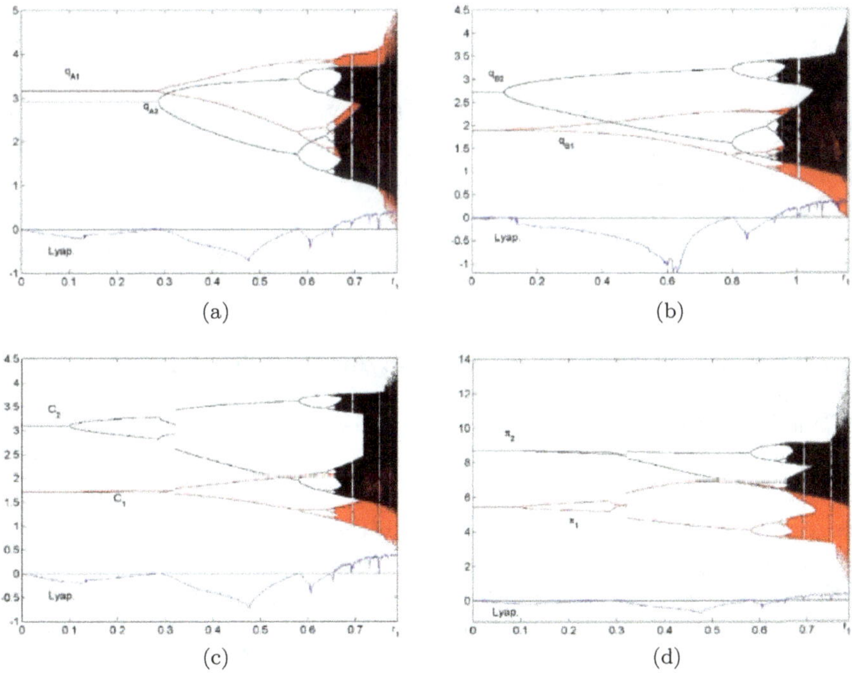

Fig. 2.16. Bifurcation diagram with θ_1 and the maximum Lyapunov. (a) the firm 1, 2 of quantities trajectory in the market A, (b) the firm 1, 2 of quantities trajectory in the market B, (c) the cost trajectory of firm 1, 2, and (d) the profit trajectory of firm 1, 2.

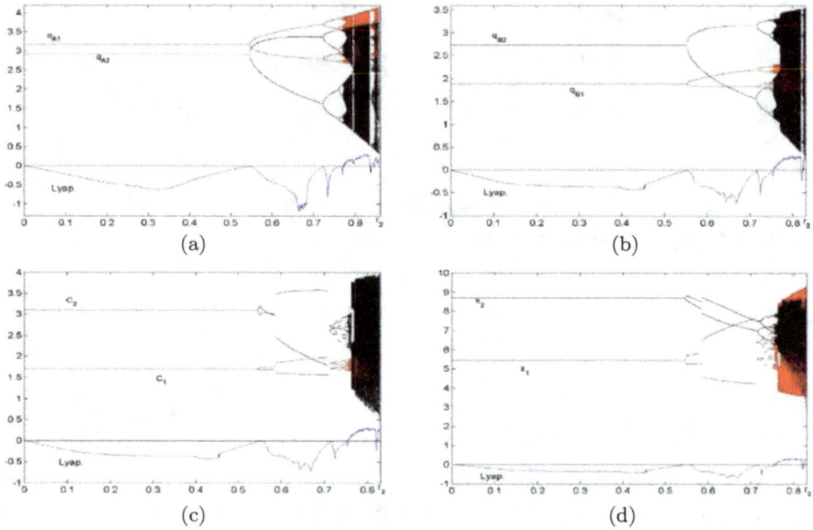

Fig. 2.17. Bifurcation diagram with θ_1 and the maximum Lyapunov. (a) the firm 1, 2 of quantities trajectory in the market A, (b) the firm 1, 2 of quantities trajectory in the market B, (c) the cost trajectory of firm 1, 2, and (d) the profit trajectory of firm 1, 2.

parameters are constant with $\theta_2 = 0.6$. As shown in Figures 2.16(a) and 2.16(b), the markets are locally stable for $\theta_1 < 0.667$ and $\theta_1 < 0.95$. Figure 2.17 plots the bifurcation diagram and the maximum Lyapunov exponents with the adjustment speed θ_2 while the other parameters are constant with $\theta_1 = 0.5$. When $\theta_1 = 0.766$, the system exhibits chaotic phenomena.

2.7 Chaotic Inflation and Unemployment with Taylor Rules

In modern capitalist societies, governments play an active role through monetary policies and taxation, in addition to many other methods such as investment in education, infrastructure, military expenditures, and provision of various social welfare. Central banks use monetary policy rules to control economies. These rules are often targeted at inflation, unemployment, and economic growth. There are trade-offs among these variables. It is a common observation that governments know, perhaps, what they want but seldom achieve what they want. Fortune is the mother of monetary policy successes in modern economies characterized by the complexity of networking with greatly reduced constraints of time and space owing to rapid globalization of digital technology. There is a well-known

Taylor rule as a guide for driving policy instruments. It guards how central banks should act in order to achieve their macroeconomic objectives. Taylor rules are referred to how central banks should determine nominal interests as economic conditions are changed. The rule was initially proposed by Taylor (1993) and Henderson and McKibbin (1993). The rule has helped central banks in practice. Taylor considered that the nominal interest rate should be related to the divergences of actual inflation from the targeted inflation rate and actual GDP from the potential GDP. The Federal Reserve should enhance interest rates when inflation is high or when employment is higher than full employment levels; on the other hand, the Federal Reserve should reduce interest rates when inflation and employment levels are low. The Taylor rule is accepted in economics in modeling monetary policy (e.g., Benhabib *et al.*, 2001; Meng and Yip, 2004; Schmitt-Grohe and Uribe, 2009; Benhabib *et al.*, 2014; and Zhang, 2019).

This section introduces a model proposed by Guevara and Escot (2021). Their model is described as follows:

$$\begin{aligned}
\pi_t &= f(u_t) + a\pi_t^e, \quad 0 \le a \le 1, \\
f &= \alpha_1 + \frac{\alpha_2}{u} + \frac{\alpha_3}{u^2} \quad \text{(the Phillips curve)}, \\
\pi_{t+1}^e &= \pi_t^e + c(\pi_t - \pi_t^e), \quad 0 \le c \le 1, \\
u_{t+1} &= -b(m_t - \pi_t) + u_t, \quad b > 0,
\end{aligned}$$

where π_t and π_t^e are the current and expected inflation rates in period t and u_t is the level of unemployment. The parameter a stands for the degree to which inflationary expectations are incorporated into current inflation; the parameter c shows the formation of adaptive expectations; the parameter m is the growth rate of money supply. The term $b(m - \pi_t)$ implies that an increase in the real amount of money increases the level of production. The system is unstable. Figure 2.18 provides the bifurcation diagram of the unemployment rate with $m(11 < m < 17)$ as the bifurcation parameter and the following specified values of the parameters and the initial conditions:

$$\begin{gathered}
\alpha_1 = -1.14, \quad \alpha_2 = 5.52, \quad \alpha_3 = 3.68, \\
a = 1, \quad b = 0.1, \quad c = 0, \\
\pi(0) = 0.5, \quad \pi^e(0) = 11, \quad u(0) = 0.8797.
\end{gathered}$$

The figure gives a typical route to chaos. As m increases, a period-2 limit cycle emerges. As the growth rate of money is further increased, a period-4

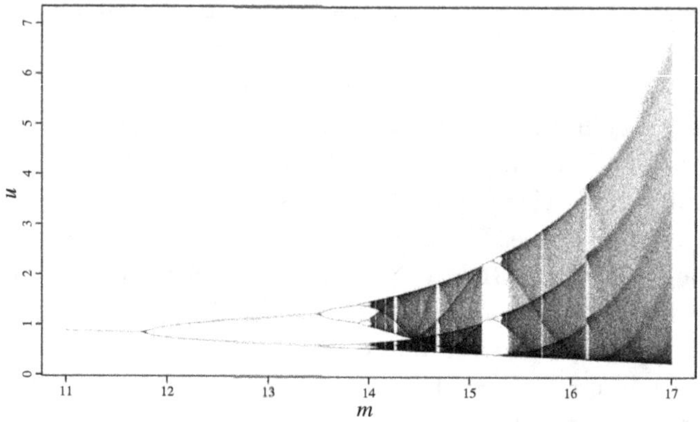

Fig. 2.18. Chaos with m as the bifurcation parameter.

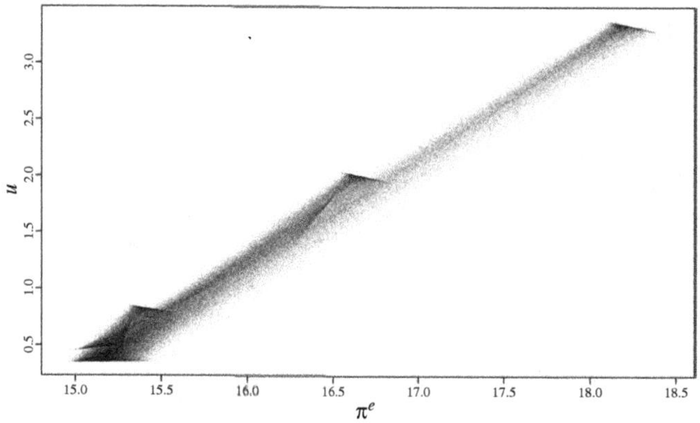

Fig. 2.19. Strange attractor in u and π^e with $m = 16$.

limit cycle appears. The cascade of bifurcations continues to increase until chaotic dynamic equilibrium. Figure 2.19 plots the behavior at $m = 16$.

Guevara and Escot applied the Taylor rule to control chaos. In this case, the Taylor rule is taken on as follows:

$$m_t = \bar{m} - k_1(\pi_t^e - \pi^*) - k_2(u_t - u^*),$$

where $\bar{m}$, k_1 and k_2 are non-negative parameters and π^* and u^* are respectively the objectives of expected inflation and unemployment. Applying chaos control mathematical methods, they specify

$$m_t = 16 - 0.07176911(\pi_t^e - 16) - 23.1343(u_t - 0.6960655).$$

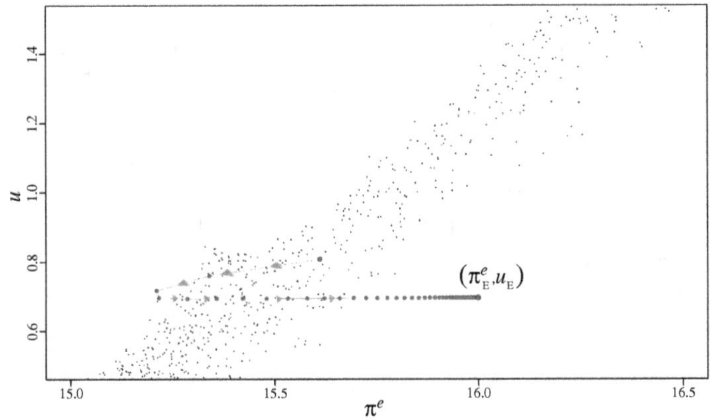

Fig. 2.20. Controlling strange attractors with the Taylor rule.

As Figure 2.20 demonstrated in Figure 2.20 — which is the same as in Figure 2.19 before the government applies the Taylor rule from $t = 400$ — the government can achieve its long-term goals as shown in the trajectory in red which moves towards the targeted points π^* and u^*

2.8 A Financial Dynamic Model with Delay

Finance is a typical field characterized by unpredictability. If finance market is predictable, one might wonder about economic meaning and sustainability of capitalist financial markets. Its unpredictability is the condition for its sustainability, like many games in life, such as gender games and football games. This section introduces a relatively simple model for financial markets examined by Ding *et al.* (2012). The study shows internal structures of a nonlinear financial system by introducing delays in the financial market models in Ma and Chen (2001a, 2001b). Delays in dynamical systems are well examined in fields like ecology and biology (e.g., Hadeler and Ruan, 2007; Su *et al.*, 2009; Zuo and Wei, 2011). Financial markets are described by motion of three variables: the interest rate $x(t)$ the investment demand $y(t)$ and the price index $z(t)$ They model the financial market with the following differential equations with delay:

$$\dot{x} = z + (y - a)x,$$
$$\dot{y} = 1 - by - x^2 + K(y(t) - y(t - \tau)),$$
$$\dot{z} = -x - cz, \; a, b, c > 0,$$

where a is the savings, b is the cost per investment, and c is the elasticity of demand of commercial market. The change in x is dependent on the surplus between investment and savings and the price. The investment demand varies according to the rate of investment, the cost of investment, and interest rate. The difference between $y(t)$ and $y(t-\tau)$ measures the impact of the time delay τ on the change rate of investment demand. The parameter K measures the effect strength. The price changes owing to the contradiction between supply and demand in commercial market and the interest rate. It should be noted that Chen [2008] studied a more general model as follows:

$$\begin{aligned}
\dot{x} &= z + (y-a)x + k_1(x(t) - x(t-\tau_1)),\\
\dot{y} &= 1 - by - x^2 + k_2(y(t) - y(t-\tau_2)),\\
\dot{z} &= -x - cz + k_3(z(t) - z(t-\tau_3)).
\end{aligned}$$

When there is no time delay, the system is well examined in the literature. For instance, its behavior is chaotic when $a = 0.9, b = 0.2$ and $c = 1.2$ (Figure 2.21). The figure is cited from Rao (2019).

In their numerical examples, Ding *et al.* introduce two perturbation parameters

$$\mu_1 = a - \frac{c-b}{bc}, \quad \mu_2 = \tau - \tau_0,$$

where τ_0 is a value of τ determined by the equilibrium conditions. The parameters are taken on as follows:

$$a = \frac{100}{11}, \quad b = 0.1, \quad c = 1.1, \quad K = 1.$$

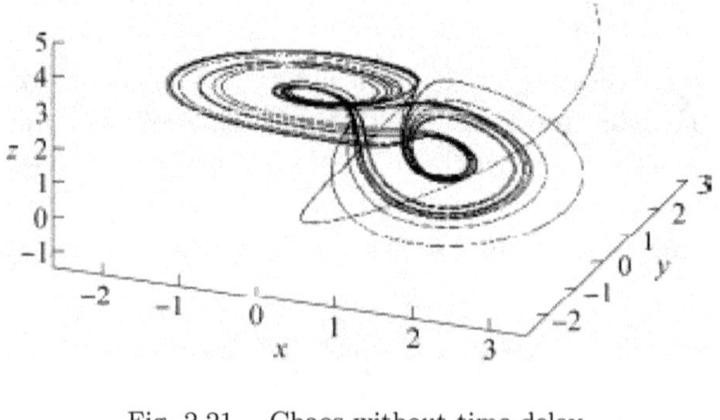

Fig. 2.21. Chaos without time delay.

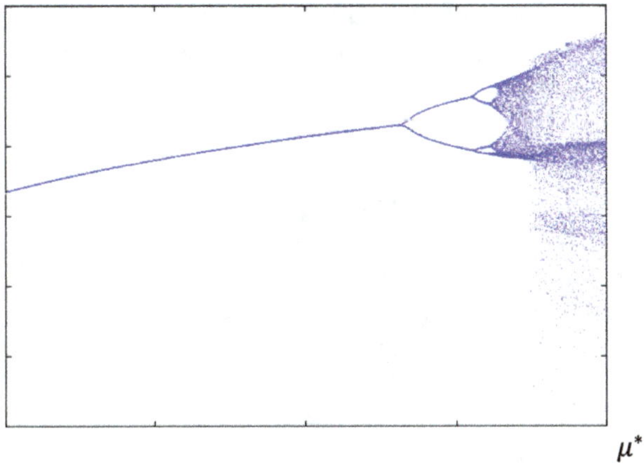

Fig. 2.22. The bifurcation diagram for $0.01 \le \mu^* \le 0.03$.

It is calculated that $\tau_0 = 1.0347$. Define a bifurcation parameter $\mu^* = -\mu_1 = -\mu_2$ Figure 2.22 displays the bifurcation diagram for $0.01 \le \mu^* \le 0.03$. The figure displays a series of period-doubling bifurcations before the system becomes chaotic.

2.9 Stock Markets with Heterogeneous Agents

Henrik Ibsen portrayed: "These heroes of finance are like beads on a string; when one slips off, all the rest follows." In the study of finance, it is commonly assumed that asset prices are determined through market interaction of utility-maximizing agents with rational or irrational expectations. It is observed that returns are related to a variety of factors, such as technology, firm size, leverage, the book value of equity, intangible assets, and the earnings/price ratio. There are studies which take account into irrational elements or the boundedly rational behavior (e.g., Day and Huang, 1990; Chiarella, 1992; Brock and Hommes, 1998; Lux, 1998). This section introduces a model by Agliari *et al.* (2018) who deal with a stock market entry model in which participation depends on an attractiveness measure related to market activity and the fundamental value of the market.

The stock market under consideration has a market maker who mediates transactions in the market by setting the stock price P_t from period to period according to the total excess demand. The market consists of market participants who behave as fundamentalists or contrarians. Let N and

n_t $(1 < n_t < 0)$ represent the total fixed number of investors and the fraction who participate in the market. Let D_t^F and D_t^C stand for the excess demand. The price setting is supposed to be described by

$$P_{t+1} = P_t + \gamma n_t N(\omega_t^F D_t^F + (1 - \omega_t^F) D_t^C),$$

where γ is the appositive parameter measuring the speed of price adjustment and ω_t^F is the proportion of the market participants who behave as fundamentalist and $(1 - \omega_t^F)$ as contrarians.

It is assumed that for the fundamentalists, the stock price converges towards its fundamental value. Orders are placed by the fundamentals

$$D_t^F = g^F(F - P_t),$$

where g^F is the reaction parameter and F is the fundamental value. Contrarians optimistically buy and pessimistically sell. Their orders are given by

$$D_t^C = g^C(P_t - F),$$

where g^C is the reaction parameter. The share of market participants is assumed

$$n_t = \frac{1}{1 + e^{-\lambda A_{t-1}}}, \quad 0 \leq \lambda < +\infty,$$

where λ is the investors' intensity of choice and A_{t-1} is the attractiveness of the market in period $t - 1$ which is defined as follows:

$$A_{t-1} = \alpha \left(\frac{\bar{D}}{P_{t-1}} - r \right) + \beta \left(\frac{P_{t-1} - P_{t-2}}{P_{t-2}} \right),$$

where α and β are positive parameters, $\bar{D}$ is the stock market's constant average dividend payments, and r reflects the return of a risk-free asset. The first bracket measures the stock market's fundamental gain potential from an investment in a risk-free asset. The second bracket measures the speculative gain potential of the stock market.

The fitness functions for two groups are defined respectively as follows:

$$\pi_t^k = D_{t-1}^k (P_t - P_{t-1}), \quad k = F, C,$$

which may be considered as "realized net profit" of each group. The fractions of each group in the population are modeled by the logit model probabilities:

$$\omega_t^k = \frac{e^{h\pi_t^k}}{e^{h\pi_t^F} + e^{h\pi_t^D}}, \quad k = F, C,$$

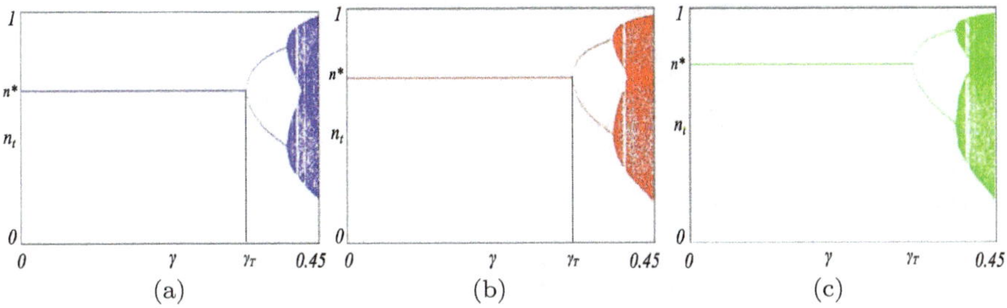

Fig. 2.23. The bifurcation diagram with γ as the bifurcation parameter. (a) $\lambda = 1$, (b) $\lambda = 1.5$, and (c) $\lambda = 2$.

where h is a non-negative parameter measuring how quickly agents switch between the two strategies. If $h = 0$, agents make no switching. If $h \to +\infty$, all agents immediately switch to the best strategy.

We have thus described the model. It can be shown that the system is given by the map with (P_t, n_t) For numerical simulation, some parameters are fixed as follows:

$$\alpha = 2.1, \quad \beta = 15, \quad D = 1, \quad F = 3, \quad r = 0.01, \quad N = 100, \quad g_F = 0.5,$$
$$g_C = 0.3.$$

Figure 2.23 illustrates a few cases of nonlinear behavior in the case of a fixed fraction by Agliari *et al.* For different values of λ the bifurcation diagrams use γ as the bifurcation parameter. The system displays chaos.

Figure 2.24 describes the motion of (P_t, n_t) and (t, P_t) for $\lambda = 1$ with a few selected values of γ.

2.10 Rent and Speculations in Housing Market

Housing and financial markets attract the attention of various people for different purposes in a contemporary world. Owing to their speculative and unstable nature and their influences on the economy and welfare of people, governments apply various policies to control these markets directly or indirectly. The previous sections introduced a few models of financial markets within which chaos appears under certain conditions. This section introduces a housing market model with rent control proposed by Schmitt and Westerhof (2022). In this approach, homebuyers are assumed to be boundedly rational and able to form expectations with learning. They can switch between extrapolative and regressive expectation rules under the

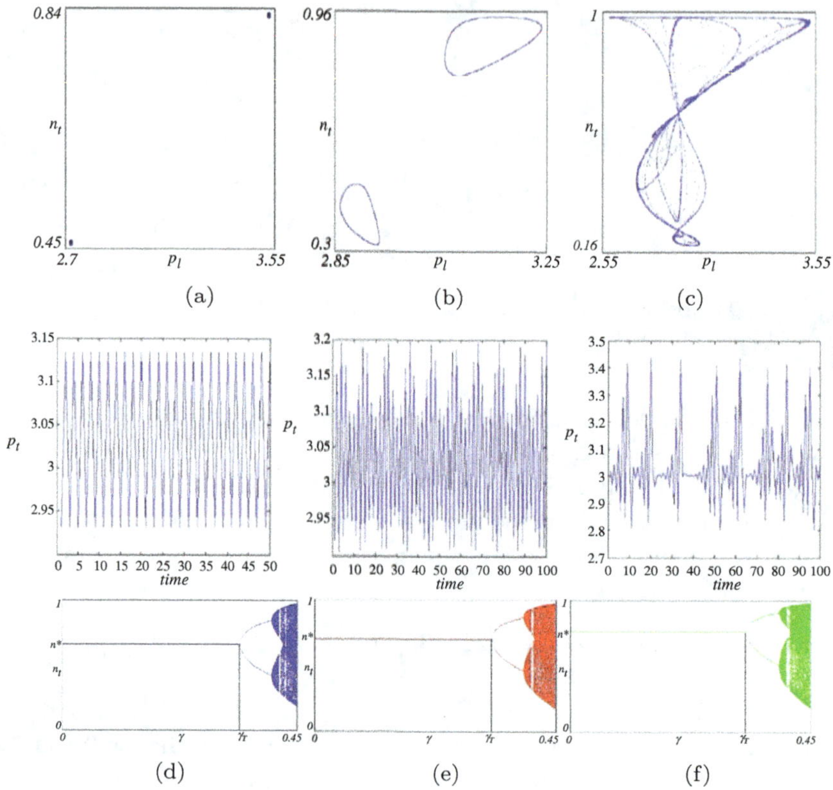

Fig. 2.24. Motion of the system bifurcated from cycles to chaos. (a) stable 2-cycle, $\gamma = 0.35$, (b) a pair of closed curves, $\gamma = 0.4$, (c) chaotic attractor, $\gamma = 0.45$, (d) $\gamma = 0.35$, (e) $\gamma = 0.35$, and (f) $\gamma = 0.35$.

influences of their past forecasting accuracy. Policymakers may use rent control to affect the rent level.

The modeling framework is for an unregulated housing market with a single price, P_t of houses which is determined by an intertemporal no-arbitrage condition and rent payments. The price is supposed to be equal to the discounted value of the next period's expected house price and rent payments. Homebuyers apply extrapolative rule which is free, and regressive expectation rule which is costly, in forming their expectations. These expectation rules are weighed by their evolutionary fitness. A rise in housing stock which is changeable due to depreciation and construction lowers the rent level. We use $E_t[P_{t+1}]$ and R_t to stand for the next period's expected house price and rent payment due at the end of the period, respectively. The house price in period P_t is determined by

$$P_t = \frac{R_t + E_t[P_{t+1}]}{1 + r + \delta}$$

where $r > 1$ stands for the risk-free interest rate and δ is the housing depreciation. The equation means that risk-neutral homebuyers are indifferent between investing their wealth in a safe asset. Schmitt and Westerhof assume that homebuyers can choose between an extrapolative expectation and a regressive expectation rule. Homebuyers' price expectations are

$$E_t[P_{t+1}] = W_t^E E_t^E[P_{t+1}] + W_t^R E_t^R[P_{t+1}],$$

where $E_t^E[P_{t+1}]$ and $E_t^R[P_{t+1}]$ are predictions generated by the extrapolative and the regressive expectation rule, respectively, and W_t^E and W_t^R are their corresponding weights.

The extrapolative expectation rule assumes that the current house price trend will continue in the following way:

$$E_t^E[P_{t+1}] = P_{t-1} + \eta \arctan\left[\frac{\chi}{\eta}(P_{t-1} - P_{t-2})\right],$$

where $\eta = 2\kappa/\pi > 0$ and $\chi > 0$ measure homebuyers' extrapolation strength. The function arctan is S-shaped, implying homebuyers' tendency to react more cautiously to large house price changes. The regressive expectation rule is specified as

$$E_t^R[P_{t+1}] = P_{t-1} + \theta \arctan\left[\frac{\phi}{\theta}(F - P_{t-1})\right],$$

where F is the fundamental house price perceived by homebuyers, $\theta = 2\lambda/\pi > 0$, and $\leq \phi \leq 1$, which measure homebuyers' expected mean reversion speed. The evolutionary fitness of expectation rules is negatively related to squared prediction errors and possible costs arising from their use:

$$A_t^E[P_{t+1}] = -\mu(P_{t-1} - E_{t-2}^E[P_{t-1}])^2,$$
$$A_t^R[P_{t+1}] = -\mu(P_{t-1} - E_{t-2}^R[P_{t-1}])^2 - \sigma,$$

where μ measures the sensitivity with regard to the past forecasting accuracy and σ is interpreted as costs for getting information about F. The weights of the two expectation rules are modeled by the exponential replicator dynamic approach:

$$W_t^E = \frac{W_{t-1}^E \exp[\varepsilon A_t^E]}{W_{t-1}^E \exp[\varepsilon A_t^E] + W_{t-1}^R \exp[\varepsilon A_t^R]},$$

$$W_t^R = \frac{W_{t-1}^R \exp[\varepsilon A_t^R]}{W_{t-1}^E \exp[\varepsilon A_t^E] + W_{t-1}^R \exp[\varepsilon A_t^R]},$$

where $\varepsilon > 0$ measures homebuyers' intensity of choice.

Under the government's influence, the rent level evolves

$$R_t = (1-\tau)R^G + \tau(\alpha - \beta H_t), \quad \alpha\beta > 0,$$

where $\leq \tau \leq 1$ measures the relative weights, R^G is the policymakers' target level, and $\alpha - \beta H_t$ is a market-demand function which reflects that the rent level tends to become higher if the stock is lower. The housing market and investment I_t in the market change according to

$$H_t = I_t + (1 - \delta H_{t-1})$$

$$I_t = \gamma P_{t-1}$$

The model construction is completed. Introducing the auxiliary variables

$$X_t = P_{t-1}, \quad Y_t = X_{t-1}, \quad Z_t = Y_{t-1}.$$

It is straightforward to show that the system is expressed by a six-dimensional map with variables P_t, X_t, Y_t, Z_t, H_t and W_t^E We now show some numerical simulation results by Schmitt and Westerhof. Figure 2.25 shows bifurcation diagrams of house prices with homebuyers' extrapolation χ as the bifurcation parameter under the following specifications of the other parameter values:

$$\alpha = 20, \quad \beta = 0.1, \quad \gamma = 0.05, \quad \delta = 0.05,$$

$$r = 0.05, \quad R_G = 10.1,$$

$$\tau = 0.2, \quad \kappa = 10, \quad \phi = 0.25, \quad \lambda = 10,$$

$$F = 100, \quad \mu = 1, \quad \sigma = 1, \quad \varepsilon = 1.$$

2.11 A Generalized Neoclassical General Equilibrium Theory with Tobin's Model and the Taylor Rule

Milton Friedman once commented: "Inflation is taxation without legislation." But Friedman has neither a proper analytical framework nor an

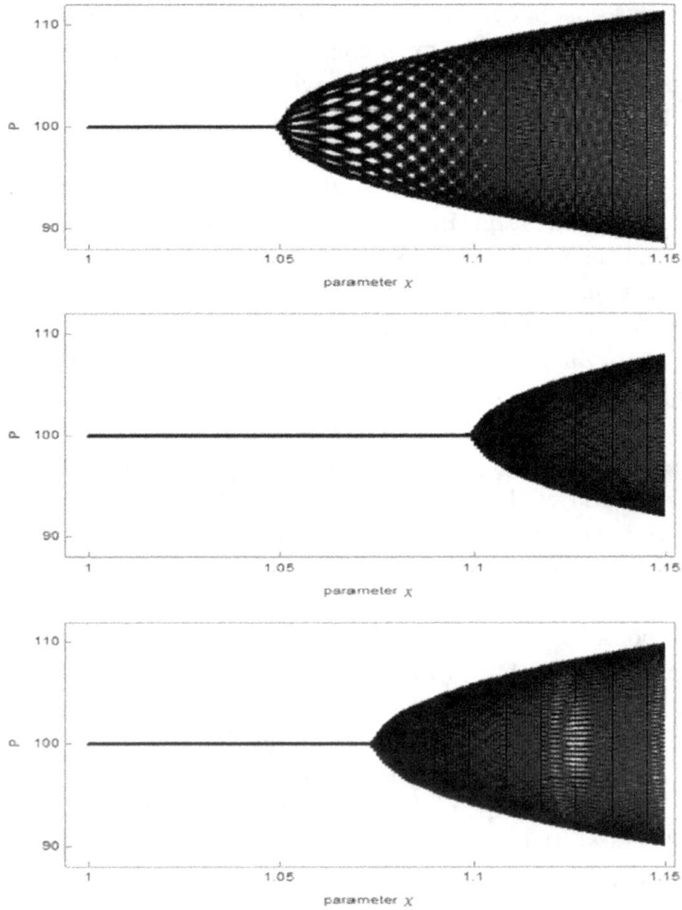

Fig. 2.25. Bifurcation diagrams of P with χ as the bifurcation parameter.

analytical tool for analyzing how the government, for instance, "steals" common people's money and re-distributes the money to them without harming rich people. This section introduces Zhang's monetary growth model with the Taylor rule by allowing all constant parameters to be time-dependent parameters (Zhang, 2020b). The model is an integration of the Solow model, the Tobin growth money with money, and the Taylor rule. This section illustrates the effects of different time-dependent exogenous periodic shocks on the monetary growth economy. It is not an easy matter to build a comprehensive model with monetary and real variables on the basis of microeconomic foundation. Tobin (1965) first proposed a formal monetary growth model by extending the Solow growth model (Solow, 1956). The Tobin growth model deals with an economy with the outside money printed by the government. Money and real capital are included in the portfolios of agents. Modeling of multiple portfolios, such as money, capital, bond, golden, and land, is difficult in theoretical economics on microeconomic foundation. In fact, Tobin failed to develop his model with an acceptable microeconomic foundation. A generalization of the Tobin model is the money in utility (MIU) function approach. Money is introduced into utility function (e.g., Patinkin, 1965; Sidrauski, 1967; Friedman, 1969; Handa, 2009). Zhang (2020b) first introduced the Taylor rule to the Solow–Tobin growth model. The Taylor rule is a well-applied assumption about how central banks determine nominal interests, based on economic conditions (e.g., Meng and Yip, 2004; Schmitt-Grohe and Uribe, 2009). The rule was proposed by Taylor (1993) and Henderson and McKibbin (1993) to deal with issues related to price stability.

We have an economy with homogenous households, one production sector (the same as in the Solow model; Solow, 1956), and government. The number of households at time t is denoted by $N(t)$ The role of government is like that in the Tobin growth model with money (e.g., Tobin, 1965; Nagatani, 1970) except about how to model money supply and demand. Capital and labor are used as inputs in production. We introduce money to utility function but neglect its possible role in production. All markets are perfectly competitive. There are three assets. They are respectively money, bond, and capital. Bond is issued by the government. Three assets are held by households. The nominal bonds pay the (positive) nominal interest rate $R(t)$.The rate is given by the Taylor rule. We use $P(t)$ to stand for the nominal price and $\pi(t)$ for the inflation rate. We have $\pi(t) = \dot{P}(t)/P(t)$ The total labor supply $N(t)$ is given by $N(t) = T(t)\bar{N}(t)$, where $T(t)$ is the work time of the representative household.

The sector's production function is taken on the following Cobb–Douglas form:

$$F(t) = A(t)K^{\alpha(t)}(t)N^{\beta(t)}(t), \alpha(t), \beta(t) > 0, \alpha(t) + \beta(t) = 1,$$

where $A(t)\alpha(t)$ and $\beta(t)$ are time-dependent. Each firm is faced with a market-determined rate of interest $r(t)$ and real wage rate $w(t)$ The marginal conditions of the industry are given by

$$r(t) + \delta_k(t) = \frac{\alpha(t)F(t)}{K(t)}, \quad w(t) = \frac{\beta(t)F(t)}{N(t)},$$

where $\delta_k(t)$ is the time-dependent depreciation rate of capital and $r(t) \equiv R(t) - \pi(t)$.

The nominal government bond held by the household is denoted by $B(t)$ The household holds money $M(t)$ The government applies the real lump-sum tax $\bar{\tau}(t)$ The household current income is

$$y(t) = r(t)(\bar{k}(t) + b(t)) + T(t)w(t) - \frac{\dot{B}(t)}{P(t)} - \frac{\dot{M}(t)}{P(t)} - \pi(t)m(t) - \bar{\tau}(t).$$

where $r(t)\bar{k}(t)$ is the interest payment, $T(t)w(t)$ is the wage payments, $\pi(t)m(t)$ is the cost of holding money, and

$$m(t) \equiv \frac{M(t)}{P(t)}, \quad b(t) \equiv \frac{B(t)}{P(t)}$$

We use $a(t)$ to stand for the total value of wealth of the representative household. That is

$$a(t) \equiv \bar{k}(t) + b(t) + m(t)$$

The disposable income is $\hat{y}(t) = a(t) + y(t)$ We use $\bar{T}(t)$ to represent the leisure time spent on leisure and T_0 the (fixed) total available time. We have

$$\hat{y}(t) = \bar{y}(t) + m(t) - \bar{T}(t)w(t) - \pi(t)m(t),$$

where

$$\bar{y}(t) \equiv (1 + r(t))(\bar{k}(t) + b(t)) + T_0 w(t) - \frac{\dot{B}(t)}{P(t)} - \frac{\dot{M}(t)}{P(t)} - \bar{\tau}(t).$$

The utility function is specified as follows:

$$U(t) = \bar{T}^{\sigma_0(t)}(t) m^{\varepsilon_0(t)}(t) c^{\xi_0(t)}(t) s^{\lambda_0(t)}(t),$$

$$\sigma_0(t)\varepsilon_0(t)\xi_0(t)\lambda_0(t) > 0.$$

where the propensity to enjoy leisure time is denoted by $\sigma_0(t)$, the propensity to hold money by $\varepsilon_0(t)$, the propensity to consume by $\xi_0(t)$, and the propensity to own wealth by $\lambda_0(t)$. Applications of this utility function to different economic issues are referred to Zhang (2005, 2008). As the disposable income is distributed to holding money, savings, and consumption, we have $(1 + R(t))m(t) + c(t) + s(t) = \hat{y}(t)$. This equation implies

$$w(t)\bar{T}(t) + \bar{\pi}(t)m(t) + c(t) + s(t) = \bar{y}(t),$$

where $\bar{\pi}(t) \equiv \pi(t) + R(t)$.

2.12 Optimal Behavior

The consumer problem is to choose current money, leisure time, consumption, and savings so that the utility is maximized. We maximize $U(t)$ to obtain the first-order conditions:

$$w(t)\bar{T}(t) = \sigma\bar{y}(t), \quad \bar{\pi}(t)m(t) = \varepsilon\bar{y}(t), \quad c(t) = \xi\bar{y}(t), \quad s(t) = \lambda\bar{y}(t),$$

where

$$\sigma \equiv \rho\sigma_0, \quad \varepsilon \equiv \rho\varepsilon_0, \quad \xi \equiv \rho\xi_0, \quad \lambda \equiv \rho\lambda_0, \quad \rho \equiv \frac{1}{\varepsilon_0 + \xi_0 + \lambda_0 + \sigma_0}.$$

We have the change as savings minus dissavings:

$$\dot{a}(t) = s(t) - a(t).$$

The original Taylor rule (Taylor, 1993) is

$$R(t) = \pi(t) + r^*(t) + 0.5(\pi(t) - \pi^*(t)) + 0.5(y(t) - y^*(t)),$$

where is $r^*(t)$ an exogenous given real interest rate, $\pi^*(t)$ is an exogenous (desired) inflation rate, $y(t)$ is the logarithm of real GDP, and $y^*(t)$ is the logarithm of an exogenous potential real GDP. The rule tells that the central bank enhances the interest rate to lower inflationary pressure when output is higher than its full-employment level or inflation is higher than its target. Instead of the original Taylor rule, this study specifies the authority's interest rate feedback rule: $R(t) = R(\pi(t), t) \geq 0$.The policy is active (passive) at an inflation rate π if $R'(\pi) > (<)1$. In particular, we generalize the rule suggested by Benhabib *et al.* (2001):

$$R(t) = q_0(t)e^{q(t)(\pi(t) - \pi^*(t))}, q_0(t), q(t), \pi^*(t) > 0,$$

in which q_0, q, and π^* are invariant in time in Benhabib *et al.* but are time-dependent in our study. Let $M(t)$ and $B(t)$ stand for, respectively, the money and the nominal bonds. The bonds of the government are paid with the nominal interest rate. The flow budget constraint of the government is

$$\dot{B}(t) = R(t)B(t) - \dot{M}(t) - P(t)\bar{\tau}(t).$$

We have thus built the model. It should be noted that it is straightforward to prove that we can simulate the model when all the parameters are time-dependent. For simplicity, let the parameters take on the following constant values:

$$\bar{N} = 50, \quad T_0 = 24, \quad \alpha = 0.33, \quad A = 1.5, \quad \pi^* = 0.01,$$

$$\bar{\tau} = 1, \quad \lambda_0 = 0.6, \quad \xi_0 = 0.1, \quad \sigma_0 = 0.18,$$

$$\varepsilon_0 = 0.005, \quad q_0 = 0.01, \quad q = 150, \quad \delta_k = 0.03.$$

The unique equilibrium point is identified as follows:

$$F = 846.1, \quad N = 362, \quad K = 3897.5, \quad R = 0.201, \quad r = 0.171,$$

$$\pi = 0.03, \quad w = 1.57, \quad m = 3.16, \quad b = 6.4,$$

$$\bar{k} = 78, \quad a = 87.5, \quad c = 14.6, \quad T = 7.24.$$

It is checked that the equilibrium point has two eigenvalues: $\{0.349, -0.234\}$ The saddle point implies that simulation is effective generally for short run. The initial conditions are as follows: $\bar{k}(0) = 77$, $\pi(0) = 0.029$. We plot the movement of the economy in Figure 2.26.

We now simulate the impact of the following oscillatory perturbations in the targeted inflation rate on the movement of the system: $\pi_0(t) = 0.01 + 0.05\sin(t)$ Figure 2.27 gives the simulation results t. The values in Figure 2.27 stand for the change rate in terms of percentage due to the parameter change with regard to the variable values in Figure 2.25. It should be noted that in the plot we use $b(t)$ to stand for the change in the amount of $b(t)$ The variable $b(t)$ passed zero before the change in the parameter, which implies infinite change rate at the point. The nominal rate of interest is oscillatory in the same period as the exogenous shock. The national labor supply and capital stock oscillate but not with the same period as the exogenous shock. This also explains why the national output does not have the same period as the exogenous shock. We see that all the variables oscillate with the exogenous periodic perturbations. We thus

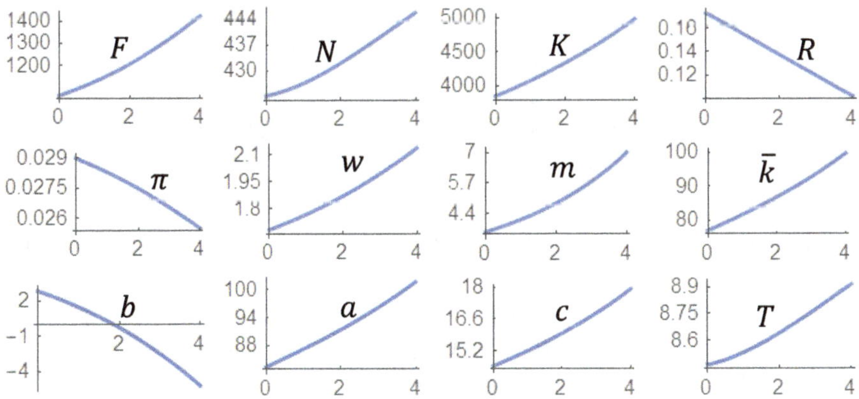

Fig. 2.26. The motion of the system with wealth and money.

Note: Horizontal axis: time; vertical axis: variable values.

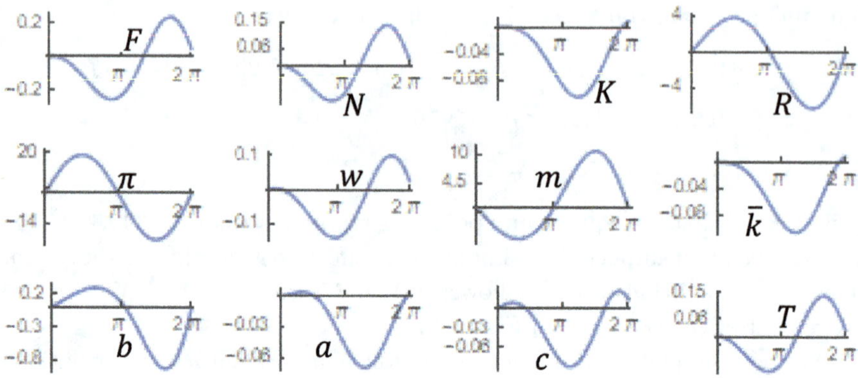

Fig. 2.27. Oscillatory perturbations in the targeted inflation rate.
Note: Horizontal axis: time; vertical axis: the changes of the variable values in percentage.

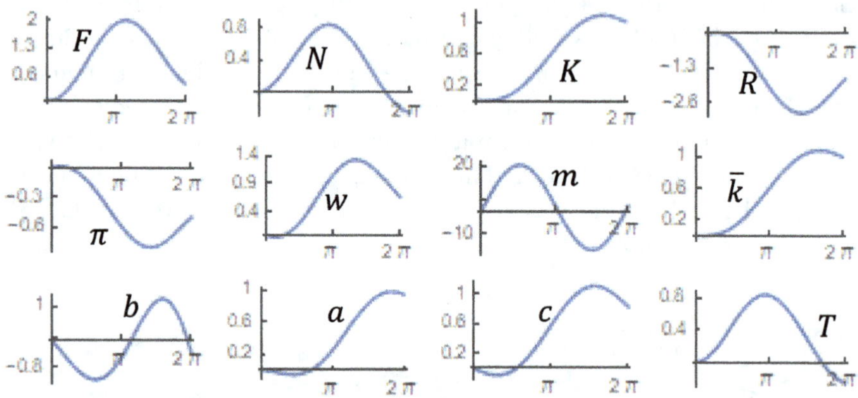

Fig. 2.28. Oscillatory perturbations in the propensity to hold money.
Note: Horizontal axis: time; vertical axis: the changes of the variable values in percentage.

conclude that the government can affect the performances of real economies by varying the targeted inflation rate.

We now simulate the impact of the following oscillatory perturbations in the propensity to hold money on the movement of the system: $\epsilon_0(t) = 0.005 + 0.001\sin(t)$ Figure 2.28 gives the simulation results. As the propensity experiences the exogenous shocks, the variables oscillate.

Chapter 3

Complexity of Economics with Capital and Wealth

Muhammad Yunus received the Nobel Peace Prize for "efforts through microcredit to create economic and social development from below" as evaluated by the Norwegian Nobel Committee. He had a faith in his own saying: "Poverty is unnecessary." The reality is that some religious or socialist state produces poverty but owing to different mechanisms. The world has given him much trust as faith is a decent will for maximizing the total welfare of humanity. Nevertheless, no properly educated economist can have such a solidified faith since Malthus warned of another possibility for mankind. Life is always full of chaos. It is not India which has mastered the English language, a group of excellent elites, and many elements of modern civilization, but China that has made the greatest achievement in escaping from poverty, led by the people who had received almost no higher education and known almost nothing about modern economics. China's economic miracle from the late 1970s tells a common sense: one can handle chaos also through faith or through ignorance. Moreover, chaos does not only imply destruction but also incubates creation. The blind faith in traditional rational economics has led human societies to suffer one disaster to another. The economic history records that neither successful Western economies nor successful East Asian economies have faithfully followed any single economic thinker. With regard to Yunus' actual achievements and validity of his approach, professionals' evaluations have been "chaotic." The will is one thing, but rational consequence is another. There is an iron law of economics, and spiritual heaven of free will — if free will exists at all. Human history has witnessed plenty of micro good wills and macro tragedies. Complexity theory shows how intricate macroeconomic consequences could be resulted from the interdependence of a few strong good wills plus a bit of human evils. This chapter uses a few theoretical models with wealth to address issues related to the complexity of economic growth. Section 3.1 applies an approach based on Ros (2000) to demonstrate a poverty trap in an extended Solow model. The model has two equilibria: a Solow-type and an unstable steady state at the level of the capital stock comparable with subsistence consumption. Section 3.2 studies the extended IS-LM model by Ma *et al.* (2017) which exhibits Hopf bifurcation. Section 3.3 shows the existence of chaos in the Keynesian dynamic model with capital accumulation and debts recently developed by Asada *et al.* (2019). Section 3.4 shows endogenous oscillations of debts in a model proposed by Matsuyama (2013). In Section 3.5, we deal with the disequilibrium macrodynamic model by Sasaki (2013). The model incorporates the three important economic mechanisms for approaching modern capitalist economies: ideas on interactions between the rate of employment and income by Goodwin, investment function by Kalecki, and the reserve-army and reserve-army-creation effects by Marx. Section 3.6 demonstrates oscillations in the reformed Solow model with two delays by Guerrini *et al.* (2019). Section 3.7 shows nonlinear phenomena in the reformed Kaldor–Kalecki growth model with capital stock's anticipation and investment lag analyzed by Liu *et al.* (2015) to show that can lead to the emergence of business cycles. Section 3.8 represents a generalized neoclassical general equilibrium theory with monopolistic and perfect competition with exogenous shocks.

3.1 Poverty Traps in an Extended Solow Model

The Solow model — fairly the Solow–Swan model — is the basic model of the basic models in neoclassical growth theory (Solow, 1956; Swan, 1956). It provides the first growth model which has still been taught in all traditionary courses in economic growth theory. There is obviously a strict assumption in the Solow model. The savings rate is fixed. Common sense tells us that savings rates vary across households as well as countries. Solow (1999) pointed out that if one is only concerned with an endogenous savings rate, it is easy to generalize the traditional model. We may consider savings rate $\hat{s}$ as a function of capital per capita $\hat{s}(k)$. In an article on transitional dynamics in the neoclassical framework, King and Rebelo (1993) used a utility function in which there is a subsistence level of per capita consumption, and the elasticity of intertemporal substitution varies over time. The model has two equilibria: a Solow-type and an unstable steady state at the level of the capital stock comparable with subsistence consumption. King and Rebelo assume that the savings rate is hump-shaped as a function of capital–labor ratio. This occurs because the elasticity of substitution rises as output increases. At low levels, savings rate rises as output increases. As the economy becomes mature, the savings rate falls. The model shows that even though the rate of interest falls as output increases, the growth rate of output does not diminish throughout the transition but has a hump-shaped path. The dynamic processes described by the King–Rebelo model can be also found in the older development literature on poverty traps. We now illustrate this approach based on Ros (2000: 60–2). The model starts with a consumption function:

$$c(t) = (y_0 - \delta_k k_0) + \bar{\xi}(y(t) - c_0),$$

where $c(t)$ and $y(t)$ are respectively per capita consumption and per capita income at time t, y_0 is subsistence income per capita, k_0 is the capital–labor ratio consistent with a subsistence level of income, δ_k is the depreciation rate of capital, and $\bar{\xi}(0 < \bar{\xi} < 1)$ is the propensity to consume out of non-subsistence income. When income per worker is at the subsistence level, savings is equal to the depreciation of capital stock, i.e., $y_0 - c = \delta_k k_0$. The corresponding savings rate is

$$\hat{s}(t) = \frac{y(t) - c(t)}{y(t)} = \hat{s}_0 - \frac{\delta^*}{y(t)'}$$

where $\hat{s}_0 \equiv 1 - \bar{\xi} > 0$ and $\delta^* \equiv \hat{s}_0 y_0 - \delta_k k_0$. The new parameter $\hat{s}_0$ is interpreted as the propensity to save out of non-subsistence income. According to the definitions, the parameter δ^* may be either positive or negative. If $\hat{s}_0 y_0 > \delta_k k_0$, δ^* is positive, implying that as income rises, the savings rate rises. If $\hat{s}_0 y_0 < \delta_k k_0$, δ^* is negative, implying that as income rises, the savings rate falls. The savings rate is a nonlinear function of the level of income per capita. The savings rate rises with income per capita if the marginal propensity to consume out of non-subsistence income is less than the average propensity to consume out of subsistence income. Otherwise, the savings rate tends to fall as income rises above the subsistence level. The per-capita output given by the neoclassical technology is denoted by $f(k)$ which equals $y(t)$ The change in per capita is the savings minus the net depreciation of capital:

$$\dot{k} = \hat{s}(t)f(k) - nk - \delta_k k = \hat{s}_0 f(k) - (n + \delta_k)k - \delta^*,$$

where n is the exogenous population growth rate. We call the above model the *generalized Solow model with poverty traps*. We see that if $\delta^* = 0$, the

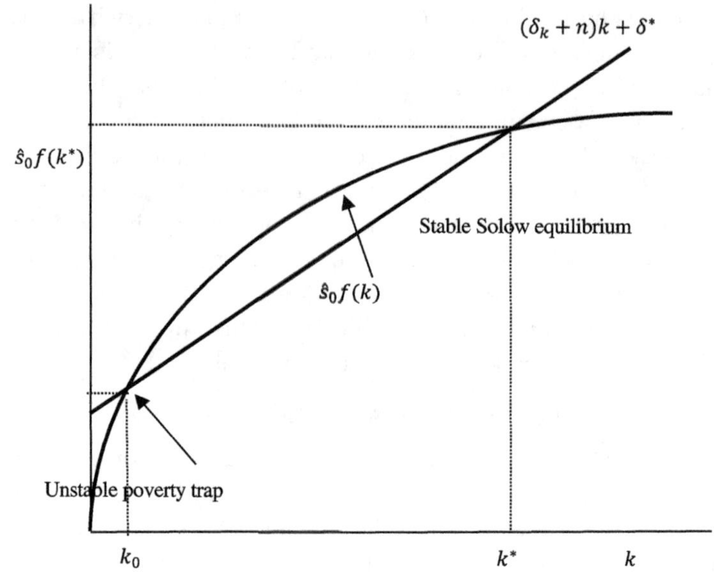

Fig. 3.1. Poverty trap in the extended Solow model.

model has the same structure as the Solow model. There are two steady states: an unstable origin and a stable equilibrium. Unlike the Solow model, where there is a unique value of capital–labor ratio, this model can yield two equilibria as shown in Figure 3.1 when $\delta^* > 0$.

In the case of $\delta^* > 0$, the equilibrium at the high-k level is like the steady state in the Solow model. The other is at the subsistence level of income. This is often referred to as poverty trap, but it is a fortune one in the sense that it is unstable. The economic system will not stay there long. Poverty may not be persistent under proper disturbances from, for instance, foreign aids and trade. This trap occurs because at low levels of capital–labor ratio, income per capita is scarcely sufficient and savings fall below depreciation. If an economy is in this type of poverty, it is easy to start rapid development because once capital–labor ratio is higher than the level k_0, it will grow fast towards a stable equilibrium. Once it reaches a high level of living standard, it is trapped because this is a stable state. The model has only one equilibrium: an unstable poverty when $\delta^* < 0$, i.e., $\hat{s}_0 y_0 < \delta_k k_0$. This situation occurs when the savings rate is too low or the subsistence income per capita is too low. If an economy is characterized by political and social instabilities, then it tends to have a low savings rate.

3.2 Business Cycles in an Extended IS-LM Model

The so-called IS-LM model is commonly included in courses on introduction in economics. Like most basic models in economics, nonlinearized versions of the model can be found in the literature. This section introduces such an extended IS-LM model by Ma *et al.* (2017) which exhibits Hopf bifurcation, or business cycles. Their simulation results confirm that the business cycle is stable within the range of most of the parameters. The stability is important as it implies the sustainability of business cycles, characterizing alternatives of recovery, prosperity, recession, and depression. The model is a combination of the Kaldor model and the traditional IS-LM model. The existence of Hopf bifurcation in the Kaldor model was identified by Zhang (1990).

The model consists of three differential equations:

$$\dot{y}(t) = \alpha(I(t) + g - S(t) - T(t)),$$
$$\dot{r}(t) = \beta(L(t) - m(t)),$$
$$\dot{m}(t) = g - T(t),$$

in which $y(t)$ is the national income, $I(t)$ is the investment, g is the government procurement, national income, $S(t)$ is the savings which is dependent on disposable income $y^D(t)$, $T(t)$ is the tax income, $r(t)$ is the interest rate, $L(t)$ is the actual demand for money, $m(t)$ is the nominal supply of money, and α and β are positive parameters. It is not difficult to interpret economically the model. A key problem in this modeling framework is that the price is fixed. An integration of the traditional monetary growth models and the IS-LM model was provided by Zhang (2021c). I also made prices endogenous and model behavior of households on microeconomic foundation (that is, maximizing utility subject to constraints). For simulation, Ma *et al.* specified the savings and money demand and government behavior functions as follows:

$$I(t) = a\frac{y(t)}{r(t)}, \quad a > 0,$$
$$L(t) = by(t) + \frac{\gamma_1}{\gamma_2 - r(t)}, \quad b, \gamma_1\gamma_2 > 0,$$
$$T(t) = \epsilon y(t), \quad 0 < \epsilon < 1,$$
$$S(t) = s(1-\epsilon)y(t), \quad 0 < s < 1.$$

If γ_2 is very large, the economy is likely to have a liquidity trap, and the demand for money is not sensitive to interest rate. The system is now rewritten as follows:

$$\dot{y}(t) = \alpha \left(a\frac{y(t)}{r(t)} + g - s(1-\epsilon)y(t) - \epsilon y(t) \right),$$
$$\dot{r}(t) = \beta \left(by(t) + \frac{\gamma_1}{\gamma_2 - r(t)} - m(t) \right),$$
$$\dot{m}(t) = g - \epsilon y(t).$$

Choose the parameters and an initial state for simulation as follows:

$$a = 0.37, \quad \alpha = 0.95, \quad \gamma_1 = 1, \quad \gamma_2 = 0.0035, \quad b = 0.0035, \quad g = 30,$$
$$s = 0.25, \quad \epsilon = 0.01, \quad y(0) = 3000, \quad r(0) = 1.494949495,$$
$$m(0) = 11.17229173.$$

Selecting β as the bifurcation parameter, Ma *et al.* numerically demonstrated that Hopf bifurcation occurs at $\beta = 6.385$. The simulation results with β as the bifurcation parameter are plotted in Figure 3.2 in which w is another variable defined as a function of the three variables.

When the value of β is lower than its bifurcation point, the system is unstable. The national economy is in disorder. When the value is much larger than its critical value, the system is convergent. Business cycles appear near the critical value. The original paper also extensively examines the stabilities of business cycles.

3.3 A Keynesian Dynamics with Capital and Debts

This section introduces the Keynesian dynamic model with capital accumulation and debts recently developed by Asada *et al.* (2019). The model neglects international trade. The paper mainly examines the analytical and numerical properties of Asada's Keynesian model (Asasa, 2012, 2014), which describes the development of a firm's real private debt, the real output, the expected rate of inflation, the nominal rate of interest, the government expenditure, and the real government debt. We first describe the model.

Let $D(t)$, $p(t)$ and $K(t)$ denote, respectively, the stock of the representative firm's nominal private debt, price level, and real capital stock. The investment expenditure of private firms which is not internally financed

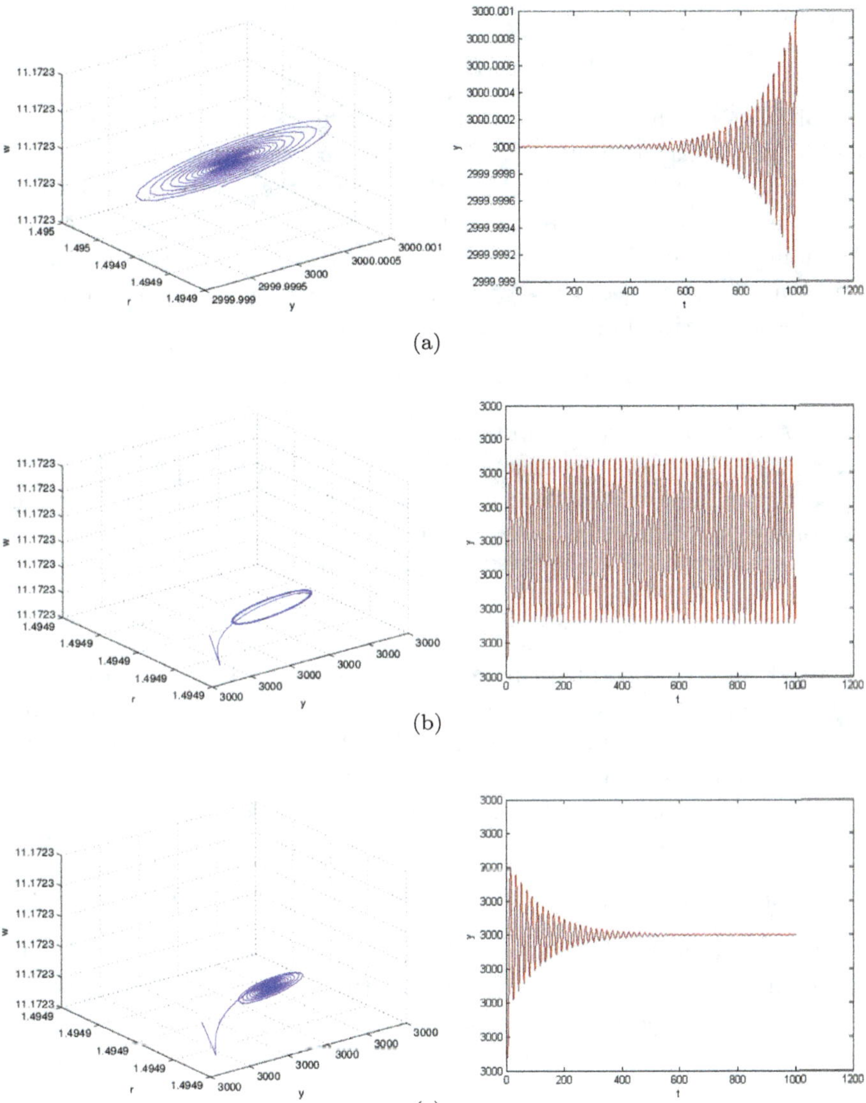

Fig. 3.2. Hopf bifurcation near $\beta = 6.385$. (a) $\beta = 5.8$; (b) $\beta = 6.385$; (c) $\beta = 7$.

must be debt financed by

$$\dot{D} = \Phi(g)pK - s_f(rpK - iD),$$

in which the parameter $s_f(0 < s_f < 1)$ is the firm's internal retention rate, $g \equiv \dot{K}/K\Phi(g)$ is the adjustment cost function of investment, $r = P/K$ is the rate of profit (P being real profit), and i is the rate of interest which is applied to the firm's private debt and is assumed to be dependent on the nominal rate of interest of the government ρ and expected rate of inflation π^e. Introduce $d \equiv D/(pK)$. Taking derivatives of d the above equation is rewritten as

$$\dot{d} = \Phi(g) - s_f(r - id) - (g + \pi)d, \tag{3.3.1}$$

where $\pi \equiv \dot{p}/p$ is the rate of inflation.

We use $Y(t)C(t)$ and $G(t)$ to denote the real output, the total consumption, and real government expenditure, respectively. We introduce the output, consumption, and expenditure per capital stock by $y = Y/K$, $c = C/K$, and $v = G/K$. The motion of y is given by

$$\dot{y} = \alpha(c + \Phi + \mathrm{v} - \mathrm{y}), \quad \alpha > 0, \tag{3.3.2}$$

where α is an adjustment parameter. Equation (3.3.2) expresses the Keynesian quantity adjustment process of the disequilibrium in the goods market. As ΦK is the real investment expenditure including the adjustment, Φ is the real investment per capital stock. The motion of the expected rate of inflation is assumed to follow a mixture of forward-looking and backward-looking inflation expectations:

$$\dot{\pi}^e = \gamma\left[\xi(\bar{\pi} - \pi^e) + (1 - \xi)(\pi - \pi^e)\right], \quad \gamma > 0, \ 0 \le \xi \le 1, \tag{3.3.3}$$

where $\bar{\pi}$ is the targeted rate of inflation set by the central bank and γ and ξ are parameters. If $\xi = 0$, the equation describes a purely adaptive inflation expectation hypothesis. The case of $\xi = 1$ implies that the publics' expected rate of inflation gravitates toward the targeted level. The parameter ξ is called credibility parameter. The rate of interest of the government changes according to

$$\dot{\rho} = \beta_1(\pi - \bar{\pi}) + \beta_2(y - \bar{y}), \quad \beta_1 > 0, \ \beta_2 > 0, \tag{3.3.4}$$

where $\bar{y}$ is the nominal value of output at the natural level of employment. The equation formalizes an interest rate monetary rule by the central bank. It basically illustrates the Taylor rule type of monetary policy.

We use B and T to denote the stock of nominal government bond and real tax. We introduce $b = B/pK$ and $\tau = T/K$. The government expenditure is as follows:

$$\dot{v} = \sigma\left[\theta(\bar{y} - y) + (1-\theta)(\bar{b} - b)\right], \quad \sigma > 0, \ 0 \leq \theta \leq 1, \qquad (3.3.5)$$

where $\bar{b}$ is the target value of b set by the government.

The authors specified some functional forms:

$$\Phi = ag^2 + g, \quad g = \frac{\kappa}{1+e^q}, \quad \beta = \frac{P}{Y}, \quad q = i - e^e - nr,$$
$$i = \rho + md, \quad r = \beta y, \quad \pi = \varepsilon(y - \bar{y}) + \pi^e, \quad \tau = \tau_1 y - T_0,$$
$$c = (1-s_1)[y - r + (1-s_f)r - \tau] + (1-s_2)id + (1-s_3)\rho b,$$

where $a, \kappa, n, m, \varepsilon, s_1, s_2, s_3,\ \tau_1$, and T_0 are parameters. The system is subjected to the following equations:

$$\frac{M}{pK} = \frac{\tilde{m}H}{pK} = \varphi(\rho)y, \; pT + \dot{B} + \dot{H} = pG + \rho B,$$

where $M = \tilde{m}(\rho)H$ is the nominal money stock, H is the high-powered money that is issued by the central bank, and $\tilde{m}(\rho) > 1$ is the money multiplier. It is easy to show that the above two equations lead to the dynamics of b

$$\dot{b} = F(d, y, \pi^e, \rho, v, b). \qquad (3.3.6)$$

We will not give explicitly F as it is a tedious combination of the parameters and functions already introduced. The dynamic system consists of six nonlinear differential equations with six variables. We specified the parameters:

$$\bar{y} = 0.2, \quad \varepsilon = 1, \quad \bar{\pi} = 0.02, \quad \beta = 0.05, \quad \beta_1 = 1, \quad \beta_2 = 0.2,$$
$$\tau_1 = 0.5, \quad T_0 = 0.02, \quad s_1 = 0.22, \quad s_2 = 0.9, \quad s_3 = 0.4, \quad s_f = 0.24,$$
$$m = 0.01, \quad n = 0.2, \quad \kappa = 0.1, \quad a = 0.1, \quad \alpha = 1, \quad \gamma = 10,$$
$$\sigma = 1, \quad \theta = 0.7, \quad \psi = 0.1e^{-\rho}.$$

Figures 3.3 and 3.4 demonstrate endogenous oscillations of the nonlinear economy when $\xi = 0.9\xi_0$, where ξ_0 is a critical value of ξ identified by the simulation.

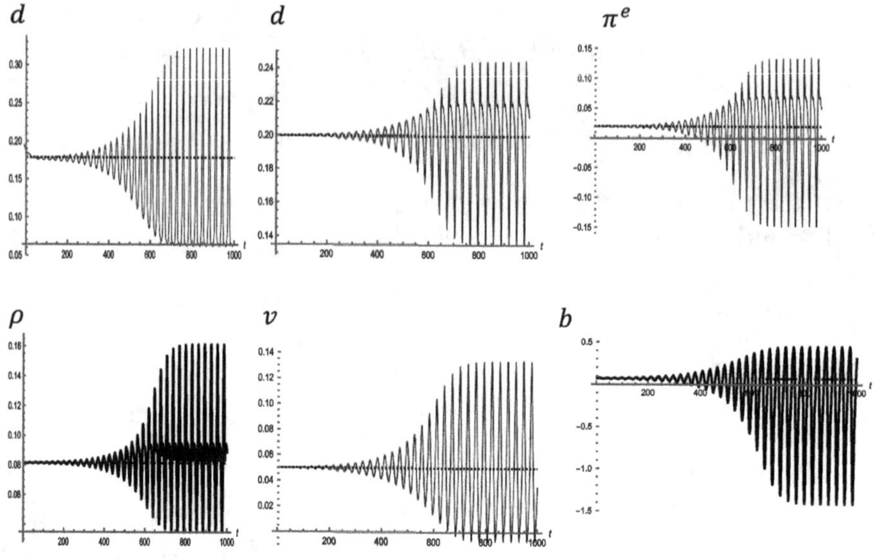

Fig. 3.3. The business cycle in the key variables.

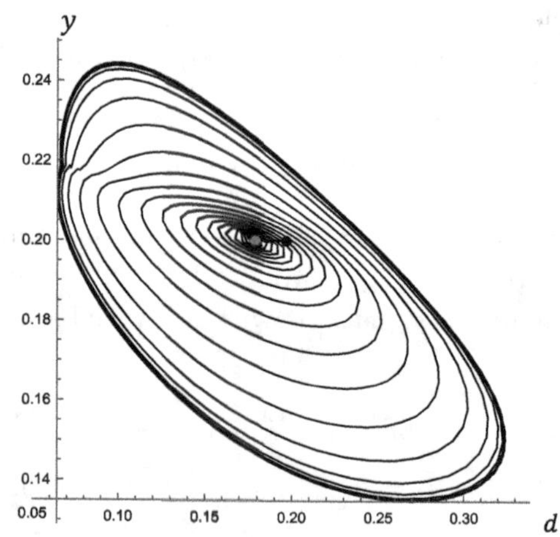

Fig. 3.4. Oscillations in the firm's debt and output.

3.4 Credit Cycles in an Extended Diamond Model

This section shows endogenous oscillations of debts in a model proposed by Matsuyama (2013). The model was reformed and analyzed by Matsuyama *et al.* (2016). This section is based on the 2016 model. Their approach is to explain the observation in macroeconomic research of financial frictions (e.g., Bernanke and Gertler, 1989). In economies with financial frictions, savings does not necessarily flow into effective investment projects. Different phenomena are observed in the literature. When an improved net worth allows more savings to flow into profitable investments, for instance, savings is redirected towards the investments that generate pecuniary externalities, resulting in further improvement of borrower net worth. This mechanism can produce the persistence of a low borrower net worth, leading to a slow recovery and prolonged recessions. Matsuyama *et al.* examine cases that not all the profitable investments have the same demand spillover effects. Some profitable may not improve the net worth of other borrowers. The deterioration of borrower net worth causes macroeconomic instabilities. An easy credit extended to the Bad projects during the boom may thus encourage a subsequent bust — a case of "successes breed crises." Mendoza and Terrones (2008) and others identified "credit booms gone bust." Kindleberger (1996) empirically observed that after a period of expansion, people tend to become more driven by euphoria, greed, and manias which increase those credits to finance tome activities of dubious characters. The current model does not assume any form of irrationality in exploring the existence of credit cycles.

The basic framework follows Diamond's overlapping generations model with two periods of lives ($t = 0, 1, 2 \ldots$). There is one commodity which can be either consumed or invested. The final goods sector uses constant returns to scale technology, $Y_t = F(K_t, L_t)$, where K_t and L_t are capital and labor inputs, respectively. It can also be written in per capita terms: $y_t = f(k_t) = F(k_t, 1)$. It is assumed that physical capital depreciates fully in one period. Perfect competitive market conditions lead to $\rho_{t+1} = f'(k_{t+1})$ and $w_t = f(k_t) - k_t f'(k_t)$. In the numerical examples, the Cobb–Douglas form used $f = Ak_t^\alpha$, $0 < \alpha < 1$. At the beginning of each period, $L_t\,(= 1)$ agents arrive and stay active for two periods: as wage earner when young and consumers when old. At the end of each period, the young agents have w_t aggregate supply of the credit in the economy. In addition to lending to the other agents in the same cohort at the gross rate of return r_t they can choose the Good (projects) and the Bad (projects). The Good projects convert one unit of the final goods at the end of the period into one unit of physical capital available for the next period with net returns ρ_{t+1}. A Bad project transforms m units of the final goods in period t into mB units of the final goods in $t + 1$, where B is the profitability of the Bad projects. Each agent needs to borrow $m - w_t$ to run a project with the rate r_{t+1}. The agents always have options of lending to the others at

r_{t+1} and of investing in the Good projects to earn ρ_{t+1}, which ensures $r_{t+1} = \rho_{t+1}$.

Some young agents may run the Bad projects. They can thus consume $mB - r_{t+1}(m - w_t)$. If they do not run the Bad projects, they consume $r_{t+1}w_t$ Hence, the young agents will run the Bad projects if and only if $B \geq r_{t+1}$ which is called the profitability constraint (PC) for the Bad projects. Even if PC holds, the agents may be unable to invest in the Bad projects owing to the borrowing constraint, which is given by $\mu mB\,(0 < \mu < 1)$. The lender would lend only up to $\mu mB/r_{t+1}$. The agents can thus borrow to run the Bad projects if $\mu mB \geq r_{t+1}(m - w_t)$, which is called the borrowing constraint (BC). For some young agents to invest in the Bad projects, both BC and PC must be satisfied. It is shown, through quite tedious processes, that the map of w_{t+1} is given by

$$w_{t+1} = T(w_t) \equiv \begin{cases} (w_t)^{\alpha} & \text{if } w_t \leq w_c, \\ \left[\dfrac{\alpha}{\mu B(1-\alpha)}\left(1 - \frac{w_t}{m}\right)\right]^{\dfrac{\alpha}{1-\alpha}} & \text{if } w_c \leq w_t \leq w_{\mu}, \\ \left[\frac{\alpha}{B(1-\alpha)}\right]^{\frac{\alpha}{1-\alpha}} & \text{if } w_t \geq \max\{w_c, w_{\mu}\}, \end{cases}$$

where

$$(w_c)^{1-\alpha} \equiv \frac{\alpha}{\mu B(1-\alpha)} \max\left\{\left(1 - \frac{w_c}{m}\right), \mu\right\}, \quad w_{\mu} \equiv m(1-\mu).$$

The problem is now to analyze the continuous piecewise smooth dynamical system with four parameters μ, α, m, and B (and $A(1-\alpha) = 1$). The authors conducted a very thorough bifurcation analysis of the problem. We just provide some numerical results. Figure 3.5 illustrates the motion of the map with $\alpha = 1/3$ and $m = 1.05$ with various initial conditions which are chosen near to their respectively close to their attractors. Only w_t is plotted because the other variables are directly calculated by the equations defined previously. It shows that the model has different types of irregular fluctuations during the transient phase even in the limited regions of the parameters. For instance, Figure 3.5 illustrates how the equilibrium trajectory asymptotically converges to a stable 3-period.

Figure 3.6 provides a typical bifurcation scenario in the parameter μB with $\alpha = 1/3$ and $m = 1.05$. Figure 3.6(b) only enlarges the boxed area in Figure 3.6(a) to demonstrate the complexity of bifurcation structures. As shown in Figure 3.6(a), decreases in μB lead to the emergence of stable 2-cycles. Further decreases in μB lead to a chaotic attractor with four

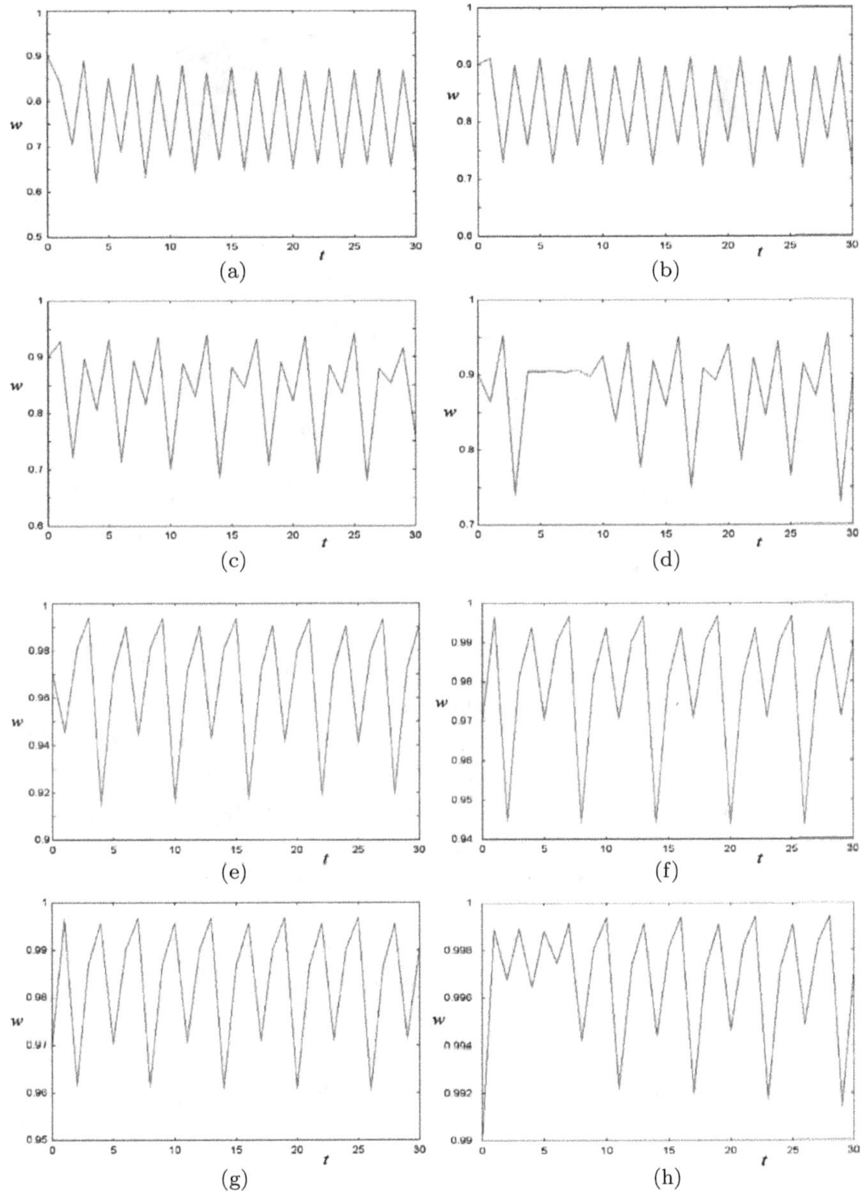

Fig. 3.5. Business cycles. (a) $\mu B = 0.2$ (2-cycle), with $w_0 = 0.9$, (b) $\mu B = 0.125$ ($G_{2,4}$), with $w_0 = 0.9$, (c) $\mu B = 0.1125$ ($G_{2,2}$), with $w_0 = 0.9$, (d) $\mu B = 0.085$ (G_1), with $w_0 = 0.9$, (e) $\mu B = 0.032$ (3-cycle), with $w_0 = 0.97$, (f) $\mu B = 0.0285$ ($G_{3,6}$), with $w_0 = 0.97$, (g) $\mu B = 0.0275$ ($G_{3,3}$), with $w_0 = 0.97$, and (h) $\mu B = 0.0245$ (G_1), with $w_0 = 0.99$.

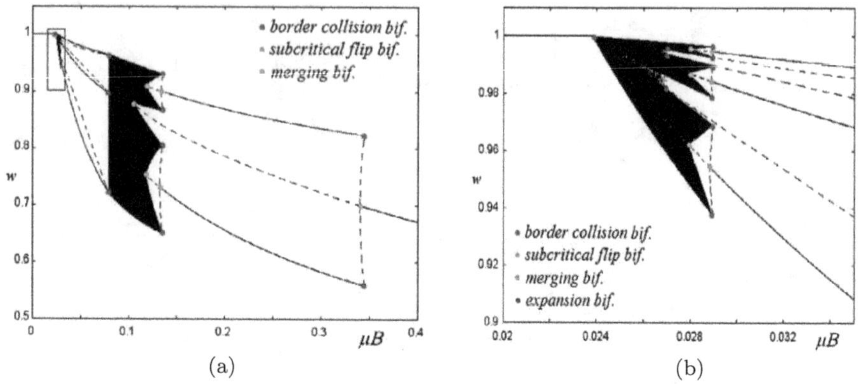

Fig. 3.6. A bifurcation scenario in the parameter μB.

intervals. Then, the chaotic attractor experiences a pairwise merging to become a chaotic attractor with two intervals. Bifurcation processes go on with further changes in the parameter.

The model shows the role of introducing Bad projects to the standard approach to economic growth. As the Bad are subject to the borrowing constraint, the agents need a high level of net worth to initiate the Bad projects. When the net worth is low, all the credit would be invested in the Good even when the Bad are more profitable than the Good. The over-investment in the Good leads to booms, resulting in an improved net worth. The agents are now able to make investment in the Bad, which would cause a decline in net worth. The whole process is nonlinearly independent. The Good seduce the Bad in booms and the Bad make the Good less profitable. In this modeling framework, persistent volatility continues under the conditions that the Bad projects may be highly profitable and the Bad projects come with an intermediate degree of pledgeability (so that the agents cannot finance them when their net worth is low, but they can when their net worth is high). The study also implies the possibility that, even in a very simplified economic system, an improvement in the financial system can increase the volatility of the national economy. Their analysis by applying the theory of piecewise smooth dynamical systems shows a much more convenient way to demonstrate the emergence of economic complexity with simple economic mechanisms than the theory of smooth dynamical systems, especially in exploring the complexity of regime switching. Many of the recent papers on economic complexity apply the mathematical tool in the paper (e.g., Deng and Khan, 2018).

3.5 Business Cycles in a Goodwin–Kalecki–Marx Model

Sasaki (2013) recently proposed a disequilibrium macrodynamic model, incorporating the three important economic mechanisms for approaching modern capitalist economies. It is based on the ideas on interactions between the rate of employment and income by Goodwin (1967), the investment function by Kalecki (1971), and the reserve-army and reserve-army-creation effects by Marx. The motion of the economy is described by three nonlinear differential equations for the rate of utilization, profit share, and the share of employment. The population is divided into capitalists and workers. Workers spend all their wages, w, and capitalists save a fraction s of their profits. Capitalists have capital K, which does not depreciate. The real savings are given by $S = srK$, where r is the rate of profit. The ratio of real savings to capital stock $g_s \equiv S/K = sr$. Let Y and L denote the real output and employment, respectively. We define the rate of capital utilization by $u = Y/Y^*$, where Y^* is the potential output. The constant u implies that the two variables grow at the same rate. The production technology is

$$Y = \min\left\{aL, \frac{u}{k}K\right\},$$

where a is (fixed) labor productivity and $k \equiv K/Y^*$, which is assumed to be constant ($= 1$) which implies that the two variables grow at the same rate. We thus have $r = mu$, where m is the profit share. The ratio $g_d \equiv I/K$ of real investment I is assumed to be a function of the profit and the rate of capacity utilization:

$$g_d = \psi m^\beta u^\gamma, \quad \psi > 0, \quad \beta \in (0,1), \quad \gamma \in (0,1).$$

When $\beta < \gamma$, the equilibrium growth is called wage-led growth, while when $\beta > \gamma$, it is called profit-led growth. It is assumed that the motion of the rate of capacity utilization is as follows:

$$\dot{u} = \alpha(g_d - g_s), \quad \alpha > 0,$$

where α is the speed of adjustment of the goods market. It implies that excess demand leads to a rise in the rate of capacity utilization, while excess supply leads to a decline. According to the definitions, we have $m = 1 - wL/pY$, where p is the price. It is straightforward to confirm

$$\frac{\dot{m}}{1-m} = \frac{\dot{p}}{p} - \frac{\dot{w}}{w} + \frac{\dot{s}}{a}.$$

The price and wage dynamics are specified as follows:

$$\frac{\dot{w}}{w} = (1-\theta)(m-m_w), \quad m_w \in (0,1),$$

$$\frac{\dot{p}}{p} = \theta(m_f - m), \quad \theta >\in (0,1), \; m_f \in (0,\,1),$$

where m_w is the target profit share set by workers and m_f is the target profit share set by firms. The parameter θ is interpreted as the relative bargaining power of firms.

Let e denote the rate of employment. We have $e = L/N$, where $N = N_0 e^{nt} n > 0$. The population grows at a constant rate n It is assumed that the workers' target profit share depends negatively on $m_w = m_w(e)$, which is interpreted as the reserve-army effect with $dm_w/de < 0$. The firms' target profit share is assumed to be constant. From $e = uK/aN$, we have

$$\frac{\dot{e}}{e} = \frac{\dot{u}}{u} + g_d - g_a - n,$$

where $g_a \equiv \dot{a}/a$. It is assumed that g_a is dependent on $e, g_a = g_a(e)\; dg_a/de > 0$.

It is straightforward to prove that the motion of the economy is given by the following three nonlinear differential equations:

$$\dot{u} = \alpha(\psi m^\beta u^\gamma - smu),$$

$$\dot{m} = -(1-m)\left[m - \theta m_f - (1-\theta)w(e) - g_a(e)\right],$$

$$\dot{e} = e\left[\alpha \frac{\psi m^\beta u^\gamma - smu}{u} + \psi m^\beta u^\gamma - g_a(e) - n\right].$$

For numerical simulation, it is required that

$$m_w(e) = \delta(1-e), \quad \delta > 0, \quad g_a(e) = \eta e, \quad \eta > 0,$$

where δ and η are parameters. For numerical simulation, let us specify the following parameter values:

$$\beta = 0.2, \quad \gamma = 0.4, \quad \psi = 0.15, \quad \eta = 0.1, \quad s = 0.6, \quad \delta = 0.5,$$
$$\theta = 0.25, \quad m_f = 0.3, \quad n = 0.015.$$

The reserve-army effect is strong. The elasticity of the investment rate with respect to the profit share is smaller than the elasticity of the investment rate with respect to the rate of elasticity utilization. The relative bargaining power of firms and the reserve-army-creation effect are weak. Figure 3.7 shows different paths of the system with $\alpha = 4$ and various

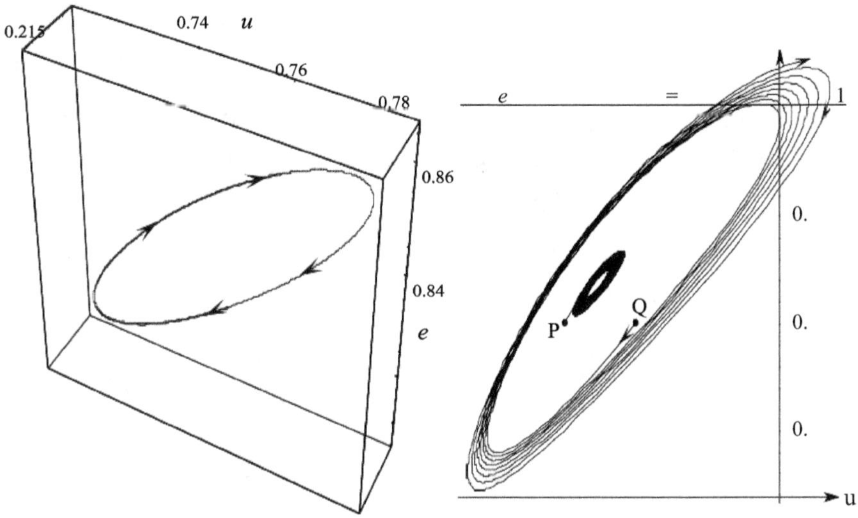

Fig. 3.7. Cyclical paths.

initial conditions. Figure 3.7(a) displays the motion with $u(0) = 0.7$, $m(0) = 0.21$, and $e(0) = 0.8$. The solution is not a completely closed orbit as the system approaches the long-term equilibrium point when the simulation runs longer. The periodic solution is unstable. Figure 3.7(b) shows that the path initiated from point P converges to the long-run equilibrium and the path from point Q diverges from the long-run equilibrium.

Figure 3.8 shows that the system has a stable limit cycle when $\alpha = 2$ and

$$\beta = 0.4, \quad \gamma = 0.2, \quad \psi = 0.2, \quad \eta = 0.1, \quad s = 0.6, \quad \delta = 0.1,$$
$$\theta = 0.25, \quad m_f = 0.3, \quad n = 0.016.$$

3.6 Oscillations in a Reformed Solow Model with Delays

The Solow model has been the prototype in neoclassical growth theory. It provides an economic mechanism of growth with endogenous wealth and physical capital. As wealth is a key force of modern economic growth, many dynamic models for economic growth and development are based on the model. Different mathematical methods are applied to examine the properties of the model and its extensions or generalizations. Guerrini *et al.* (2019) recently introduced two delays into the model. Delays are mentioned

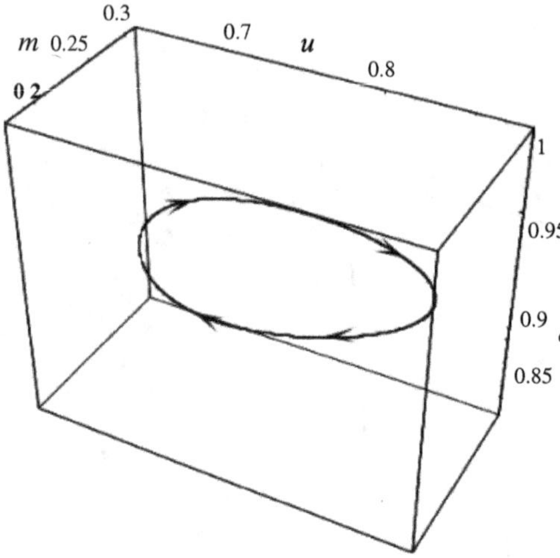

Fig. 3.8. Stable business cycles.

and analyzed in the literature on economic growth (e.g., Kalecki, 1935; Kydland and Prescott, 1982; Zak, 1999; Szydlowski and Kwawiec, 2004). Gu *et al.* (2005) took account of two delays in a growth model. The model presented in the following is closely related to this model. We now show how this traditional model with unique stable equilibrium displays oscillations owning to time delays in production and depreciation. It is demonstrated that the production delay has a stabilizing effect, and the depreciation has a destabilizing effect in a single delay model. Cyclic fluctuations emerge via Hopf bifurcation. We now introduce the model and some results from numerical simulation.

The capital accumulation is given by

$$\dot{k}(t) = sf(k(t-\tau_1)) - \delta k(t-\tau_2),$$

where k is the per capita capital, f is the per capita output, and s and δ are savings rate and depreciation rate, respectively. The parameters τ_1 and τ_2 are called gestation delay in the production process and depreciation delay, respectively. We specify

$$f = k^{0.5}, \quad s = 0.3, \quad \delta = 0.1, \quad \tau_1 = 35.2, \quad \tau_2 = 34.$$

Business cycles emerge in the reformed Solow model as shown in Figure 3.9. Analyses of the model are referred to in the original study.

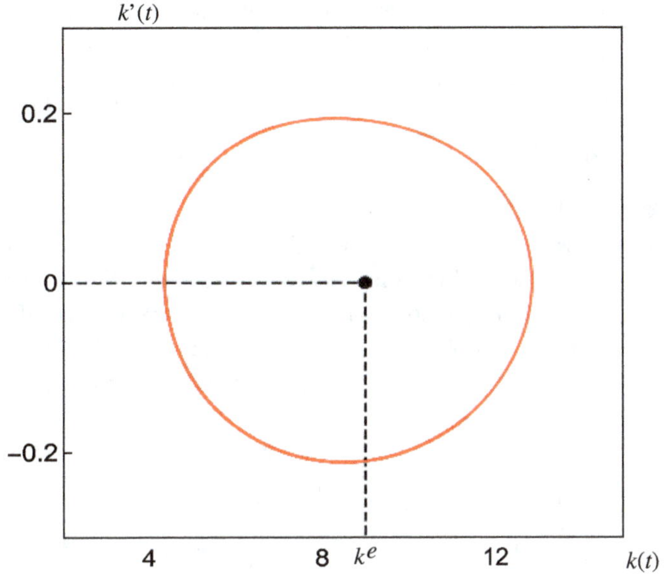

Fig. 3.9. Cycles generated in the Solow model by delays.

3.7 A Reformed Kaldor–Kalecki Growth with Expectation and Delay

It has been previously demonstrated that expectations and delays lead to nonlinear phenomena. This section introduces another study by Liu *et al.* (2015) to show that capital stock's anticipation and investment lag can lead to the emergence of business cycles. The model consists of three differential equations:

$$\dot{Y}(t) = \alpha(I(Y(t), \quad R(t), K(t+\tau)) - S(Y(t), R(t))),$$
$$\dot{R}(t) = \beta(L(t) - \bar{M}),$$
$$\dot{K}(t) = I(Y(t-\tau), \quad R(t-\tau), \quad K(t-\tau)) - dK(t),$$

in which Y is the gross production, K is the capital stock, I is the investment, national income, S is the savings, R is the interest rate, $L(t)$ is the actual demand for money, $\bar{M}$ is the supply of money, d is the depreciation rate of capital, and α and β are positive parameters. Here, $\tau > 0$ is investment delay or expected time of capital stock, and $K(t+\tau)$ stands for the expected capital stock. The numerical simulations of the functional forms and parameter values are specified as follows:

$$I = \frac{1+\exp(Y)}{\exp(Y)} - 0.1R - 0.2K, \quad L = 0.05Y + \frac{0.0005}{R - 0.001},$$
$$S = 0.2Y + 0.1R, \quad \alpha = 2, \quad \beta = 1.5, \quad d = 0.1, \quad \bar{M} = 0.05.$$

When $\tau = 0$, the system has a locally asymptotically stable equilibrium point. As τ is increased, the system loses stability. Figure 3.10 displays the bifurcation diagram with the delay as the parameter. When the delay is low, the system has a unique equilibrium. When it is increased, it first loses stability and periodic solutions appear. As the delay is further increased, the system is stabilized before it loses stability again (Figures 3.11 and 3.12).

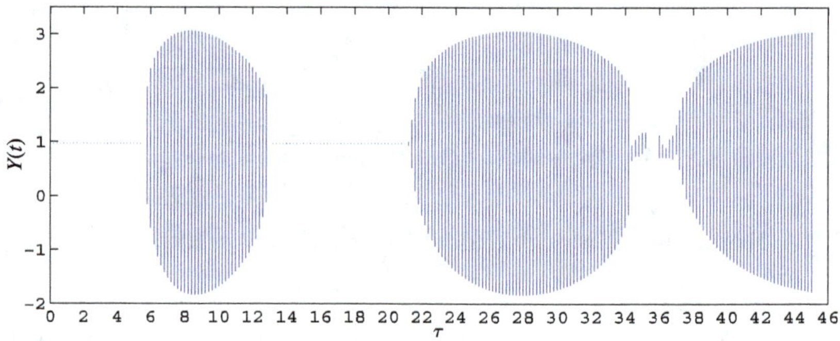

Fig. 3.10. Bifurcation with the delay parameter.

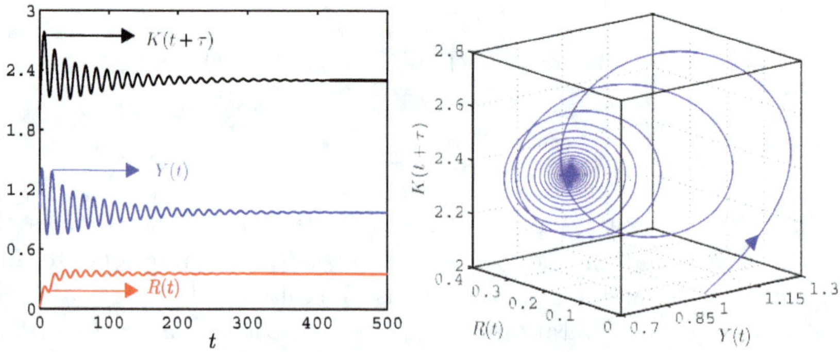

Fig. 3.11. The behavior before the system loses its stability at $\tau = 5$.

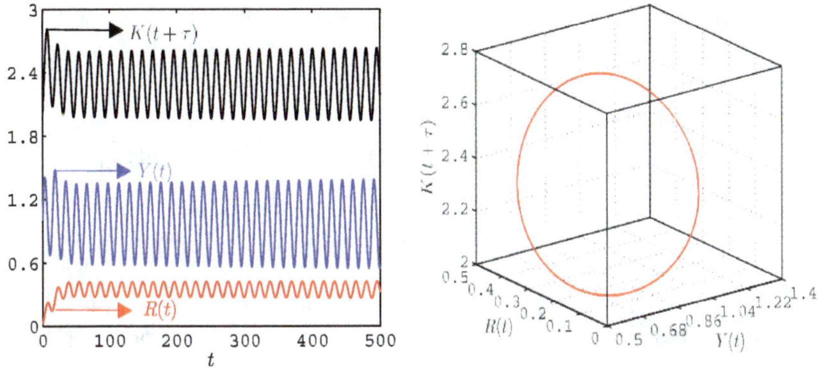

Fig. 3.12. Persistent business cycles at $\tau = 5.65$.

3.8 Neoclassical General Equilibrium Theory Generalized with Monopolistic and Perfect Competition

This section shows the appearance of endogenous oscillations by introducing a neoclassical growth model with perfect and monopolistic competition proposed by Zhang (2020c). The model determines income and wealth distribution on the basis of Walrasian general equilibrium theory, neoclassical growth theory, and Dixit–Stiglitz monopolistic competitive theory. Modern economies are characterized by different types of consumers, different kinds of goods and services, and different market structures. Moreover, these different forces and their relations are changeable over time. Dynamic general equilibrium is influenced by Walrasian general equilibrium theory (e.g., Walras, 1874; Arrow and Debreu, 1954; Arrow and Hahn, 1971; Mas-Colell *et al.*, 1995). Capital accumulation and final goods production with perfect competition are according to neoclassical growth theory (e.g., Solow, 1956; see also Burmeister and Dobell, 1970). Intermediate goods sector is modeled according to the Dixit–Stiglitz model with monopolistic competition (e.g., Dixit and Stiglitz, 1977; see also Krugman, 1979).

The economy is composed by J groups of people, indexed by $j = 1, \ldots, J$. People are classified due to levels of human capital and preferences. Variables $T_j(t)$ represent the work time of household j. The total labor force $N(t)$ is given by

$$N(t) = \sum_{j=1}^{J} h_j(t) T_j(t) \bar{N}_j(t),$$

in which $h_j(t)$ and $\bar{N}_j(t)$ are respectively the level of human capital and the population of group j. This paper treats $\bar{N}_j(t)$ and $h_j(t)$ as exogenous time-dependent coefficients.

We use $K(t)$, $\tilde{N}(t)$, and $F(t)$ to represent the capital input, labor input, and output of the final goods sector. We use the Cobb–Douglas production function as follows:

$$F(t) = AK^{\alpha(t)}(t)\tilde{N}^{\beta(t)}(t), \quad 0 < \alpha(t), \quad \beta(t) < 1, \quad \alpha(t) + \beta(t) = 1,$$

in which $A(t), \alpha(t)$, and $\beta(t)$ are time-dependent coefficients. Capital good is used as numeraire. Physical capital is depreciated at a rate $\delta_k(t)$. The wage rate $w(t)$ and rate of interest $r(t)$ are exogenously given to the sector. The first-order conditions for maximizing profit are

$$R(t) = \frac{\alpha(t)F(t)}{K(t)}, \quad w(t) = \frac{\beta(t)F(t)}{\tilde{N}(t)}, \quad w_j(t) = h_j(t)w(t)$$

in which $w_j(t)$ is the wage rate of household j and $R_\delta(t) \equiv r(t) + \delta_k(t)$.

Let $\bar{k}_j(t)$ denote group j's household wealth. The total profit in the middle goods sector is equally shared between the households. Variable $\pi_j(t)$ denotes the profit shared by household j. The current income of household j is

$$y_j(t) = r(t)\bar{k}_j(t) + h_j(t)T_j(t)w(t) + \pi_j(t).$$

Variable $\hat{y}_j(t)$ represents household j's disposable income. It is the current disposable income and the value of wealth: $\hat{y}_j(t) = y_j(t) + \bar{k}_j(t)$. Household j distributes the disposable income between savings $s_j(t)$ consuming final goods $d_j(t)$ and consuming middle goods $\tilde{c}_j(\varepsilon, t)$. Variable $\tilde{c}_j(\varepsilon, t)$ is the amount of variety ε consumed by household j. Let variety ε distribute within the range from 0 to $n\varepsilon \in [0, n]$ Following Dixit and Stiglitz (1977; see also Spence, 1976; Tirole, 1988), we define composite goods as follows:

$$c_j(t) = \left(\int_0^{n(t)} \tilde{c}_j^{\bar{\theta}(t)}(\varepsilon, t)d\varepsilon\right)^{1/\bar{\theta}(t)}, \quad 1 > \bar{\theta}_j(t) > 0,$$

where $\bar{\theta}(t)$ is a positive parameter. Let the price of $\tilde{c}_j(\varepsilon, t)$ be denoted by $\tilde{p}(\varepsilon, t)$. The disposable income is spent on savings, consuming final goods, and consuming middle goods. We have the budget constraint as follows:

$$d_j(t) + \int_0^n \tilde{p}(\varepsilon, t)\tilde{c}_j(\varepsilon, t)d\varepsilon + s_j(t) = \hat{y}_j(t).$$

We use $\bar{T}_j(t)$ to denote the leisure time and T_0 (fixed) available time for household j. The time constraint is expressed by $T_j(t) + \bar{T}_j(t) = T_0$. From this equation, we have

$$\hat{y}_j(t) = R(t)\bar{k}_j(t) - h_j(t)\bar{T}_j(t)w(t) + W_j(t),$$

where $R(t) \equiv 1 + r(t)$, $W_j(t) \equiv h_j(t)T_0 w(t) + \pi_j(t)$. The budget becomes

$$h_j(t)\bar{T}_j(t)w(t) + d_j(t) + \int_0^{n(t)} \tilde{p}(\varepsilon,\, t)\,\tilde{c}_j(\varepsilon,\, t)d\varepsilon + s_j(t) = \bar{y}_j(t),$$

in which $\bar{y}_j(t) \equiv R(t)\bar{k}_j(t) + W_j(t)$.

Utility function $U_j(t)$ has taken on the following form:

$$U_j(t) = \bar{T}_j^{\sigma_{0j}(t)}(t)c_j^{\chi_{0j}(t)}(t)d_j^{\xi_{0j}(t)}(t)s_j^{\lambda_{0j}(t)}(t),$$
$$\times\, \sigma_{0j}(t),\, \xi_{0j}(t),\, \lambda_{0j}(t),\, \chi_{0j}(t) > 0,$$

in which $\chi_{0j}(t)$ is the propensity to consume intermediates, $\xi_{0j}(t)$ is the propensity to consume final goods, $\sigma_{0j}(t)$ is the propensity to use leisure time, and $\lambda_{0j}(t)$ is the propensity to save. We use the two-stage method to analyze the behavior of households. In the first stage, consider a price $p(t)$ for $c_j(t)$. The budget is then

$$h_j(t)w(t)\bar{T}_j(t) + d_j(t) + p(t)c_j(t) + s_j(t) = \bar{y}_j(t). \tag{3.8.1}$$

The optimal solution is expressed as

$$h_j(t)w(t)T_j(t) = \sigma_j(t)\bar{y}_j(t),\, d_j(t) = \xi_j(t)\bar{y}_j(t),$$
$$p(t)c_j(t) = \chi_j(t)\bar{y}_j(t),\, s_j(t) = \lambda_j(t)\bar{y}_j(t),$$

in which

$$\sigma_j(t) \equiv \rho_j(t)\sigma_{0j}(t),\, \xi_j(t) \equiv \rho_j(t)\xi_{0j}(t),\, \chi_j(t) = \rho_j(t)\chi_{0j}(t)$$
$$\lambda_j(t) \equiv \rho_j(t)\lambda_{0j}(t),\, \rho_j(t) \equiv \frac{1}{\sigma_{0j}(t) + \xi_{0j}(t) + \chi_{0j}(t) + \lambda_{0j}(t)}.$$

The second-stage maximization is to optimize $c_j(t)$ by deciding $\tilde{c}_j(\epsilon, t)$ under the constraint:

$$\int_0^{n(t)} \tilde{p}(\varepsilon,\, t)\tilde{c}_j(\varepsilon,\, t)d\varepsilon = p(t)c_j(t).$$

The optimal solution is given by

$$\tilde{c}_j(\varepsilon,t) = \chi_j(t)\bar{y}_j(t)\tilde{p}^{\gamma(t)}(\varepsilon,t)P_j^{-1}(t),\ p(t) = P_j(t)^{\frac{1}{\bar{\theta}(t)\,\gamma(t)}},$$

where

$$\gamma(t) \equiv \frac{1}{\bar{\theta}(t)-1} P_j(t) \equiv \int_0^n \tilde{p}^{\bar{\theta}(t)\,\gamma(t)}(\varepsilon,\, t)\, d\varepsilon.$$

Savings minus dissavings is the change in the household's wealth:

$$\dot{k}_j(t) = s_j(t) - \bar{k}_j(t).$$

We now describe the middle goods sector which is characterized by monopolistic competition. There is no middle goods which has an attribute very close to any given attribute of any other product. No firm considers the possible impacts of its decisions on any other firm. Market equilibrium of demand and supply implies

$$\sum_{j=1}^{J} \tilde{c}_j(\varepsilon,t)\bar{N}_j(t) = x(\varepsilon,t),$$

where $x(\varepsilon,\, t)$ is the output level of variety ε All the firms for middle goods have the same cost function. The labor force employed in production $l(\varepsilon,\, t)$ is linearly related to output:

$$l(\varepsilon,\, t) = \tilde{\alpha}(t) + \tilde{\beta}(t)x(\varepsilon,\, t).$$

where $\tilde{\alpha}(t)$ is a fixed cost and $\tilde{\beta}(t)$ is a positive parameter. The middle goods sector's total labor force $N_x(t)$ is

$$N_x(t) = \int_0^{n(t)} l(\varepsilon,\, t)\, d\varepsilon.$$

Producer ε's profit is

$$\bar{\pi}(\varepsilon,t) = \tilde{p}(\varepsilon,t)x(\varepsilon,t) - (\tilde{\alpha}(t) + \tilde{\beta}(t)x(\varepsilon,\, t))w(t).$$

The symmetry means that all the firms in the sector produce the same quantity at the same price. We apply the shorthand notation:

$$x(t) = x_j(\varepsilon,t), \quad \pi(t) = \bar{\pi}(\varepsilon,t), \quad \tilde{p}(t) = \tilde{p}(\varepsilon,t), \quad \text{for all } \varepsilon.$$

It is straightforward to check

$$\bar{\pi}(t) = (\tilde{p}(t) - \tilde{\beta}(t)w(t))\, \tilde{p}^{\gamma(t)}(t)M(t) - \tilde{\alpha}(t)w(t),$$

in which

$$M(t) \equiv P_j^{-1}(t) \sum_{j=1}^{J} \chi_j(t)\, \bar{y}_j(t) \bar{N}_j(t).$$

The first-order condition (i.e., $\partial \bar{\pi} / \partial \tilde{p} = 0$) leads to the fixed-markup pricing rule:

$$\tilde{p}(t) = \frac{\tilde{\beta}(t) w(t)}{\bar{\theta}(t)}.$$

Hence,

$$\bar{\pi}(t) = \vartheta(t) w^{1+\gamma(t)}(t) M(t) - \tilde{\alpha}(t) w(t),$$

in which

$$\vartheta(t) \equiv \left(\frac{1}{\bar{\theta}(t)} - 1 \right) \tilde{\beta}(t) \left(\frac{\tilde{\beta}(t)}{\bar{\theta}(t)} \right)^{\gamma(t)}.$$

The profit share of household j is given by

$$\pi_j(t) = \frac{\mu_j(t) n(t) \bar{\pi}(t)}{\bar{N}_j(t)},$$

where $n(t)\bar{\pi}(t)$ implies the total profit of the sector and share distribution is given as

$$\sum_{j=1}^{J} \mu_j(t) = 1, \quad \mu_j(t) \geq 0.$$

3.9 Demand and Supply of Final Goods

The output of the final goods sector is equal to the change in capital stock plus the total consumption and depreciations of capital stock, thus we get

$$\dot{K}(t) = F(t) - \sum_{j=1}^{J} d_j(t) \bar{N}_j(t) - \delta_k(t) K(t).$$

The national wealth $\bar{K}(t)$ is the sum of the wealth values of all the households:

$$\bar{K}(t) = \sum_{j=1}^{J} \bar{k}_j(t) \bar{N}_j$$

We also have $\bar{K}(t) = K(t)$.

Input factors are fully employed:

$$\tilde{N}(t) + N_x(t) = N(t),$$

where $N_x(t) = n(t)l(t)$

We now show some numerical simulation results. The parameters are first taken on the following constant values:

$$\begin{array}{ccccc} T_0 = 24, & \bar{\theta} = 0.4, & \delta_k = 0.05, & A = 1.4, & n = 200, \\ \alpha = 0.35, & \tilde{\alpha} = 0.01, & \tilde{\beta} = 0.05, & \bar{N}_1 = 10, & \bar{N}_2 = 40, \\ \bar{N}_3 = 100, & h_1 = 4, & h_2 = 1.5, & h_3 = 1, & \mu_1 = 0.3, \\ \mu_2 = 0.3, & \mu_3 = 0.4, & \lambda_{01} = 0.7, & \chi_{01} = 0.1, & \xi_{01} = 0.2, \\ \sigma_{01} = 0.2, & \lambda_{02} = 0.65, & \chi_{02} = 0.1, & \xi_{02} = 0.2, & \sigma_{02} = 0.25, \end{array}$$

$$\lambda_{03} = 0.6, \quad \chi_{03} = 0.15, \quad \xi_{03} = 0.25, \quad \sigma_{03} = 0.3.$$

With the initial condition, $z_1(0) = 0.07$, $\bar{k}_2(0) = 90$, and $\bar{k}_2(0) = 46$, the motion of the system is illustrated in Figure 3.13.

The system has a unique stable equilibrium. We now show how various exogenous periodic shocks cause business cycles with reference to the growth path identified in the previous section. We use a variable to stand for the change rate of the variable in percentage due to changes in the value of a given parameter. We deal with the impact on the economy when the

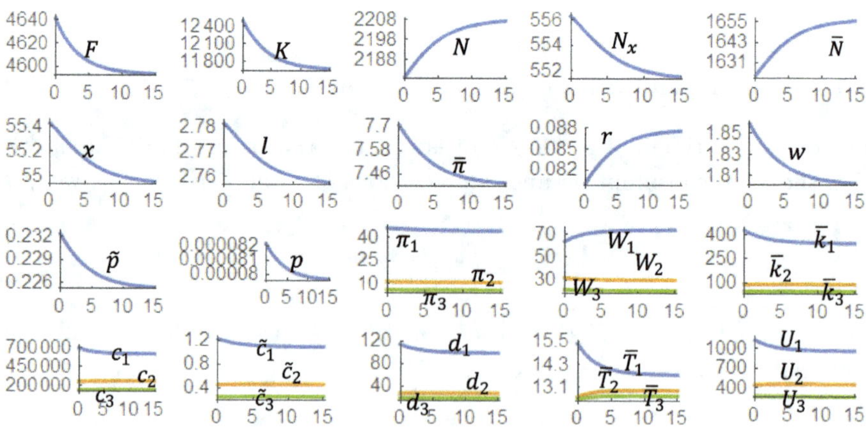

Fig. 3.13. The motion of the economic system.

Note: Horizontal axis: time; vertical axis: the variable values.

elasticity of substitution between two varieties is exogenously oscillated as follows:

$$\bar{\theta}(t) = 0.4 + 0.02\,\sin(t).$$

Figure 3.14 shows the simulation result. We see that all the variables are periodic. The amplitudes of group 1's oscillations in the total income, wealth, and work hours are much larger than the other two groups' amplitudes.

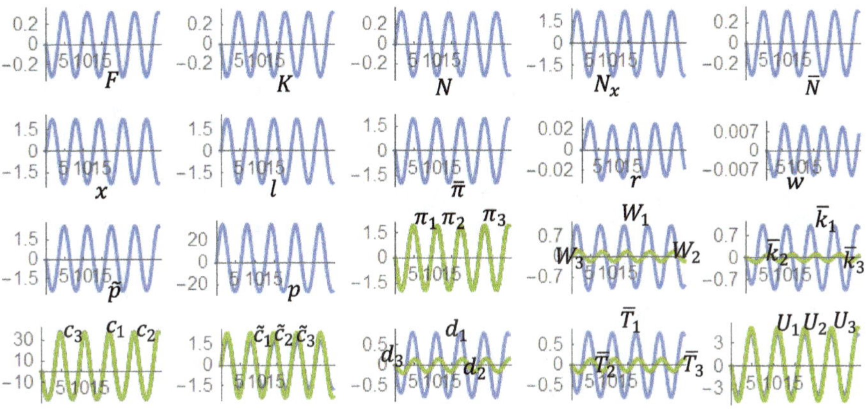

Fig. 3.14. Oscillations in the elasticity of substitution between two varieties.

Note: Horizontal axis: time; vertical axis: the changes of the variable values in percentage.

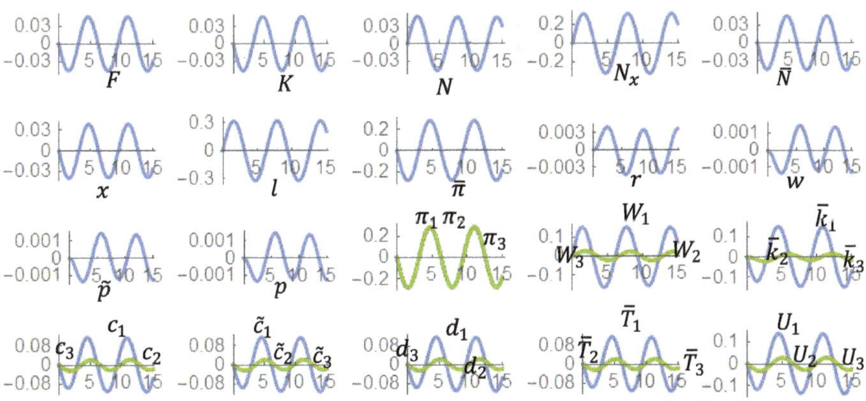

Fig. 3.15. Oscillations in the fixed labor cost of the middle goods.

Note: Horizontal axis: time; vertical axis: the changes of the variable values in percentage.

We deal with the impact on the economy when the fixed labor cost of the middle goods firm is exogenously oscillated as follows:

$$\tilde{\alpha}(t) = 0.01 + 0.01\ \sin(t).$$

Figure 3.15 shows the simulation result. As in real business cycle theory, changes in costs bring about business cycles. The amplitudes of group 1's oscillations in the total income, wealth, consumption of middle goods, and work hours are much larger than the other two groups' amplitudes.

Chapter 4

Nonlinear Population Dynamics

Gender relationships are complicated and have increasingly become more unpredictable and chaotic in association with modernization (Engels, 1981/1884; Greenwood, 2019). There is chaos in contemporary family systems across countries (Ward, 1995). "The idea that women were oppressed throughout history is an appalling theory," Jordon Peterson expressed the modern viewpoint. Over history, in highly "civilized" societies with traditional technologies, man and woman had strict division of labor and consumption. Napoleon Bonaparte had the opinion perhaps commonly held by French men of his time: "Women are nothing but machines for producing children." Adam Smith said: "Men, like animals, naturally multiply in proportion to the means of their subsistence." Malthus pointed out that "in proportion to" might not be valid. This simple discovery led Malthus to depict a quite different world of economic evolution with population. Emmeline Pankhurst believed: "You must make women count as much as men; you must have an equal standard of morals; and the only way to enforce that is through giving women political power so that you can get that equal moral standard registered in the laws of the country. It is the only way." Liz Truss asked for the financial power of women: "Economics and finance is the final frontier for women; it's the last thing they will conquer because controlling finance is at the heart of everything in government."

Population causes complex phenomena in economies. This chapter presents a few nonlinear population dynamics. Section 4.1 introduces a population dynamic model constructed by Haavelmo in continuous form. Its discrete form was examined by Stutzer (1980) by applying modern mathematics for one-dimensional mappings. It is an early model that shows economic chaos from a simple economic model. Section 4.2 represents the nonlinear OLG model with endogenous fertility and old age support proposed by Chakrabarti (1999). Section 4.3 presents period doubling cascades in a traditional prey–predator modeling framework developed by Gupta *et al.* (2014). Section 4.4 studies the discrete prey–predator model with chaos by Chen and Chen (2012). Section 4.5 represents the existence of nonlinear phenomena in a spatial extension of the classical prey–predator model with time delay in prey by Rao (2018). Section 4.6 represents the ecological model by Ruiz-Herrera (2017) that explores the effects of carryover effects (COEs) — any process that in one season that affects, non-lethally, individuals in the following seasons — on population dynamics. Section 4.6 provides a model of generalized neoclassical general equilibrium theory with generalized Malthusian theory.

4.1 Chaos in a Generalized Malthusian Growth Model

The model is constructed by Haavelmo in continuous form. Its discrete form was examined by Stutzer (1980) by applying modern mathematics for one-dimensional mappings (see Zhang, 2005, Section 12.2). First, consider a macroeconomic growth model proposed by Haavelmo (1954):

$$\dot{N} = N\left(a - \frac{\beta N}{Y}\right), \quad a, \beta > 0, Y = AN^{\alpha} A > 0, \;\; 0 < \alpha < 1, \tag{4.1.1}$$

where N is the population, $Y = AN^{\alpha}$ is the real output, and a, β, α, and A are the parameters. If we replace time derivatives by first differences and accept discrete time, then Eq. (4.1.1) becomes

$$N_{t+1} = N_t \left[(1+a) - \frac{\beta N_t^{1-\alpha}}{A}\right],$$

which is further simplified as

$$x_{t+1} = (1+a)x_t\left(1 - x_t^{\frac{1}{2}}\right) = F(x_t; a, 0.5), \tag{4.1.2}$$

in which the new variable x_t is defined by the transformation

$$N_t = \left[\frac{A(1+a)}{\beta}\right]^{1/(1-\alpha)} x_t,$$

with $\alpha = 1/2$. It can be shown that none of the qualitative properties of the system are affected by the particular choice of $0 < \alpha < 1$. The term chaotic dynamics refers to the dynamic behavior of certain equations F which possess the following: (a) a non-degenerate n-period point for each $n \geq 1$ and (b) an uncountable set $S \in J(= [0, 1])$ containing no periodic points and no asymptotically periodic points. The trajectories of such points wander around in J "randomly."

For each value of a, equilibrium points are given by the intersection of the graph of $F(x_t; a)$ with the 45-degree line. For each value of a, there are two equilibria $x_0 = 0$ and $x_0 = \{a/(1+a)\}^2$. The point $x_0 = 0$ is unstable and repels nearby points. The local stability of the other can be determined by linearization at the equilibrium. We have

$$F'(x_0; a) = 1 - \frac{a}{2} = \theta(a). \tag{4.1.3}$$

The eigenvalue $\theta(a)$ determines the local stability of x_0. When $0 < \theta < 1$, x_0 attracts nearby points in an exponential, monotonic fashion. When $0 > \theta > -1$, x_0 attracts nearby points in a damped oscillatory manner. When $\theta = 1$, x_0 is neither stable nor unstable. Finally, if $|\theta| > 1$, x_0 is unstable. These behaviors occur when $0 < a < 2$, $2 < a < 4$, $a = 4$, and $4 < a < 5.57$, respectively. When the equilibrium is stable, i.e., $a < 4$, the trajectory starting at any point always approaches it. In this region, a traditional comparative statics analysis shows that an increase in the parameter a will increase x_t for sufficiently large t. If $4 < a < 5.57$, trajectories don't approach the equilibrium but are bounded by and 1. In fact, as the parameter a exceeds 4, the unstable equilibrium point bifurcates into two stable points of period two, i.e., into a stable periodic orbit of length 2. The 2-period cycle becomes unstable for values of a in excess of about 4.8, and each 2-period point bifurcates into two 4-period points, producing a stable cycle of length four denoted by $\{x^4_{01} x^4_{02} x^4_{03} x^4_{04}\}$. Figure 4.1 illustrates the phenomenon.

This pitchfork bifurcation process continues as the parameter a increases, producing non-degenerate orbits of length $2k(k = 2, \ldots)$. These orbits are called harmonics of the 2-period orbit. It can be shown that all the harmonics occur prior to the parameter a reaching 5.54, although how much prior to this value is not known. Thus, the range of a, within which a stable orbit of length k first appears and later becomes unstable and bifurcates to a $2k$-period orbit, decreases in length as the parameter a increases to a limiting value $a_c < 5.54$. The range of $a_c < a \leq 5.75$ is termed the chaotic region. As the parameter a enters this region, even stranger behavior can occur. For example, a 3-period orbit exists at values of a near 5.540. This, then gives rise to orbits of periods $3k(k = 2, \ldots)$ via the pitchfork process just described. In fact, if we can locate the 3-period orbit, a remarkable theorem of Li and Yorke (1975) demonstrates that for any $F(x_t; a)$ in which a non-degenerate 3-period orbit arises, there must also exist non-degenerate points of all periods, as well as an uncountable set

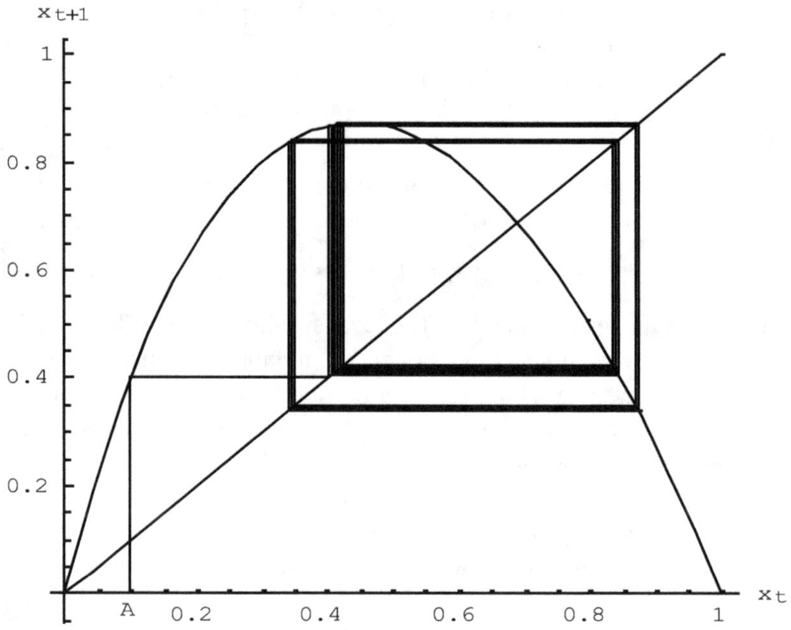

Fig. 4.1. The 4-period orbit for $a = 4.9$.

of periodic (not asymptotically periodic) points whose trajectories wander "randomly" throughout the domain of F. Our dynamic economic system satisfies the requirements in the Li–Yorke theorem for some values of a. This guarantees the existence of chaotic behavior as illustrated in Figure 4.2.

The existence of chaos implies that no one can precisely know what will happen in society in the future, except that it will be changing. To illustrate why no one precisely foresees the consequences of the intervention policy, let us try to find out what happens to the chaotic system when it starts from two different but very near states. In Figure 4.3, we consider the case of $a = 5.75$. Let us consider two cases of $x_0 = 0.400$ and $x_0 = 0.405$ over 100 years. The two behaviors are varied over time.

We calculate the difference $x_t[0.400] - x_t[0.405]$ between the path started at $x_0 = 0.400$ and the one at $x_0 = 0.405$ over 100 years, as demonstrated in Figure 4.4.

In summary, as the autonomous growth rate a exceeds a certain value, the steady state ceases being approached monotonically, and an oscillatory approach occurs. If a is increased further, the steady state becomes unstable

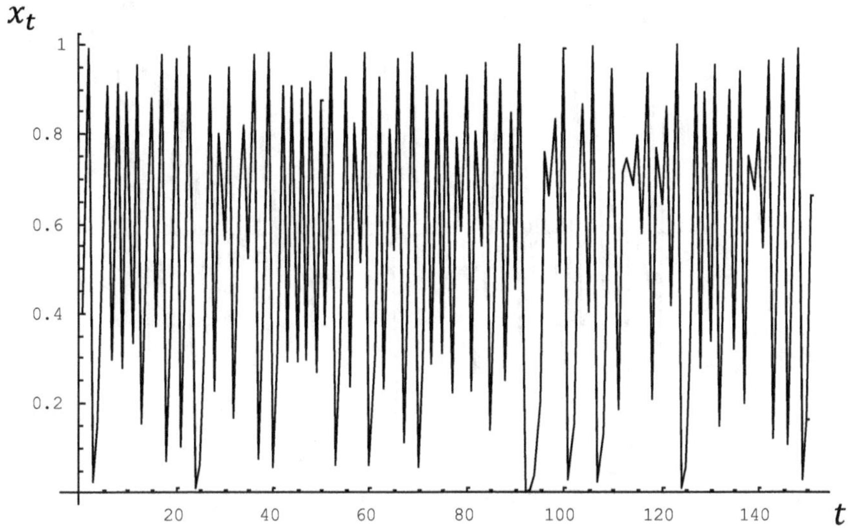

Fig. 4.2. The existence of chaos for $a = 5.75$ with $x_0 = 0.4$.

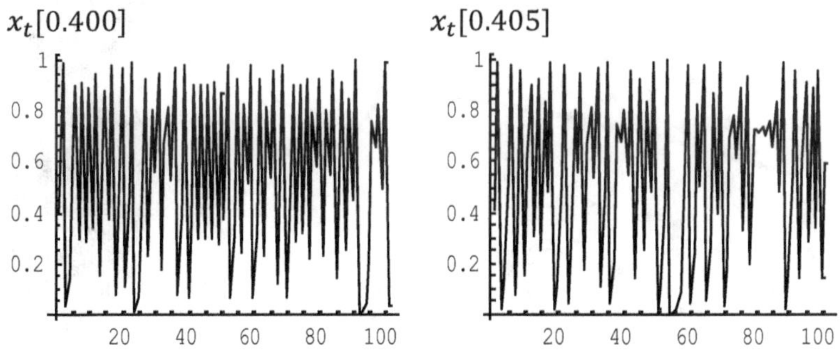

(a) (b)

Fig. 4.3. The dynamics with different initial conditions, $a = 5.75$. (a) $x_0 = 0.400$. (b) $x_0 = 405$.

and repels nearby points. As a increases, one can find a value of a where the system possesses a cycle of period k for arbitrary k (see Figure 4.5). Also, there exists an uncountable number of initial conditions from which emanate trajectories that fluctuate in a bounded and aperiodic fashion and are indistinguishable from a realization of some stochastic (chaotic) process.

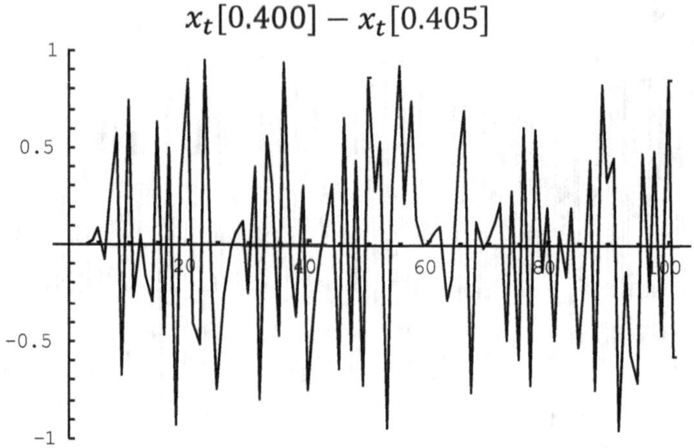

Fig. 4.4. Small differences at the beginning signify much.

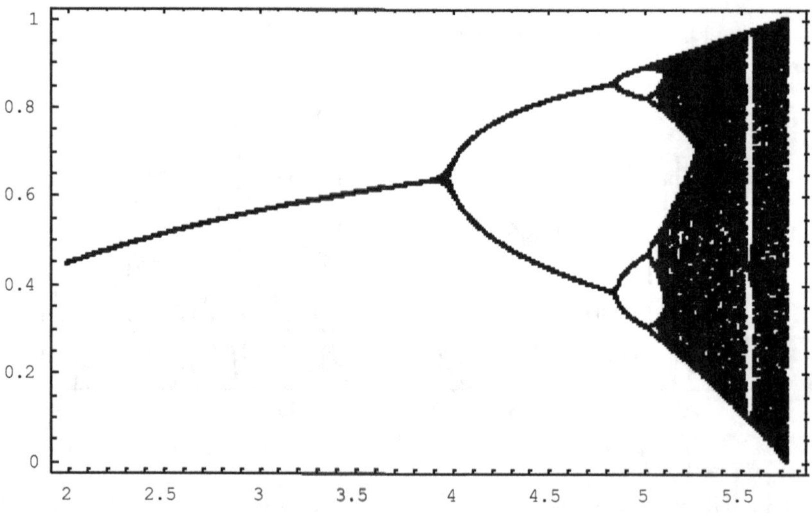

Fig. 4.5. The map of bifurcations for $a \in [2, 5.75]$.

4.2 Economic Dynamics with Endogenous Fertility and Old Age Support

This section introduces endogenous fertility and old age support into the OLG model proposed by Chakrabarti (1999) (see also Zhang, 2006b,

Chapter 7). In the literature of microeconomic-based population, two assumptions about population growth and economic conditions are made; the first is to assume that children are consumption goods and appear in the utility function of the parents; the second is to assume that children are valued as a source of old age support. The first approach is accepted by, for instance, Barro and Becker (1989), Becker *et al.* (1990), Galor and Weil (1999); the second approach by, for instance, Raut and Srinivasan (1994). Chakrabarti tried to combine the two ideas within the same framework. This assumption is made based on the observation that countries with more developed financial markets or better social security programs tend to have lower population growth rates than those that do not. For instance, in developing countries, children often start contributing to the family income while living at home and prior to adulthood. Here, we assume that individuals give a constant fraction of their income to their parents in the form of old age support and that parents incur a time cost of raising children which is increasing with the number of children.

The number of young agents at time t is denoted by $N(t)$ and there are $N(-1)$ agents in the initial old generation. The initial old generation is endowed with an aggregate initial capital stock of $K(0) > 0$. All young agents are identical and they are endowed with one unit of labor when young and have no other endowments of goods or assets at any date. There is a single good in the economy, which is produced using capital and labor as inputs. For simplicity, it is assumed that individuals care only about old age consumption, denoted by c; their lifetime consumption utility is given by $u(c)$, which is assumed to be increasing in c, and concave. Agents work and raise children when young and are retired when old. Young agents remit a fraction, μ, of their income to their parents as old age support and save the rest which is equal to $(1 - \mu)$ of the income. Each young agent decides to have $n(t)$ children. The time cost of raising children, $\gamma(n(t))$, satisfies $\gamma(0) = 0$, $\gamma' > 0$, and $\gamma'' \geq 0$. All agents take the wage rate, $w(t)$, at period t as given. The savings $s(t)$ is given by $s(t) = (1 - a)w(t)(1 - \gamma(n(t)))$. Old age consumption is thus given by

$$c(t + 1) = r(t + 1)s(t) + an(t)w(t + 1)(1 - \gamma(n(t + 1))),$$

where r is the rate of interest. Let K stand for the capital stock. The intensive production function is given by $f(k)$, where $k \equiv K/N(1 - \gamma)$. Assume that the production function is of the CES form:

$$f(k) = (\alpha k^{\rho} + \beta)^{1/\rho}, \quad \alpha\beta > 0, \ -\infty < \rho < 1.$$

Each unit of the consumption good saved at time t becomes one unit of capital at time $t+1$. The capital is used in production and it depreciates completely in the production process. We have $K(t+1) = s(t)N(t)$. The labor and capital markets are perfectly competitive. The marginal conditions are

$$r(t) = f'(k(t)) = \alpha k^{\rho-1}(t)[\alpha k^{\rho}(t)+\beta]^{1/\rho-1},$$

$$w(t) = f(k(t)) - k(t)f'(k(t)) = \beta[\alpha k^{\rho}(t)+\beta]^{1/\rho-1}, \quad t \geq 0.$$

The young agent's problem is to maximize $u(c(t+1))$ by choosing $n(t)$ subject to

$$c(t+1) = (1-a)r(t+1)w(t)(1-\gamma(n(t))) \\ + an(t)w(t+1)(1-\gamma(n(t+1))).$$

With w and r as given, the problem of optimization has an interior optimum determined by

$$-(1-a)r(t+1)w(t)\gamma'(n(t)) + aw(t+1)(1-\gamma(n(t+1))) = 0.$$

By the definition, we have $K(t+1) = N(t+1)[1-\gamma(n(t+1))]k(t+1)$. In the remainder of this section, we specify

$$\gamma(n(t)) = cn^2(t), \quad z(t) \equiv \frac{\alpha}{\beta}k^{\rho}(t).$$

With the above preparations, we get two equations for the motion of the system:

$$z(t+1) = a\frac{1-cn^2(t)}{2cn^2(t)}, \tag{4.2.1}$$

$$1-cn^2(t+1) = a_0\frac{(z(t)+1)^{\frac{1}{\rho}-1}}{n^{1-\frac{2}{\rho}}(t)}(1-cn^2(t))^{1-\frac{1}{\rho}}, \tag{4.2.2}$$

where $a_0 \equiv (1-a)(a/2\alpha c)^{-1/\rho}$. If $\rho > 0$, then the system has a unique solution. It is proved that if $\rho > 0$ and sufficiently large (with fixed a, α), then we have the following: (i) there is a critical value of c, denoted by c^*, such that for $c > (<) c^*$, the fixed point is a saddle (sink) and (ii) at $c = c^*$, a flip bifurcation occurs. Thus, for c in a neighborhood of c^*, periodic solutions of period 2 can be observed. As demonstrated in Figure 4.6, there are four possible cases.

These cases can be numerically tested as follows:

For Figure 4.6(a),

a	c	α	ρ	(z_1^*, n_1^*)	(z_2^*, n_2^*)
0.1	0.25	0.5	−0.5	(0.965, 0.443)	(58.592, 0.058)

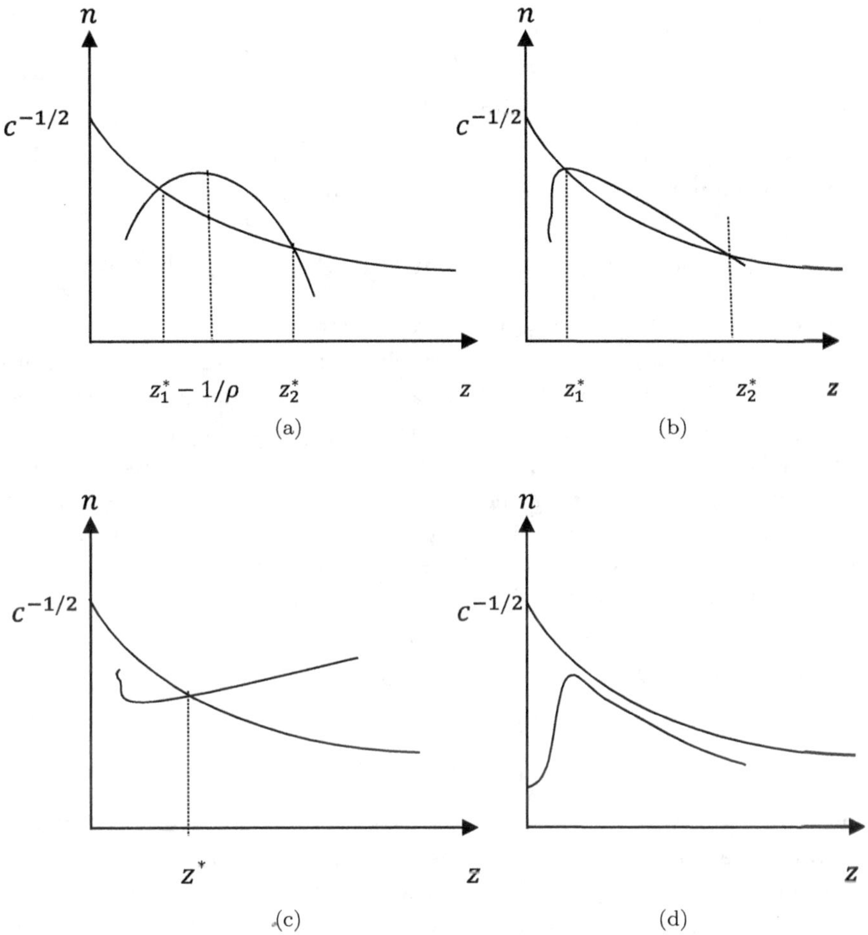

Fig. 4.6. Fixed points for $\rho <$. (a) Two fixed points: $z_1^* \leq -1/\rho < z_2^*$. (b) Two fixed points: $-\frac{1}{\rho} < z_1^* < z_2^*$. (c) Unique fixed point: $z^* > -1/\rho$ (d) No existence of fixed point.

For Figure 4.6(b),

a	c	α	ρ	(z_1^*, n_1^*)	(z_2^*, n_2^*)
0.1	0.25	0.5	−2	(0.884, 0.463)	(4.469, 0.210)

For Figure 4.6(c),

a	c	α	ρ	(z_1^*, n_1^*)
0.1	0.25	0.6062	−4	(1.418, 0.369)

For Figure 4.6(d),

a	c	α	ρ
0.1	0.1	0.6	−4

It is straightforward to check the eigenvalues for the above examples. Further examination of the model is referred to Chakrabarti.

4.3 Period Doubling Cascades of Prey–Predator Model

This section presents a study on a prey–predator, or Lotka–Volterra, type model for conservation of ecological resources through taxation with nonlinear harvesting. Prey–predator models are a key model in mathematical biology and applied in various fields of social sciences. The model presented in the following is developed by Gupta *et al.* (2014). The model applies the harvesting function by Agnew (1979) to a traditional prey–predator model. In a contemporary world, human efforts are required to sustain the co-existence of animals. Fishing is a typical example. The present model is also influenced by the literature on the economics of renewable resource management and harvesting (e.g., Clark, 1976, 1985).

Gupta *et al.* (2014) proposed the following dynamic model:

$$\dot{x}(t) = xg(x) - y\bar{p}(x) - h(x, E),$$

$$\dot{y}(t) = y(-d + \theta\bar{p}(x)), \quad x(0), \quad y(0) > 0,$$

where $x(t)$ and $y(t)$ are the densities of prey and predator, $g(x)$ is the per capita net prey growth in the absence of predator, $\bar{p}(x)$ represents the functional response of predator, θ is the conversion rate, d is the natural death rate of predator, and E is the effort applied to harvest the prey population. The functions $\bar{p}(x)$ and $g(x)$ are specified as

$$\bar{p}(x) = \frac{ax}{m + x}, \quad g(x) = r\left(1 - \frac{x}{k}\right),$$

in which r is the intrinsic growth rate of prey population, k is the environmental carrying capacity, a is the encounter rate of predator to prey, and m is the half of saturation constant.

The harvesting function is specified as

$$h(x, E) = \frac{qEx}{sC_0^{-1} + E + bsx},$$

where $E = sV$ with s being a proportionality constant and V is the number of identical vessels per unit area, used for the harvesting of population, C_0

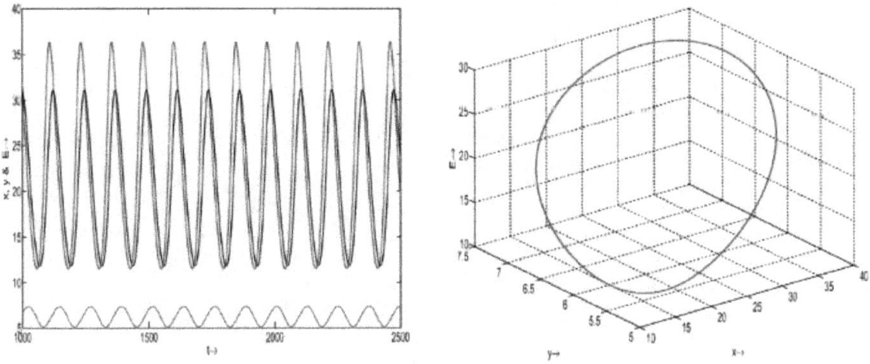

(a) (b)

Fig. 4.7. Stable business cycles at $T = 2$.

measures the degree of competition between the vessels, q is the catchability coefficient, and s is the proportionality constant for handling time. The effort changes according to

$$\dot{E} = n\left(\frac{(p-T)h}{E} - c\right)E,$$

where p is the profit, T is the tax rate, c is the cost per unit biomass, and n is an adjustment parameter.

The authors first investigate the stability of various equilibrium points, Hopf bifurcation around axial equilibrium points and around interior equilibrium points. In the following numerical illustrations, the parameter values are chosen:

$$a = 0.25, \quad r = 0.25, \quad k = 100, \quad m = 10, \quad d = 0.05, \quad p = 3, \quad \theta = 0.3,$$
$$q = 0.3, \quad C_0 = 1, \quad b = 1, \quad s = 1, \quad c = 0.15, \quad n = 1.$$

The tax rate is chosen as the bifurcation parameter. Figure 4.7 displays business cycles when $T = 2$. In the figure (and ones in the rest of this section), the red curve stands for prey population, the green curve for predator population, and the black curve for the effort applied for harvesting. Further increases in the tax rate lead to more complicated behavior of the system. It is also shown that small differences in the initial states result in complete paths of evolution (Figures 4.8 and 4.9).

Figure 4.10 illustrates how different initial states lead to long-term differences in the behavior of the system and provides the bifurcation diagram for $2.25 \leq T \leq 2.06$. In Figure 4.10(a), green and red curves show

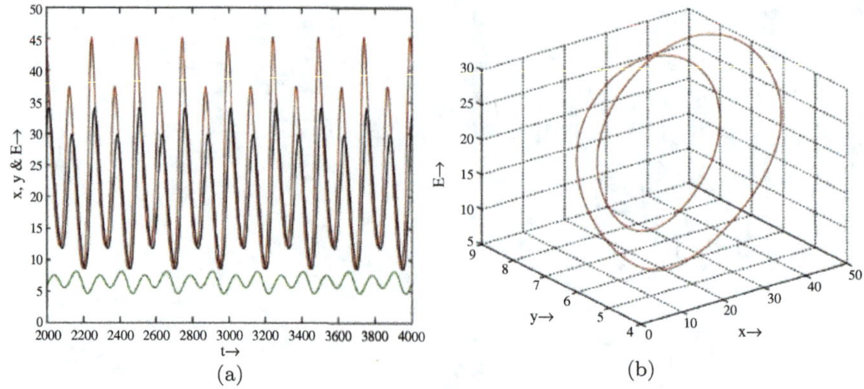

Fig. 4.8. Period-2 business oscillations at $T = 2.03$.

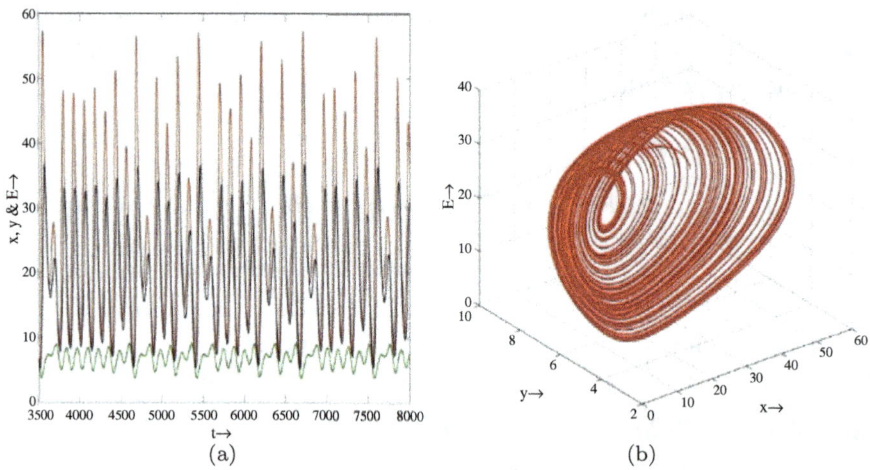

Fig. 4.9. Economic chaos at $T = 2.06$.

the prey population with two different initial states but the same parameter values (at $T = 2.06$). Figure 4.10(b) is the bifurcation diagram with the tax as the bifurcation parameter. The vertical axis is the prey population.

4.4 Chaos in a Discrete Prey–Predator Model

The previous section shows business cycles and chaos in a continuous prey–predator model. This section introduces a discrete prey–predator model

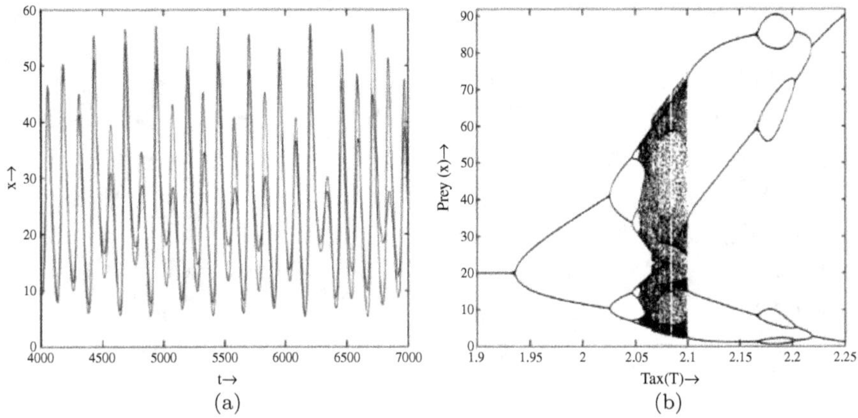

Fig. 4.10. Behavior with differential initial states and bifurcation diagram.

with chaos. The study is based on Chen and Chen (2012). They examined the dynamics of a discrete singular biological economic system. The model is a discretization of a differential-algebraic equation system for a ratio-dependent prey–predator system like in the previous section.

Let u_n and v_n stand for the densities of prey and predator populations in period n The discrete singular prey–predator system is formed as

$$\begin{aligned} u_{n+1} &= u_n + \delta u_n(r_1 - \epsilon v_n), \\ v_{n+1} &= v_n + \delta v_n \left(r_2 - \theta \frac{v_n}{u_n} - \alpha \bar{e}_n \right), \\ m &- \bar{e}_n(p v_n - c_1), \end{aligned}$$

where r_1, r_2, ϵ, θ, and c_1 are positive constants, $\bar{e}_n$ is the harvesting effort, $\alpha \bar{e}_n v_n$ is the harvesting of predator population, δ is the step size, α is the harvesting cost per unit harvesting effort, p is the harvesting reward per unit harvesting effort, and m is the economic profit per unit harvesting effort. Introduce

$$x_n \equiv \frac{\theta}{\epsilon} u_n, \quad y_n \equiv \epsilon v_n, \quad e_n \equiv \epsilon \bar{e}_n, \quad c \equiv \frac{\epsilon c_1}{p}, \quad \mu \equiv \frac{\alpha \epsilon m}{p}.$$

The original model is rewritten as

$$\begin{aligned} x_{n+1} &= x_n + \delta x_n(r_1 - y_n), \\ y_{n+1} &= y_n + \delta y_n \left(r_2 - \frac{y_n}{x_n} - e_n \right), \\ \mu &= e_n(y_n - c). \end{aligned}$$

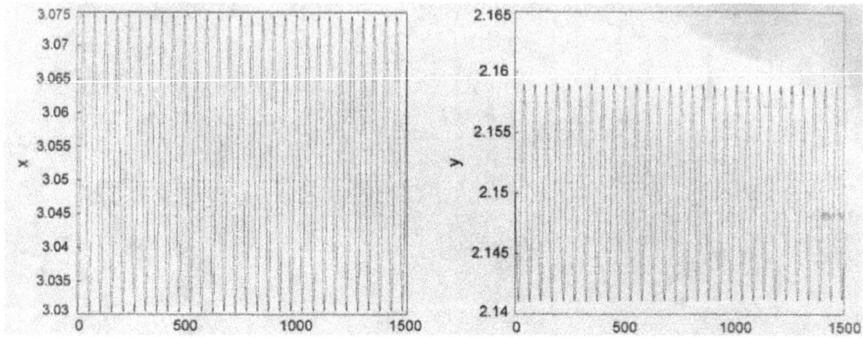

(a) (b)

Fig. 4.11. Business cycles.

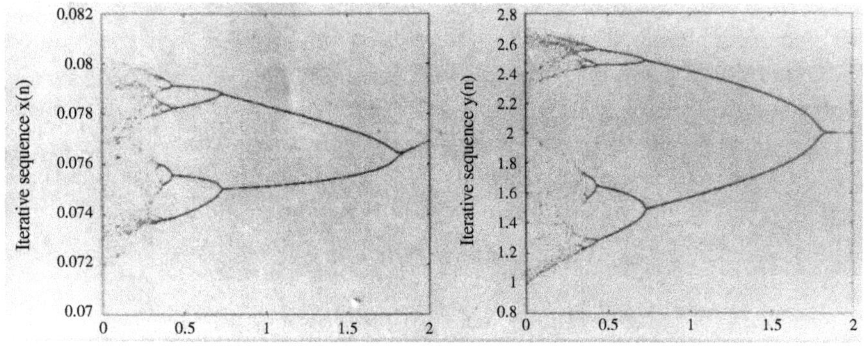

(a) (b)

Fig. 4.12. Bifurcation diagram with the bifurcation parameter μ.

Chen and Chen studied this transformed discrete singular system. They demonstrated flip and Neimark–Sacker bifurcation in the system. Figure 4.11 demonstrates business cycles when

$$r_1 = 2.15, \quad r_2 = 1, c = 1, \quad \delta = 01, \quad \mu = 0.34.$$

Figure 4.12 shows the bifurcations in the two variables with μ as the bifurcation parameter.

$$r_1 = 2, \quad r_2 = 27.9999, \quad c = 1, \quad \delta = 0.1.$$

4.5 Spatial Pattern of Prey–Predator Model with Delay in Prey

The prey–predator model is one of the most important models in biology and ecology to deal with population dynamics. It is an effective tool for exploring chains of survival, such as food chains, food webs, and biochemical network structures (e.g., Kuang, 2003; Murray, 2003; Maiti *et al.*, 2007). Karl Marx's theory of class struggle was explained by this modeling framework. It is not difficult to see that through proper introduction of behavioral mechanisms in human societies, the modeling framework has great potential for exploring the complexity of human interactions. Economics has a great deal to learn from insights from this modeling framework. For instance, the role of space in cultural formation, racial relations, and populations of races is rarely addressed in economic theory. The time between fertilization and birth in population control is a politically important variable in many countries. Pre-determined four-year elections in America should have influences on, large scales or small oscillations, global business cycles. An important question, but seldom addressed in theoretical economics, is whether space or diffusion stabilizes or destabilizes socioeconomic systems. East Asian (rice-based) highly populated cultures are naturally different from American civilization because of population densities before the recent development of digital technologies. Nomadic and Han Chinese people were a kind of prey and predator relationship before modern weapons were diffused (which disabled the invasive power of nomadic peoples). This section introduces a spatial extension of the classical model with time delay in prey.

The model, on which this section is based, is proposed by Rao (2018). It should be noted that Zhang (1988a, 1989a) applied nonlinear partial differential equations to urban economics in similar systems. It is a delayed Monod–Haldane-type predator–prey system with diffusion in both prey and predator. Let $N(x,t)$ and $P(x,t)$ stand for prey and predator population densities within the habitat $\Omega = (0,\pi)$, respectively, as follows:

$$\frac{\partial N(x,t)}{\partial t} = D_1 \Delta N + rN(1 - N(t-\tau)) - \frac{PN}{a + bN + N^2}, \quad x \in \Omega, \ t > 0,$$

$$\frac{\partial P(x,t)}{\partial t} = D_2 \Delta P + P\left(-d + \frac{N}{a + bN + N^2}\right), \quad x \in \Omega, \ t > 0,$$

$$\frac{\partial N(x,t)}{\partial x} = \frac{\partial P(x,t)}{\partial x} = 0, \ x \in \partial\Omega, \ t > 0,$$

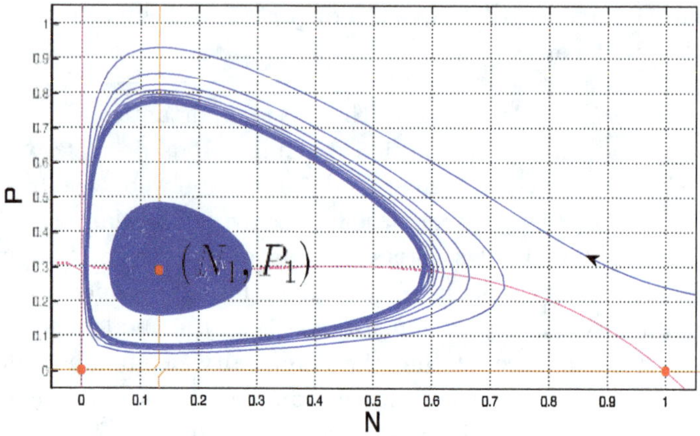

Fig. 4.13. Existence of cycles without delay.

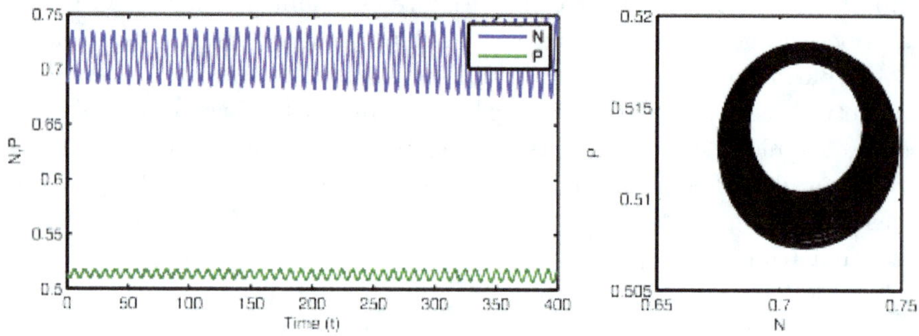

Fig. 4.14. Existence of cycles with delay and without diffusion.

$$N(x,\theta) = N_0(x,\theta) \geq 0, \quad P(x,\theta) = P_0(x,\theta) \geq 0, \quad \theta \in [-\tau, 0], \ t > 0,$$

where r, d, a, and b are the parameters, the delay parameter τ in gray is considered as the negative feedback of prey, Δ is the Laplacian operator, and D_1 and D_2 are diffusion coefficients of prey and predator, respectively. The zero-flux boundary conditions imply no migration between the system and the outside world.

We first cite a result on the existence of cycles when diffusion reaction is neglected, $D_1 = D_2 = 0$. The rest parameters are specified as

$$a = 0.3, \quad r = 1, \quad b = 0.1, \quad d = 0.4, \quad D_1 = D_2 = \tau = 0.$$

Figure 4.13 displays the existence of a stable limit cycle.

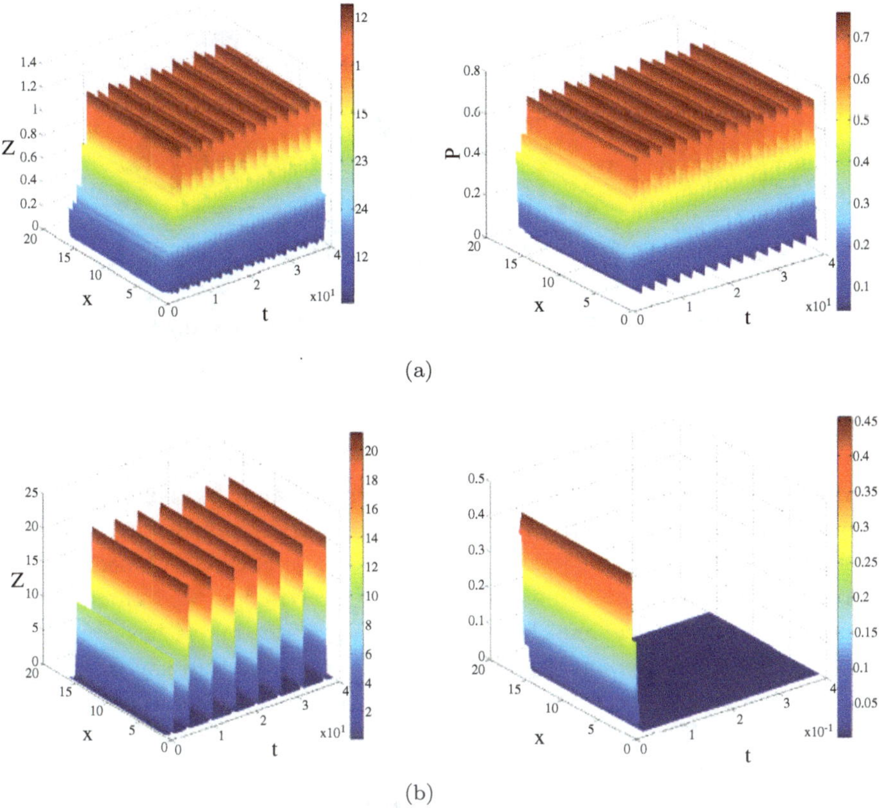

Fig. 4.15. Existence of cycles with delay and diffusion. (a) $D_2 = 0.1$; populations of two species are oscillating. (b) $D_2 = 2$; Large diffusion rate of predator species population and the extinction of predator species.

Figure 4.14 shows the existence of a stable cycle when the parameters are taken on the following values:

$$a = 1.2, \quad r = 1, \quad b = 0.1, \quad d = 0.4, \quad \tau = 1.77, \quad D_1 = D_2 = 0.$$

Figure 4.15 shows the existence of cycles with diffusion reaction of the two species with the following parameter values:

$$a = 0.35, \quad r = 1, \quad b = 0.1, \quad d = 0.72, \quad \tau = 1.3, \quad D_1 = 0.05.$$

4.6 Carryover Effects on Population

Ruiz-Herrera (2017) recently proposed an ecological model that explores the effects of carryover effects (COEs) — any process that in one season that

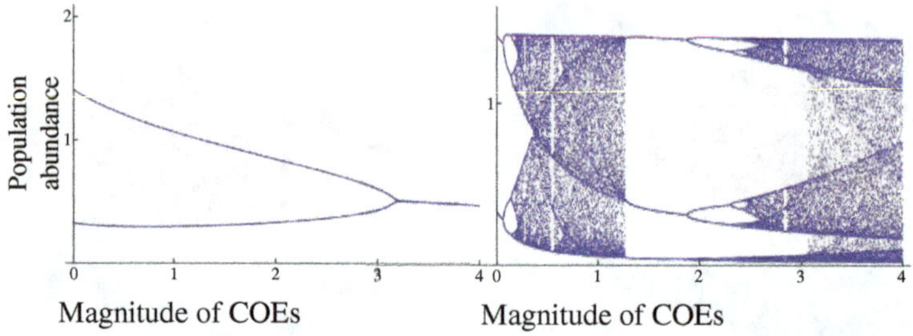

$F = e^{2.7(1-N_{nb})}$, $S = 0.7/(1 + hN_{nb})$ $F = e^{2.7(1-N_{nb})}$, $S = 0.7/(1 + hN_{nb}^5)$

Fig. 4.16. Population and magnitudes of COEs.

affects, non-lethally, individuals in the following seasons — on population dynamics. COEs can change both reproduction and survival rates. For instance, modern romanticism and economic development are globally associated with declining birth rates and aging. For many species, the behaviors of individuals depend on resources, territories, and climates. In China, for instance, the one-child policy, even abolished now, has continued to affect the Chinese population structure. Some COEs are key factors for migratory species. Ruiz-Herrera focused on examining the stabilizing or destabilizing role of OCEs.

The study is concerned with a biological population with a life cycle divided into two seasons: a breeding period and the remainder. The seasons may not be the same. Let $Nb(t)$ and $Nnb(n)$ denote respectively the population abundance at the end of the breeding and non-breading. A simple season model, which is widely applied in the literature of seasonal populations, is defined by

$$N_{nb}(n+1) = s(N_b(n))N_b(n), \tag{4.6.1}$$

$$N_b(n+1) = N_{nb}(n+1)f(N_{nb}(n+1)), \tag{4.6.2}$$

where s is the survival rate in the non-breeding season and f is the growth rate during the breeding period.

In order to introduce COEs, Ruiz-Herrera replaced the growth rate with a map $F(N_{nb}(n+1), hN_b(n))$, where the parameter h measures the magnitude of the COE on the birth rate and $F(N_{nb}(n+1), 0) = f$. We thus replace Eq. (4.6.2) with

$$N_b(n+1) = N_{nb}(n+1)F(N_{nb}(n+1),\ hN_b(n)). \tag{4.6.3}$$

Similarly, the survival rate is replaced by $S(N_b(n), hN_{nb}(n))$. We have

$$N_{nb}(n+1) = S(N_b(n), hN_{nb}(n))N_b(n). \tag{4.6.4}$$

A few numerical simulations with Eqs. (4.6.3) and (4.6.4) illustrate how COEs can affect the dynamics of the population (Figure 4.16).

4.7 Generalized Neoclassical General Equilibrium Theory with Generalized Malthusian Theory

This section confirms the existence of business cycles in the model of economic growth and population change with discrimination against women proposed by Zhang (2020d). The model deals with dynamic interdependence between wealth accumulation and endogenous birth and mortality rates with gender discrimination. The basic mechanisms for population changes are influenced by the Barro–Becker fertility choice model and the Haavelmo population model (Haavelmo, 1954). The production technology and markets are framed with general equilibrium theory with capital accumulation. There are many studies on economic growth and birth rates (Barro and Becker, 1989; Galor and Weil, 1996; Hock and Weil, 2012). There are also studies on quality–quantity trade-offs on children (Galor and Weil, 1999; Bosi and Seegmuller, 2012). There are formal models on economic growth and mortality rates (e.g., Kirk, 1996). Markets are perfectly competitive. Depreciation rate of capital is denoted by $\delta_k(t)$ Input factors are fully utilized. Savings is made by households. The population is composed of male and female populations. A family is composed of husband, wife, and children. All the families are identical. Man and woman are denoted with subscript indexes $q = 1$ and $q = 2$, respectively. We use $N(t)$ to stand for the adult population of each gender. Let $T_q(t)$ and $\bar{T}_q(t)$ stand for work time and time spent on taking care of children of gender q. We use $N_q(t)$ to represent the qualified labor force of gender q. We have

$$N_q(t) = h_q(t)T_q(t)N(t).\ \bar{N}(t) = N_1(t) + N_1(t),$$

where $h_q(t)$ is gender q's level of human capital and $\bar{N}(t)$ is total labor supply employed in time t for production. We use $K(t)$ and $F(t)$ to stand for capital input and output levels. Production function is specified as

$$F(t) = A(t)K^{\alpha(t)}(t)\bar{N}^{\beta(t)}(t), \quad \alpha(t), \beta(t) > 0, \quad \alpha(t) + \beta(t) = 1.$$

Labor and capital are paid for their marginal products. Firms earn zero profits. We use $w(t)$ to represent the wage rate per unit of qualified work time in fair labor market where workers earn their marginal value of labor. There is a fraction $\phi(t)$ of women's fair share of the gender's labor taken away by firms from women. The rate $\phi(t)$ is called the discrimination rate against women. As Maria Bartiromo emphasized, "Most women outlive their spouses. Divorce remains at record rates. It's important for a woman to be able to control her finance." This study does not involve the complexity of marriage and divorce dynamics. The total cost of the female labor force due to discrimination is $\phi(t)h_2(t)T_2(t)N(t)$.

Profit maximization yields the following marginal conditions:

$$r(t) + \delta_k(t) = \frac{\alpha(t)F(t)}{K(t)},$$

$$w_1(t) = \frac{\beta(t)h_1(t)F(t)}{\bar{N}(t)},$$

$$w_2(t) = \frac{\beta(t)h_2(t)F(t)}{\bar{N}(t)},$$

where $w_q(t)$ is the wage rate per unit of work time by gender q:

$$w_1(t) \equiv w(t), \quad h_1(t), \quad w_2(t) \equiv (1 - \phi(t))w(t)h_2(t).$$

The family decides on five variables: leisure time, work time, consumption level of commodity, number of children, and savings. We use $\bar{k}(t)$ to represent wealth per family. We have $\bar{k}(t) = K(t)/N(t)$. The family's current income $y(t)$ from interest income and wage payments is

$$y(t) = r(t)\bar{k}(t) + w_1(t)T_1(t) + w_2(t)T_2(t).$$

The family's disposable income is the sum of the current income and the value of wealth: $\hat{y}(t) = y(t) + \bar{k}(t)$. Let $n(t)$ and $p_b(t)$ stand for birth rate and cost of birth, respectively. Parents spend time and the following cost on their children: $p_b(t) = n(t)\bar{k}(t)$. The relation between fertility rate and the parent's time on raising children is specified as follows:

$$\bar{T}_q(t) = \theta_q(t)n(t), \quad \theta_q(t) \geq 0.$$

The disposable income is used up for savings $s(t)$, consumption of goods $c(t)$, and bearing children $p_b(t)$. The budget constraint implies

$$p(t)c(t) + s(t) + \bar{k}(t)n(t) = \hat{y}(t).$$

The leisure time of gender q is presented by $\tilde{T}_q(t)$. The available time T_0 is used for work, children care, and leisure. The time constraint for each worker is $T_q(t) + \bar{T}_q(t) + \tilde{T}_q(t) = T_0$. The budget is rewritten as follows:

$$p(t)c(t) + s(t) + \bar{k}(t)n(t) + \bar{T}_1(t)w_1(t) + \bar{T}_2(t)w_2(t) + \tilde{T}_1(t)w_1(t) + \tilde{T}_2(t)w_2(t) = \bar{y}(t),$$

in which

$$\bar{y}(t) \equiv (1 + r(t))\bar{k}(t) + (w_1(t) + w_2(t))T_0.$$

We thus have

$$c(t) + s(t) + \tilde{w}(t)n(t) + \tilde{T}_1(t)w_1(t) + \tilde{T}_2(t)w_2(t) = \bar{y}(t), \tag{4.7.1}$$

where

$$\tilde{w}(t) \equiv \bar{k}(t) + h(t)w(t), \quad h(t) \equiv \theta_1(t)h_1(t) + (1 - \phi(t))\theta_2 h_2(t).$$

The utility is a function of $c(t), s(t)$, $\tilde{T}_q(t)$, and $n(t)$ as follows:

$$U(t) = c^{\xi_0(t)}(t)s^{\lambda_0(t)}(t)\tilde{T}_1^{\sigma_{01}(t)}(t)\tilde{T}_2^{\sigma_{02}(t)}(t)n^{\upsilon_0(t)}(t),$$

where $\xi_0(t)$ is the propensity to consume, $\sigma_{0q}(t)$ is the gender q's propensity to use leisure time, $\lambda_0(t)$ is the propensity to have wealth, and $\upsilon_0(t)$ is the propensity to have children. Marginal conditions for maximizing the utility subject to Eq. (4.7.1) imply

$$c(t) = \xi(t)\bar{y}(t), \quad s(t) = \lambda(t)\bar{y}(t), \quad \tilde{T}_q(t) = \frac{\sigma_q(t)\bar{y}(t)}{w_q(t)},$$

$$n(t) = \frac{\upsilon(t)\bar{y}(t)}{\tilde{w}(t)}, \tag{4.7.2}$$

where

$$\xi(t) \equiv \rho(t)\xi_0(t)\lambda(t) \equiv \rho(t)\lambda_0(t), \; \sigma_q(t) \equiv \rho(t)\sigma_{q0}(t),$$

$$\upsilon(t) \equiv \rho(t)\upsilon_0(t)\rho(t) \equiv \frac{1}{\xi_0(t) + \lambda_0(t) + \sigma_{10}(t) + \sigma_{20}(t) + \upsilon_0(t)}.$$

Let $n(t)$ and $d(t)$ represent birth rate and mortality rate, respectively. The population change rate is birth rate minus mortality rate

$$\dot{N}(t) = (n(t) - d(t))N(t).$$

The mortality rate is as follows:

$$d(t) = \frac{\bar{\upsilon}(t)N^{b(t)}(t)}{\bar{y}^{a(t)}(t)},$$

in which $\bar{\upsilon}(t) \geq 0$, $a(t) \geq$. We thus have

$$\dot{N}(t) = \left(\frac{\upsilon(t)\bar{y}(t)}{\tilde{w}(t)} - \frac{\bar{\upsilon}(t)N^{b(t)}(t)}{\bar{y}^{a(t)}(t)}\right)N(t).$$

Change in the family's wealth is savings minus dissavings:

$$\dot{\bar{k}}(t) = s(t) - \bar{k}(t) = \lambda(t)\bar{y}(t) - \bar{k}(t).$$

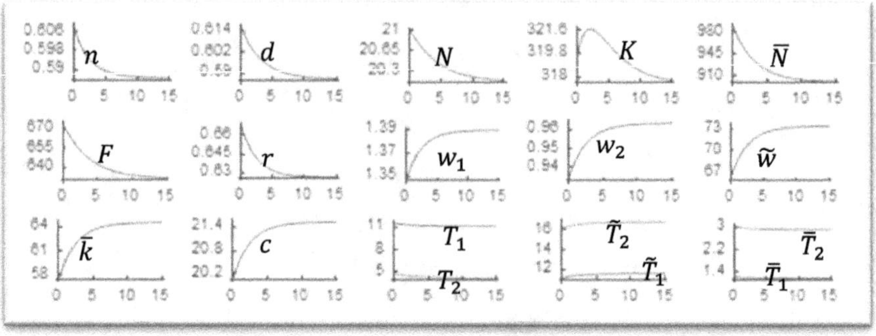

Fig. 4.17. Motion of the economy without perturbations.
Note: Horizontal axis: time; vertical axis: the variable values.

Output is used for net savings and depreciation of capital stock. We have

$$S(t) + C(t) - K(t) + \delta_k(t)K(t) = F(t), \tag{4.7.3}$$

where $S(t) - K(t) + \delta_k(t)K(t)$ is the sum of the net savings and depreciation and

$$S(t) \equiv s(t)N(t), \quad C(t) \equiv c(t)N(t), \quad K(t) \equiv \bar{k}(t)N(t).$$

We built the model. We choose $\delta_k = 0.05$ and $T_0 = 24$. The other parameters take on the following values:

$$\alpha = 0.34, \quad \lambda_0 = 0.6, \quad \xi_0 = 0.2, \quad \upsilon_0 = 0.4, \quad \sigma_{10} = 0.15,$$

$$\sigma_{10} = 0.15, \quad A = 1,$$

$$a = 0.4, \quad b = 0.5, \quad h_1 = 3, \quad h_2 = 2.6, \quad \theta_1 = 2,$$

$$\theta_2 = 5, \quad \bar{\upsilon} = 1, \quad \phi = 0.2.$$

The discrimination rate is 0.2. Initial conditions are $z(0) = 1.6$, $N(0) = 21$. Figure 4.17 shows the simulation result. Simulation shows the existence of a unique stable equilibrium.

To show the impact of discrimination against women, we now simulate a case in which the discrimination rate against women periodically oscillates:

$$\phi(t) = 0.2 + 0.05\sin(t).$$

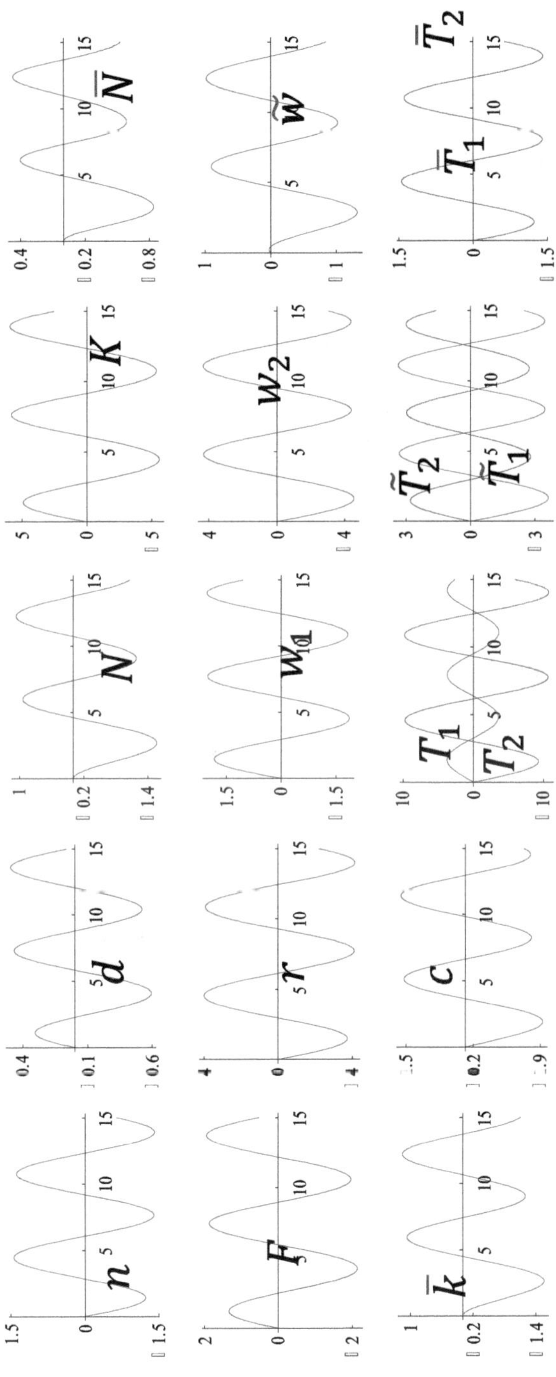

Fig. 4.18. The discrimination rate against women oscillates periodically.

Note: Horizontal axis: time; vertical axis: the changes of the variable values in percentage.

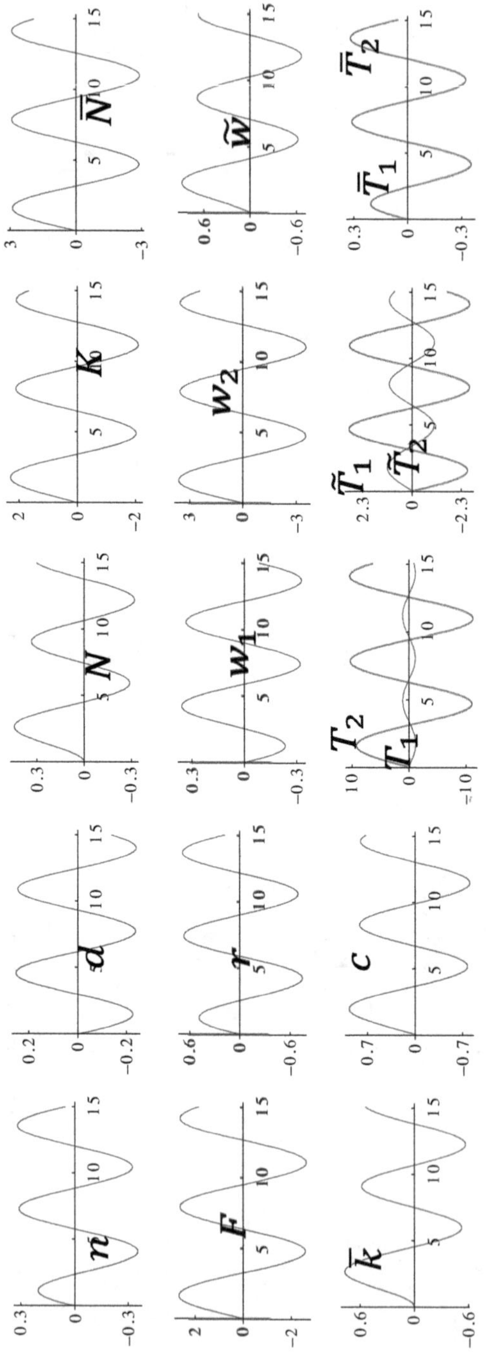

Fig. 4.19. Women's human capital oscillates periodically.

Note: Horizontal axis: time; vertical axis: the changes of the variable values in percentage.

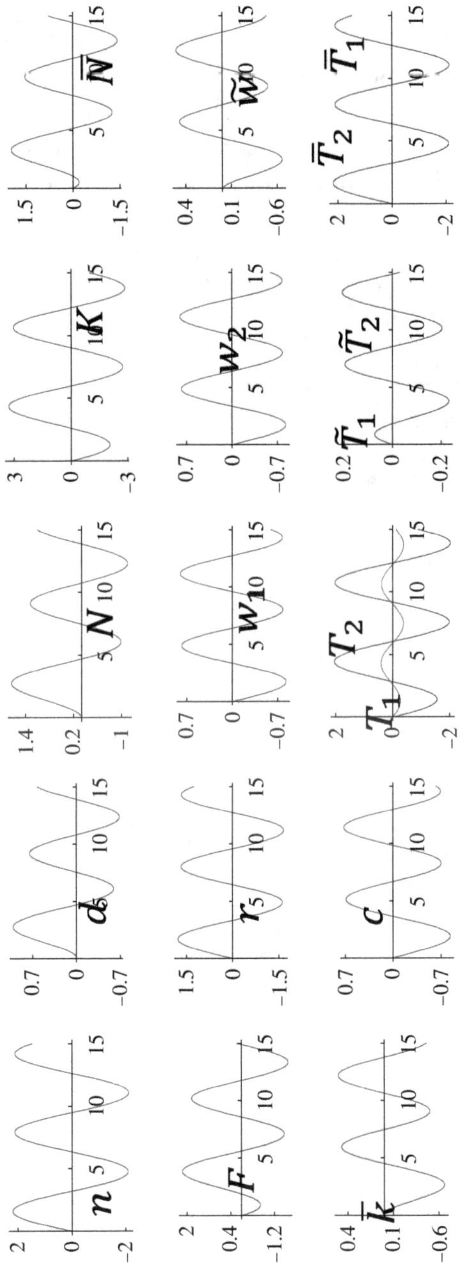

Fig. 4.20. The propensity to have children oscillates periodically.

Note: Horizontal axis: time; vertical axis: the changes of the variable values in percentage.

Figure 4.18 plots the simulation results. We see that periodic oscillations in the discrimination lead to business cycles in our model.

Traditional neoclassical economic theory holds that gender inequalities associated with human capital gap will wither away as an economy experiences high economic growth. Stotsky (2006: 18) points out: "The neoclassical approach examines the simultaneous interaction of economic development and the reduction of gender inequalities. It sees the process of economic development leading to the reduction of these inequalities and also inequalities hindering economic development." We now allow the mother's human capital to oscillate periodically as follows:

$$h_2(t) = 2.6 + 0.1 \sin(t).$$

Figure 4.19 plots the simulation results. Birth rates oscillate as the female population's human capital oscillates.

We now study an oscillated propensity to have children as follows:

$$\upsilon_0(t) = 0.4 + 0.02 \sin(t).$$

Figure 4.20 plots the simulation results.

Chapter 5

Technological Changes and Human Capital Accumulation

Adam Smith held that the large gains in the productivity of labor have their origins in the large part of the skill, dexterity, and judgment, which are consequences of the division of labor. The opportunities and incentives to which workers respond in their investment in human capital are not seriously considered by classical economists such as Smith, Ricardo, and Marx. The omission was perhaps not so much misleading as it might appear, given the role of innovation and education in economic development when the classical economists were constructing their theories. Nancy Pearcey described the exchange value of knowledge in American society: "America is a knowledge-based society, where information counts as much as material resources. Therefore, those with the power to define what qualifies as knowledge — to determine what are the accepted facts — wield the greatest social and political power." It is not general knowledge but socially or politically or economically valuated knowledge that profit-energized American society is good.

What American computer scientist Alan Perils said are applicable to interpret international relations among nations: "Fools ignore complexity. Pragmatists suffer it. Some can avoid it. Geniuses remove it," "One man's constant is another man's variable," "Symmetry is a complexity-reducing concept (co-routines include subroutines); seek it everywhere," "It is easier to write an incorrect program than understand a correct one"; "If you have a procedure with the parameters, you probably missed some," and "Often it is the means that justify the ends: Goals advance technique and technique survives even when goal structures crumble." These insights are useful, in visionary and structural senses, to understand the history of international trade. Benjamin Franklin said: "No nation was ever ruined by trade." This observation looks so true for American economy during the period of his lifetime. In recent years, America has experienced increasing protectionism. Heath Edward argued: "Protectionism is the institutionalization of economic failure." It is not difficult to show that an economy may benefit by strengthening protectionism. Robert Mundell (1932–2021) — who received the 1999 Nobel Prize in economics for his works in monetary economics and is commonly considered the father of the euro as he laid the groundwork for his introduction through his pioneering work in money and supply-side economics — reflected: "In my early days, I wrote my dissertation for MIT at the London School of Economics, really under James Meade, but my dissertation was five chapters on the theory of capital movement, but it didn't mention money." The Euro region did not last and had little sign to prove what Mundell reasoned about. We are living within the middle of global chaos that the lifepath frequently turns out against what one has rationally expected. This chapter is concerned with models with endogenous changes and human capital accumulation, which exhibit nonlinear phenomena. Section 5.1 represents the model by Zhang (2006a) which explains path-dependent economic growth. The model synthesizes Solow's physical capital accumulation, Arrow's learning-by-doing, and Uzawa's learning-by-education growth models within a comprehensive framework. It is well known that the neoclassical growth theory based on the Solow growth model focuses accumulation of physical capital as an engine of growth, while the neo-Schumpeterian growth theory stresses innovation. Section 5.2 shows oscillations between the Solowian and Schumpeterian economies in the model proposed by Matsuyama (1999). Declining hours of work during one's lifetime is a well-observed phenomenon among developed economies. In recent years, there are many models proposed to explain the economic mechanisms of endogenous labor supply in association with economic development. Section 5.3 represents a new-growth-theory model for cycles of works by Iong and Irmen (2021). Section 5.4 shows homoclinic bifurcation in the modified Romer growth model proposed by Bella (2017). Section 5.5 shows the existence of chaos in the Uzawa–Lucas model identified by Bella *et al.* (2017). Section 5.6 studies the dynamical behavior of the model for a two-stage Cournot duopoly game with R&D spillover effect and product differentiation proposed by Zhou *et al.* (2019). The original paper study investigates the behavior of the model, applying Jury criterion, central manifold theorem, norm form theory, as well as numerical simulation. Section 5.7 introduces the model by Agliari *et al.* (2018), which is based on the cobweb demand–supply framework with costly innovators and free imitators. Section 5.8 introduces the international trade model with product cycles and growth cycles by Iwaisako and Tanaka (2017). Section 5.9 provides the model of generalized neoclassical general equilibrium theory which integrates Uzawa two-sector, Uzawa–Lucas two-sector, and Onik–Uzawa multi-country models within a comprehensive framework.

5.1 A Generalized Solow–Uzawa Model with Poverty and Education

One of the first seminal attempts to render technical progress endogenous in growth models was initiated by Arrow (1962). He emphasized one aspect of knowledge accumulation: learning by doing. Uzawa (1965) introduced a sector specifying creating knowledge into growth theory. The education sector utilizes labor and the existing stock of knowledge to produce new knowledge, which enhances the productivity of the production sector. Zhang (2006a, Section 3.2) synthesized Solow's physical capital accumulation, Arrow's learning-by-doing, and Uzawa's learning-by-education growth models within a comprehensive framework. It provides another economic mechanism of path-dependent economic development in the literature on economic growth.

The economy has one production sector, subindexed by i, and one education sector, subindexed by e. The system has a homogenous and fixed national labor force, N The labor force is distributed between economic activities, teaching, and studying. We select commodity to serve as numeraire. We assume that wage rates are identical among all professions.

We use $F(t)$, $K(t)$, and $H(t)$ to denote the output level of the production sector, the national capital stocks, and the level of human capital of the population. Market-determined wage rate and rate of interest are respectively $w(t)$ and $r(t)$. We express labor force and capital stocks employed by sector j respectively, as $N_j(t)$ and $K_j(t)$. Production is to combine qualified labor force, $H^m(t)N_i(t)$, and physical capital, $K_i(t)$. Most aspects of our model are the same as the OSG model. The production process is described by

$$F(t) = AK_i^{\alpha}(t)(H^m(t)N_i(t))^{\beta}, \quad A, \alpha, \beta > 0, \ \alpha + \beta = 1.$$

The marginal conditions are given by

$$r(t) = (1-\tau)\alpha A k_i^{-\beta}(t), \quad w(t) = (1-\tau)\beta A H^m(t) k_i^{\alpha}(t),$$

where $k_i \equiv K_i/H^m N_i$ and τ is the tax rate on the product level. We denote per capita wealth by $k(t)$ where $k(t) \equiv K(t)/N$ Per capita current income is given by $y(t) = r(t)k(t) + w(t)$. The per capita *disposable income* is given by $\hat{y}(t) = y(t) + k(t)$. Maximizing the following utility function

$$U(t) = c^{\xi}(t)s^{\lambda}(t), \quad \xi, \lambda > 0, \ \xi + \lambda = 1$$

subject to $c(t) + s(t) = \hat{y}(t)$ yields the optimal solution: $c(t) = \xi\hat{y}(t)$ and $s(t) = \lambda\hat{y}(t)$. The change in the household's wealth is equal to the savings minus the wealth sold at time t i.e.,

$$\dot{k}(t) = s(\hat{y}(t)) - k(t) = \lambda\hat{y}(t) - k(t).$$

We propose the following human capital accumulation through Arrow's learning-by-doing and Uzawa's learning-by-education models:

$$\dot{H} = \frac{\upsilon_e K_e^{\alpha_e}(H^m N_v)^{\beta_v}(H^m N_e)^{\beta_e}}{N} + \frac{\upsilon_i F}{N H^{\pi}} - \delta_h H,$$

where N_e is the number of students, $\delta_h(> 0)$ is the depreciation rate of human capital, and υ_e, υ_i, α_e, β_v, and β_e are non-negative parameters. We assume that the students and teachers are paid by the government's tax income at the same wage rate as the wage rate of workers. We assume that the economy has a fixed ratio of the population who are getting education in a university: $N_e = n_e N$. Assume that the total tax income is used for paying the students, teachers, and the capital stocks employed by the university. The government spends $w(t)N_e$ amount of money on students. Obviously, this assumption is strict. A way to relax this assumption without increasing the analytical complex of the model is to assume that each individual spends a given amount of time on education. The time distribution is given by $T_i + T_e = T$, where T is the fixed available time, T_i is the work time, and T_e is the time as a student. The student gets free education but does not receive any wage. The budget for paying teachers and the capital stocks of the university is given by

$$w(t)N_v(t) + r(t)K_e(t) = \tau F(t) - w(t)N_e.$$

The university distributes its total resource $\tau F(t) - w(t)N_e$ to the teachers $N_v(t)$ and the capital stocks $K_e(t)$ in such a way that the output of the university $v_e K_e^{\alpha_e}(H^m N_v)^{\beta_v}(H^m N_e)^{\beta_e}$ will be maximized. The university's problem is formed as follows:

$$\operatorname{Max} v_e K_e^{\alpha_e}(H^m N_v)^{\beta_v}(H^m N_e)^{\beta_e}$$

subject to the budget. The solution is given by

$$K_e = \frac{\alpha_e(\tau F - wN_e)}{(\alpha_e + \beta_v)r}, \quad N_v = \frac{\beta_v(\tau F - wN_e)}{(\alpha_e + \beta_v)w}.$$

Labor force and capital stocks are fully employed $N_i + N_e + N_v = N$ and $K_i + K_e = K$. We described the model.

We now examine multiple equilibrium points by simulation. We specify the parameters as follows:

$$\alpha = 0.35,\ N = 1,\ A = 2,\ N_e = 0.06,\ \tau = 0.08,\ \lambda = 0.7,\ \alpha_e = 0.7,$$

$$\beta_e = 0.7,\ \beta_v = 0.7,\ \nu_e = 1.8,\ \nu_i = 0.02,\ \delta_h = 0.08,\ \pi = 0.3,\ m = 0.8.$$

The system has two equilibrium points:

$$(k_1, H_1) = (17.858,\ 2.226)(k_2, H_2) = (10.401,\ 19.509).$$

The one with lower levels of human capital and per capita wealth is stable; the other is unstable, also as analytically proved. Figure 5.1 depicts the vector field and the steady states of the dynamic system. As shown in Figure 5.1, an economy with a low level of human capital, even if it was initially rich, tends to converge to the stable equilibrium with low standard

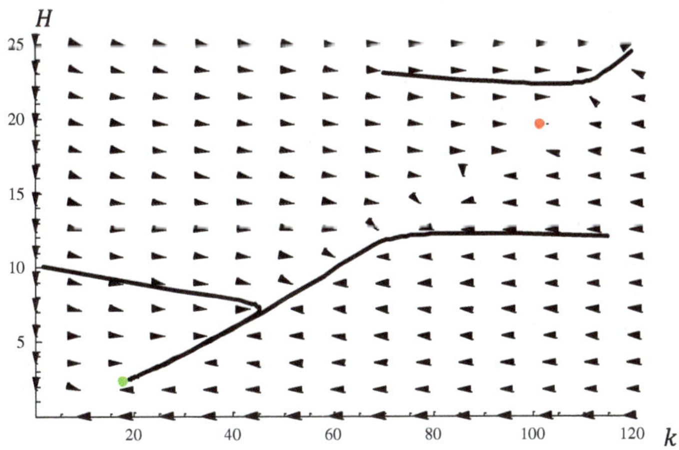

Fig. 5.1. Path-dependent economic evolution.

of living and low-level human capital. An economy with high level of human capital, even if it was initially poor, tends to experience sustained growth. This nonlinear dynamic system has path-dependent features. Here, we can see the significance of cultural value for education. Japanese-, Korean-, and Chinese-dominated economies like Singapore and Taiwan could have sustained economic growth irrespective of their initial poor conditions in the 1960s, mainly because of their cultural values on education, rather than due to high savings rates. In the 1950s, no one could have foreseen the rapid economic development of East Asia because few economists recognized the significance of education in economic development and fewer knew the validity of rationalism in classical Confucianism for modern economies. In the literature on economic growth and development published in the 1960s and 1970s, capital accumulation is the main engine of economic development. Economists failed to properly interpret the economic evolution of these regions because they did not properly examine the cultural values of education in this region.

We simulate three paths of the economy with the initial values:

$$(k_0, H_0) = (1.5, 10), \quad (k_0, H_0) = (115, 12), \quad (k_0, H_0) = (70,\ 23). \quad (5.1.1)$$

The paths with $(k_0, H_0) = (1.5, 10)$ and $(k_0, H_0) = (115, 12)$ converge to the low levels of human capital and per capita wealth. It is interesting to note that the path with $(k_0, H_0) = (115, 12)$ starts with high level of wealth. But its level of human capital is not improved over time. As decreasing returns dominate this path, its prosperity does not last long. The path with $(k_0, H_0) = (70, 23)$ will grow infinitely because the increasing return to scale dominates the economic evolution. Indeed, this kind of infinite growth will not happen in reality as our model neglects many other significant factors, such as endogenous population change, negative externalities such as pollution, and limitations of natural resources, which are neglected in this model.

As far as qualitative features of economic development are concerned, Figure 5.1 provides some insights into the difference in the economic development in Mainland China and Taiwan during the period of 1950–1980 — I depict this difference without any mathematical equation (Zhang, 2003, 2021a). The two areas started the economic development with similar economic conditions but different average educational levels. Before the economic reform in 1978 started in Mainland China, the living conditions and educational achievements in the two Chinese societies had been enlarging. It is only in recent years that Mainland China has begun to explore the opportunities for economic development. Structurally, mainland China's political and economic system had devaluated modern (Western) education so that no sector in the society could have explored the potential benefits of increasing returns offered by the Western civilization. Both cultural values and political systems matter in our "neoclassical" model — I call this model neoclassical in the sense that except for the utility function, all the assumptions accepted in this study were developed and accepted in the literature of neoclassical economic growth theory developed in the 1950s and 1960s.

We now conduct a comparative dynamic analysis. Let us consider the case that the expenditure on education is reduced from 8 percent of the GDP to 7 percent: $\tau : 0.08 \Rightarrow 0.07$. Figure 5.2 shows the simulation results — the points with larger sizes are the new steady states and the other two points with smaller sizes are the old steady states. The two steady states shift as follows:

$$(k_1, H_1) : (17.858, 2.226) \Rightarrow (14.758, 1.718),$$

$$(k_2, H_2) : (101.401, 19.509) \Rightarrow (230.783, 53.417).$$

We see that the new stable steady state has lower levels of human capital and per capita wealth, but the new unstable steady states have much higher levels of k and H It seems promising with the new education policy because the new unstable steady state of higher k and H is much better than the old unstable one. Nevertheless, the economy with the discouraging policy has more chances to the traditional trap than to the economic miracle.

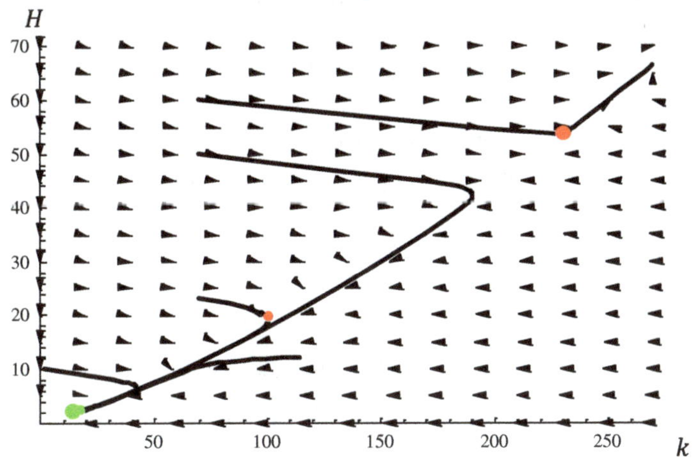

Fig. 5.2. The path-dependent development as the education is discouraged.

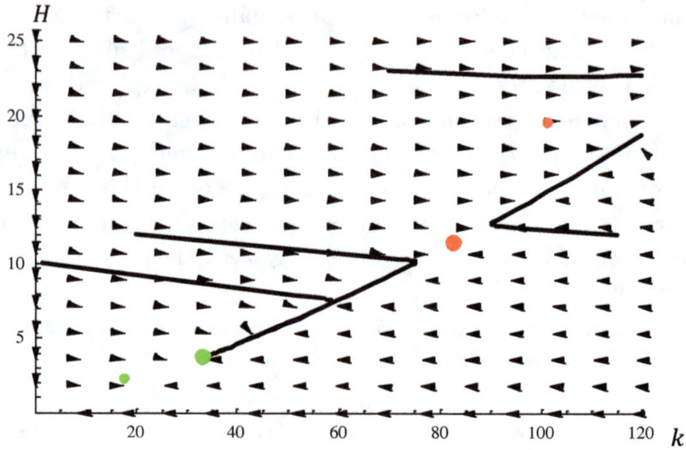

Fig. 5.3. An increase in the propensity to save.

For instance, we start from Eq. (5.1.1). As demonstrated in Figure 5.2, all the paths with these initial conditions end up in the poverty trap. But in Figure 5.1, the path with $(k_0, H_0) = (70, 23)$ exhibits the economic miracle. This example shows that the discouraging policy deprives the society from development opportunity. The "chance" for development is loss due to the new policy. As shown in Figure 5.2, for the economy to experience sustained growth, the economy must have a much higher initial level of human capital than in the case of $\tau = 0.08$. Hence, if the society reduces its investment in education, it will have much less opportunities to experience sustained economic growth, even though heavy investment in education will not guarantee sustainable development of the nonlinear system in certainty.

We increase the propensity to save. Let us consider the case that the propensity to save is increased from 0.7 to 0.73, that is, $\lambda : 0.7 \Rightarrow 0.73$. Figure 5.3 shows the simulation results — the points with larger sizes are the new steady states and the other two points with smaller sizes are the old steady states. The two steady states shift as follows:

$$(k_1, H_1) : (17.858, 2.226) \Rightarrow (14.758, 1.718),$$

$$(k_2, H_2) : (101.401, 19.509) \Rightarrow (230.783, 53.417).$$

We see that the new stable steady state has higher levels of human capital and per capita wealth, but the new unstable steady state has lower levels of k and H. Figure 5.3 depicts the impact of change in λ on the dynamics of the system.

Our simulation results demonstrate the path-dependent characteristics of the nonlinear system. Some of the assumptions should be relaxed. Indeed, our analysis does not rely on the specified production and utility functions.

5.2 Oscillations between the Solowian and Schumpeterian Economies

The neoclassical growth theory based on the Solow growth model focuses on accumulation as an engine of growth, while the neo-Schumpeterian growth theory stresses innovation. Recently, Matsuyama (1999; see also Zhang, 2006b, Section 5.5) proposed a model to capture these two mechanisms within the same framework. The model generates an unstable balanced growth path, and the economy achieves sustainable growth cycles, moving back and forth between the two phases: one is characterized by higher output growth, higher investment, no innovation, and a competitive market structure, and the other by lower output growth, lower investment, high innovation, and a more monopolistic structure.

There is a single final good, taken as a numeraire; it is competitively produced and can either be consumed or invested. Let $K(t-1)$ be the final good left unconsumed in period $t-1$ and made available for use in production in t. Labor is supplied inelastically in amount N. Labor goes directly into final goods production. Capital $K(t-1)$ must be first converted into a variety of differentiated intermediate products; these intermediates are aggregated into the composite by a symmetric CES. The final goods production function is

$$Y(t) = A_0 N^{1/\sigma} \int_0^{Z(t)} x^{\alpha}(z,t)dz, \quad \alpha = 1 - \frac{1}{\sigma},$$

where $x(z,t)$ is the input of variety z in period t, $\sigma \in (1,\infty)$, and $[0, Z(t)]$ is the range of intermediates available at t. The market structure of the intermediate sector is described as follows. Prior to t, the economy developed all the intermediates in the range, $[0, Z(t-1)]$, with $Z(0) > 0$. These old intermediates are manufactured by converting a units of capital into one unit of an intermediate and sold competitively in t. In addition, the intermediates of variety $z \in [Z(t-1), Z(t)]$ may be introduced and sold exclusively by their innovators in t. Innovating new intermediates requires F units of capital per variety. The process of manufacturing new intermediates requires a units of capital per output. Let $r(t)$ denote the price of capital. The marginal cost of manufacturing intermediates in t is equal to $ar(t)$. The old products are supplied at the marginal costs

$$p(z,t) = p^c(t) = ar(t), \quad z \in [0, Z(t-1)].$$

All the new products are sold at

$$p(z,t) = p^m(t) = \frac{a\sigma}{\sigma - 1} r(t), \quad z \in [Z(t-1), Z(t)].$$

Since all the intermediates enter symmetrically in the final goods production, we have

$$\frac{x^c(t)}{x^m(t)} = \left[\frac{p^c(t)}{p^m(t)}\right]^{-\sigma} = \alpha^{-\sigma},$$

where $x(z,t) = p^c(t), z \in [0, Z(t-1)]$ and $p(z,t) = p^m(t), z \in [Z(t-1), Z(t)]$. The one-period monopoly enjoyed by the innovator yields the monopoly profit: $\pi = p^m x^m - r(ax^m + F)$ at t. The profit is negative if and only if $x^m(t) < (\sigma - 1)F/a$. The free entry conditions ensure

$$ax^m(t) \le (\sigma - 1)F, \quad Z(t) \ge Z(t-1),$$
$$[ax^m(t) - (\sigma - 1)F][Z(t) - Z(t-1)] = 0.$$

The resource constraint on capital in t is given by

$$K(t-1) = ax^c(t) Z(t-1) + (ax^m(t) + F)(Z(t) - Z(t-1)).$$

Under the conditions so far, the above constraint becomes

$$ax^c(t) = a\sigma_0^{-\sigma} x^m(t) = \min\left\{\frac{K(t-1)}{Z(t-1)}, \theta\sigma F\right\},$$

$$Z(t) = Z(t-1) + \max\left\{0, \frac{K(t-1)}{\sigma F} - \theta Z(t-1)\right\},$$

where $\theta \equiv \sigma^{1-\sigma}$. The total output is

$$Y(t) = \begin{cases} A\left[\theta\sigma F Z(t-1)\right]^{\frac{1}{\sigma}} K^{\alpha}(t-1) & \text{if } K(t-1) \le \theta\sigma F Z(t-1), \\ AK(t-1) & \text{if } K(t-1) > \theta\sigma F Z(t-1), \end{cases}$$

where we use

$$A \equiv \frac{A_0}{a}\left(\frac{aN}{\theta\sigma F}\right), \int_0^{Z(t)} x^{\alpha}(z,t)\,dz = (x^c(t))^{\alpha} Z(t-1)$$
$$+ (x^m(t))^{\alpha}(Z(t) - Z(t-1)).$$

If $K(t-1)/Z(t-1) \leq \theta\sigma F$, the resource base of the economy, K, is too small relative to the number of the existing products, Z, and there is no innovation. The economy in this situation is called the *Solow regime.* If $K(t-1)/Z(t-1) > \theta\sigma F$, some new products are introduced; the economy is said to be in the *Romer regime.* To close the model, it is assumed that the economy carries over a constant fraction of its output to the next period, i.e., $K(t) = sY(t)$, where s is a constant. Set $k(t) = K(t)/\theta\sigma F Z(t)$. Then, the system can be expressed as the one-dimensional difference equation:

$$k(t) = f(k(t-1)) = \begin{cases} sAk^{\alpha}(t-1), & \text{if } k(t-1) \leq 1, \\ \dfrac{sAk(t-1)}{1+\theta(k(t-1)-1)}, & \text{if } k(t-1) > 1. \end{cases}$$

The critical value of k, denoted by $\bar{k}(=1)$, which separates the Solow and Romer regimes is equal to one. If $sA < 1$, the system has a unique steady state, $k^* = (sA)^{\sigma} < \bar{k}$. Without innovation, all goods are competitively supplied and the economy does not grow: the steady is a *neoclassical stationary path.* If $sA > 1$, the steady state, given by $k^{**} = 1 + (sA-1)/\theta > \bar{k}$, is in the Romer regime. New products are introduced steadily, and K and Z grow at the same rate. It is a *balanced growth path,* characterized by $K(t+1) = sAK(t)$. Figure 5.4 depicts the case of $sA < 1$. For any initial condition, after at most one period, innovation stops and the economy is trapped in the Solow regime.

Figure 5.5 illustrates the case of $1 < sA < \theta - 1$. The equilibrium point k^{**} is locally unstable because of $f'(k^{**}) < -1$. The interval $[f^2(k^{**}), f(k^{**})]$ represents the trapping region, i.e., the region that the economy enters eventually and once entered will never leave. The trapping region covers both the Solow and Romer regimes. If the economy starts with a small k_0, the economy may stay in the Solow regime for some periods but eventually accumulates enough capital to enter the Romer regime, and innovation begins. The economy begins cycling between the two regimes. Formally, it can be proved that if $1 < sA < \theta - 1$, there are period-2 cycles, and $k(t)$ fluctuates forever between the Solow and Romer regimes for almost all initial conditions. In the case of $> \theta - 1$, $-1 < f'(k^{**}) < 0$.

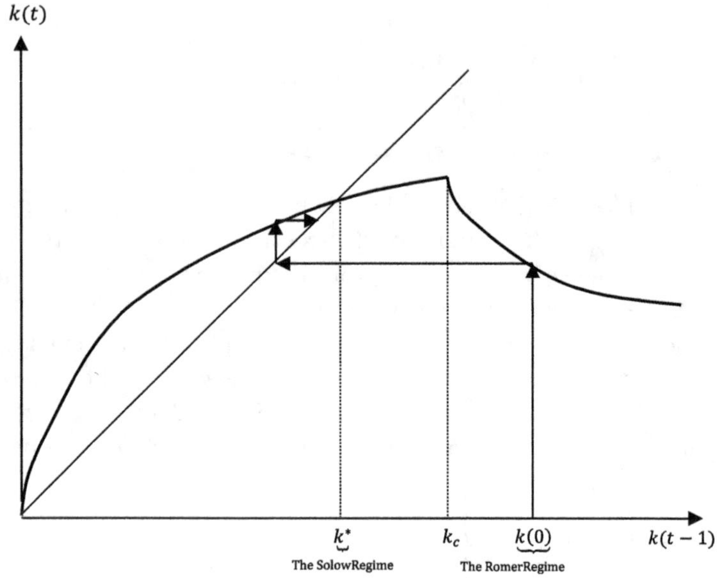

Fig. 5.4. Growth governed by the Solow mechanism with $sA < 1$.

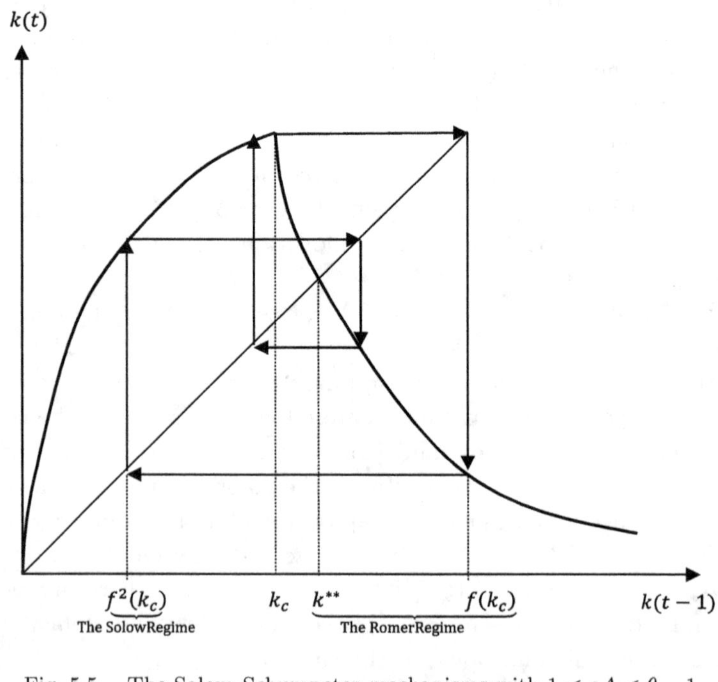

Fig. 5.5. The Solow–Schumpeter mechanisms with $1 < sA < \theta - 1$.

The steady state is globally stable. In the long term, the economy will forever stay in the Romer regime.

5.3 Cycles of Work Hours Explained by New Growth Theory

Declining hours of work during one's lifetime is a well-observed phenomenon among developed economies. Keynes foresaw this long-tern trend long time ago. In recent years, there are many models proposed to explain the economic mechanisms of endogenous labor supply in association with economic development. This section introduces a model by Iong and Irmen (2021), which is influenced by Boppart and Krusell (2020) and Matsuyama (1999).

The economy consists of a household sector with overlapping two-period lived individuals, a production sector of monopolistically competitive firms which produce differentiated varieties of a consumption good, and a research sector which are specified in innovating new consumption goods. Time is discrete, $t = 0, 1, \ldots$. The young people supply labor for production and research. There is an asset market where bonds and ownership shares in the firms of the production sector are traded. At the beginning of each period, all assets are held by the old generation. The old sell their ownership shares to the young to finance their consumption. The economy has L_t young and L_{t-1} old individuals. The number of young individuals between two adjacent periods grows at a fixed rate g_L. A young person supplies labor, gets wage, saves, consumes goods, and enjoys leisure. An old person sells his wealth to pay for consumption. Let c_t^y, c_{t+1}^o, $l_t (\in [0,1])$, and s_t stand for consumption when young, consumption when old, leisure time, and savings, respectively. We use h_t as a unit of labor supply when young, that is, $h_t = 1 - l_t$. The utility function has taken on the following form:

$$U_t = \ln c_t^y + \ln \left(1 - \varphi (1 - l_t) (c_t^y)^{\frac{v}{1-v}}\right) + \beta c_{t+1}^o, \tag{5.3.1}$$

where parameter $\varphi > 0$ measures the strength of disutility of labor, $\beta \in (0,1)$ is the discount factor, and $v \in (0,1)$ implies that consumption and leisure are complementary. Let $x_t^y (j)$ and $x_{t+1}^o (j)$ represent consumption good j Bundles of differentiated consumption goods are given by

$$c_t^y = A_t^{\sigma - \frac{1}{\alpha}} \left\{ \int_0^{A_t} \left[x_t^y (j)\right]^\alpha dj \right\}^{\frac{1}{\alpha}}, \quad c_{t+1}^o = A_{t+1}^{\sigma - \frac{1}{\alpha}} \left\{ \int_0^{A_{t+1}} \left[x_{t+1}^o (j)\right]^\alpha dj \right\}^{\frac{1}{\alpha}},$$

where $\sigma > 1$ and $\alpha \in (0, 1)$ are parameters and A_t is the number of available consumption goods at t. The parameter σ is a taste for variety. The parameter α measures the elasticity of substitution between any pair of existing consumption good varieties. The optimal behavior is decided by a two-stage budgeting procedure. First, it allocates its spending across the differentiated consumption goods available when young and old. Second, it determines labor supply and consumption profile. It is well known in new growth theory that the first stage determines

$$x_t^y(i) = \frac{p_t(j)^{-\frac{1}{1-\alpha}} c_t^y}{A_t^{\sigma-\frac{1}{\alpha}} \left\{ \int_0^{A_t} p_t(i)^{-\frac{\alpha}{1-\alpha}} di \right\}^{\frac{1}{\alpha}}},$$

$$x_{t+1}^0(i) = \frac{p_{t+1}(j)^{-\frac{1}{1-\alpha}} c_{t+1}^0}{A_{t+1}^{\sigma-\frac{1}{\alpha}} \left\{ \int_0^{A_{t+1}} p_{t+1}(i)^{-\frac{\alpha}{1-\alpha}} di \right\}^{\frac{1}{\alpha}}}.$$

At this stage, the two expenditure functions in period t are given by $P_t c_t^y$ and $P_t c_t^o$ where the price index is defined as

$$P_t = A_t^{\frac{1}{\alpha}-\sigma} \left\{ \int_0^{A_t} p_t(i)^{-\frac{\alpha}{1-\alpha}} di \right\}^{\frac{1}{\alpha}}.$$

We use $w_t > 0$ to represent the wage per hour and $R_{t+1} > 0$ the interest factor paid per unit saved. The problem is to maximize U_t in Eq. (5.3.1) subject to

$$P_t c_t^y + P_t s_t \le w_t h_t,$$
$$P_{t+1} c_{t+1}^0 \le R_{t+1} P_t s_t.$$

We will not give the expressions of the solution as we are mainly concerned about the construction of the model, and the meanings of the parameters are provided.

There are A_t firms which equal the number of available consumption goods at t as each firm possesses the blueprint and a perpetual patent for the exclusive production of variety $j \in [0, A_t]$. All firms produce with the same linear production function: $x_t(j) = h_{x,t}(j)$, where $h_{x,t}(j)$ is the working hours that firm j employs. Firm j's profit is

$$\pi_t(j) = p_t(j) x_t(j) - w_x(j) h_{x,t}(j),$$

where $x_t(j) = L_{t-1}(j) x_t^o(j) + L_t(j) x_t^y(j)$. The price is decided at $p_t = p_t(j) = w_t/\alpha$ set by all firms. All firms thus supply the same quantity, i.e., $x_t = x_t(j)$, $x_t^o = x_t^o(j)$, and $x_t^y = x_t^y(j)$. The profit for each firm: $\pi_t = (1 - \alpha) p_t x_t$. These profits are paid as dividends to old individuals. The total amount of work hours $H_{x,t} = A_t h_{x,t} = A_t x_t$.

We now describe the research sector. As in Jones (1995), the representative has a technology available for creativity:

$$A_{t+1} = A_t + \frac{H_{A.t}}{a} A_t^{\psi}, \quad a > 0, \ 0 < \psi < 1.$$

We use v_t to stand for the revenue from selling a blueprint of a newly created variety. We have the profit for firm: $v_t - w_t a / A_t^{\psi}$, where a/A_t^{ψ} is the amount of hours worked in the research sector required to invent one new variety. The equilibrium condition under free entry

$$v_t \leq w_t a A_t^{\psi}, \quad \text{with} = \text{if } A_t > 0.$$

We have a few equilibrium conditions:

$$L_t = L_1 (1 + g_L)^{t-1}, \ P_t c_t^y L_t + P_t c_t^o L_{t-1} = p_t A_t x_t, \ H_{x,t} + H_{A,t} = h_t L_x.$$

In the asset market at t the ownership shares of existing and new varieties, which have the same price v_t, are traded. A market valuation of shares requires

$$v_t = \frac{\pi_{t+1}}{R_{t+1}} + \frac{\pi_{t+2}}{R_{t+1} R_{t+2}} + \cdots,$$

where π_j is the dividend paid to the shareholders in the future. We rewrite the above equation as follows:

$$\frac{v_{t+1}}{v_t} + \frac{\pi_{t+1}}{v_t} = R_{t+1}.$$

The equilibrium conditions for savings and ownership shares are $s_t L_t = v_t A_{t+1}$. Normalize the prices by choosing $P_t = 1$ for all t. The authors examine the transitional dynamics of the economy by following the motion of a new variable: $z_t = L_t / A_t^{\eta}$, where $\eta = 1 - \psi + v(\sigma - 1) > 0$. The authors identified a value z_c such that if $z_t \leq z_c$, then the economy is said to be in Regime 0 (in which there is no research activity), and if $z_t > z_c$, then the economy is said to be in Regime 1 (in which research is active). The authors also examined the properties of the economy and provided numerical examples to demonstrate the existence of business cycles with z_1 as the bifurcation parameter and $z_c = 1$ and $g_L = 0.006$. Figure 5.6 shows the motion of z_t when $\psi - v(\sigma - 1) = -2$. All the variables experience cycles over history.

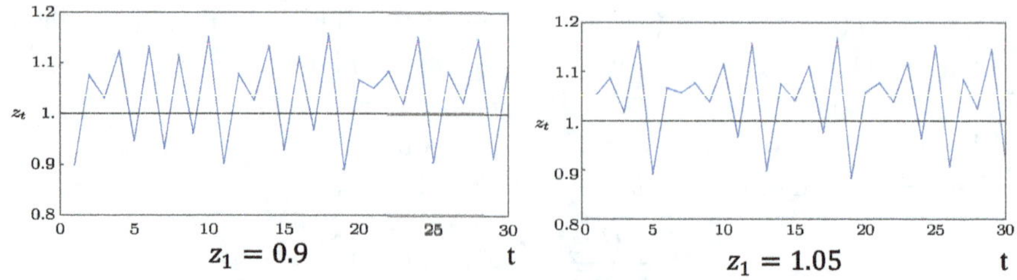

Fig. 5.6. Cycles with research and without research.

5.4 Homoclinic Bifurcation in a Modified Romer Growth Model

The 2018 Nobel Prize in economics was awarded to Romer because of his work "for integrating technological innovations into long-run macroeconomic analysis." His core work for the prize is his 1990s paper *Endogenous Technological Change*, which has played an important role for the development of new economic growth — the mainstream of explaining America's golden period of economic growth. The determinacy of the equilibrium is examined from local perspectives, studying the saddle-path dynamics only in the vicinity of the steady-state solution. It has become evident that local analysis is not able to provide a complete picture of the full dynamics of a nonlinear dynamic model. The presence of a saddle-path does not exclude the possible existence of a more complicated dynamic phenomenon in the large. The Romer model has been extended and generalized in different directions. There is a huge number of publications directly or indirectly related to the paper (which had been cited over 36000 times even by 2021). The original model does not exhibit complicated nonlinear phenomena concerned in this book. A recent reformation of the model proposed by Bella (2017) leads to homoclinic bifurcation. Bella derived "the parametric configuration that allows for the emergence of a double-pulse homoclinic orbit, and the rise of globally indeterminate solutions, in the same area where local determinacy was found. Our results confirm that irregular patterns and oscillating solutions can be obtained along a subsidiary homoclinic orbit, in presence of a so-called Belyakov degeneracy, at which the periodic loop starts to double, so that the system might perpetually oscillate (with different periods of the generated cycles) around the long run equilibrium, perhaps without ever attaining the steady state again, being thus finally confined in an outer stationary trapping region." This section introduces some key points of Bella's work.

The modified version of the Romer model is much influenced by Benhabib and Farmer (1994) and Slobodyan (2007). Economy has a continuum of firms. The production is carried out by two sectors: one sector producing capital goods and the other being devoted to do research. Firms in the final goods sector are characterized by perfect competition, while the market for intermediate is monopolistic. Production function of final goods has taken on the following form:

$$Y(t) = h^{\alpha} L^{\beta} \left(\int_0^A x(i)^{\gamma/\xi} \, di \right)^{\xi}, \quad \alpha, \beta, \gamma > 0, \;\; \alpha + \beta + \gamma = 1,$$

where h is the amount of skilled workers employed in the production sector, L is the amount of unskilled labor, and $x(i)$ is the unit of intermediate goods indexed by an increased level of knowledge, A In this model, the total amount of skilled workers in the economy is 1. The parameter $\xi \geq 1$ allows a degree of complementarity among intermediate capital goods, which extends the original Romer model. It is assumed that in equilibrium all intermediate goods are equally supplied, i.e., $x(i) = \bar{x}$, for all i. The total capital stock is given by $K = \eta \int_0^A x(i) \, di = \eta A \bar{x}$, where η measures the units of intermediates. We now have

$$Y = \eta^{-\gamma} h^{\alpha} L^{\beta} A^{\xi - \gamma} K^{\gamma}.$$

We thus have physical capital accumulation:

$$\dot{K}(t) = Y(t) - C(t), \tag{5.4.1}$$

where $C(t)$ is the total amount of consumption.

The profit $\pi(i)$ of firm i is given by

$$\pi(i) = p(i) \, x(i) - r\eta x(i),$$

where $p(i)$ is the price and r is the interest rate. The price is given by $p(i) = \partial Y / \partial x(i)$. From the optimal condition for firm i, we have $r = p/\eta$. Under these conditions, we have the optimal profit:

$$\pi = \frac{\eta(\xi - \gamma)}{\gamma} r \bar{x}.$$

Knowledge accumulation is specified as

$$\dot{A} = \delta(1 - h) A, \tag{5.4.2}$$

where $(1-h)$ is the amount of skilled workers enrolled in the research sector and δ is a positive parameter. Under free entry, the price of new goods P_A produced in the research sector must equal the net present value of profits:

$$P_A = \int_0^\infty \pi(\tau)e^{-\int_t^\tau r(s)ds}d\tau.$$

With the above conditions, we have the motion of P_A as follows:

$$\dot{P}_A = rP_A - \pi. \tag{5.4.3}$$

The model applies the standard CES utility function to describe preferences. Consumption is determined by

$$\max \int_0^\infty \frac{C^{1-\sigma}-1}{1-\sigma}e^{-\sigma t}dt,$$

subject to Eqs. (5.4.1)–(5.4.3) and $1 \neq \sigma$. Introducing $q = C/K$. Bella shows that the dynamics is described by the following three differential equations:

$$\begin{aligned} \dot{r}(t) &= F_r(r,h,q), \\ \dot{h}(t) &= F_h(r,h,q), \\ \dot{q}(t) &= F_q(r,h,q). \end{aligned} \tag{5.4.4}$$

We don't provide explicit functional forms of F_j because we have already introduced the model. The rest of this section illustrates some interesting properties of Eq. (5.4.4). After some complicated transformation, the local behavior is described as three variables (x, y, z) as functions of (r, h, q). Under

$$(\alpha, \beta, \gamma, \delta, \xi, \rho, \sigma) = (0.33, 0.01, 0.46, 0.023, 2.7, 0.01, 2.2)$$

the behavior of (x, y, z) is illustrated in Figure 5.7. We don't present the units as the transformations are too complicated to provide an explicit interpretation of (x, y, z). The numerical simulation shows that under commonly accepted parameter values in the literature of new growth theory, the dynamic system may exhibit "a rich setoff different outcomes, going from the stable solution implied by the homoclinic orbit to the saddle equilibrium, passing through the rise of homoclinic cycles with different period length, and finally leading to the possible emergence of a chaotic attractor" (Bella, 2017). It is noted that Bella and Mattana (2018) examine nonlinear behavior in the well-known Lucas–Uzawa two-sector growth model with endogenous human capital.

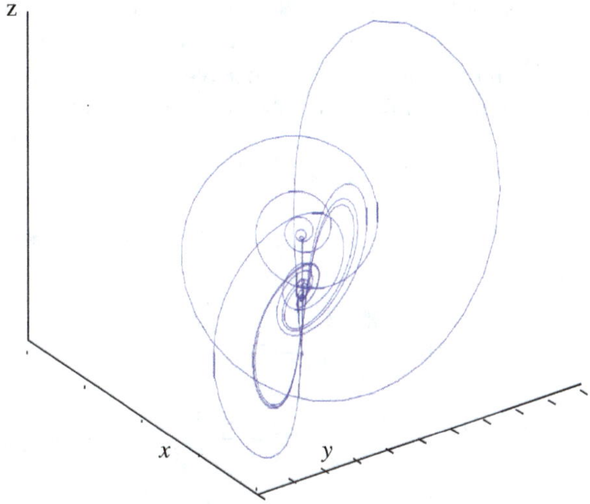

Fig. 5.7. The double-pulse homoclinic orbit.

An important study on education and economic growth with formal modeling is the Uzawa–Lucas model (Uzawa, 1965; Lucas, 1988). The Uzawa–Lucas model deals with growth and human capital accumulation with formal education. The model has great influences on the development of theoretical research (e.g., Zhang, 2017). Benhabib and Perli (1994) examined further analytical properties of Lucas' 1988. Bella *et al.* (2017) identified Shilnikov chaos in the Lucas model. This section shows some simulation results by Bella *et al.*

5.5 Chaos in the Uzawa–Lucas Model

We first describe the Lucas model reformed by Benhabib and Perli and then show numerical illustrations and introduce the simulation results. Formally, the Lucas model is constructed as follows:

$$\max_{c(t),u(t)} \int_0^\infty \frac{c^{1-\sigma}-1}{1-\sigma} e^{-\rho t} dt$$

$$\text{subject to } \dot{k} = Ak^\beta (uh)^{1-\beta} h^\gamma - c,$$

$$\dot{h} = \delta h(1-u),$$

and positive initial conditions. Here, c is the consumption, k is the physical capital, h is the human capital, u is the work hours, $1-u$ is the hours devoted to accumulating human capital, γ is a positive externality parameter, and A, β, σ, δ and ρ are parameters. Introduce

$$x \equiv kh^{(1-\beta-\gamma)/(\beta-1)}, \quad q \equiv \frac{c}{k}.$$

Benhabib and Perli showed that the motion of the Lucas model is described by the following three nonlinear differential equations:

$$\dot{x} = Ax^{\beta}u^{1-\beta} + \frac{\delta\,(1-\beta-\gamma)}{\beta-1}\,(1-u)\,x - qx,$$

$$\dot{u} = Ax^{\beta}u^{1-\beta} + \frac{\delta\,(\beta-\gamma)}{\beta}\,u^2 + \frac{\delta\,(1-\beta-\gamma)}{\beta-1}u - qu,$$

$$\dot{q} = q^2 + A\frac{(\beta-\sigma)}{\sigma}x^{\beta-1}u^{1-\beta}q - \frac{\rho}{\sigma}q.$$

Bella *et al.* (2017) examined some nonlinear phenomena which were not identified in previous studies. They showed that bifurcations occur on the parametric hypersurface as shown in Figure 5.8 under some additional conditions. The parameters β, and σ are taken on wide ranges of values.

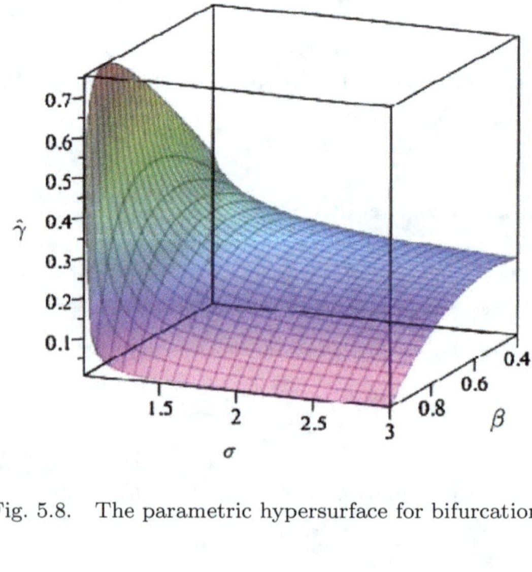

Fig. 5.8. The parametric hypersurface for bifurcations.

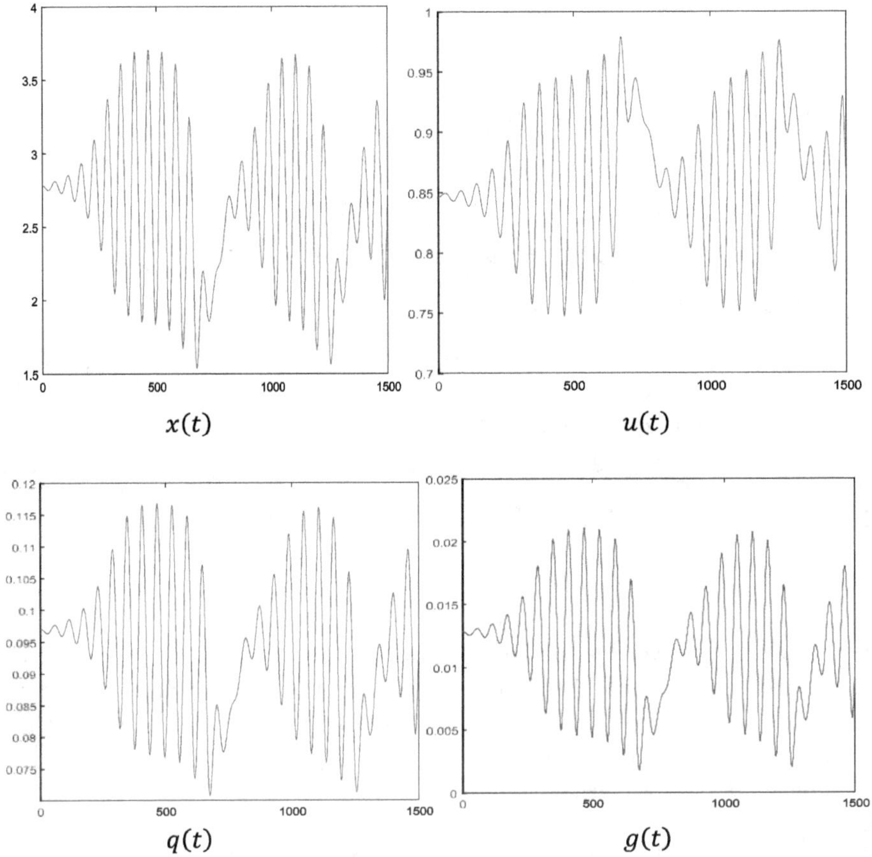

Fig. 5.9. Irregular time-dependent motion of the economy.

Let variable g denote the growth rate of the economy. Figure 5.9 shows irregular time-dependent behavior of the economy with the following parameter values:

$$A = 0.2, \quad \beta = 0.5, \quad \delta = 0.05, \quad \gamma = \frac{1}{3}, \quad \rho = 0.02297, \quad \sigma = 2.5.$$

The authors also varied γ near the value in Figure 5.9. Figure 5.10 shows how the system oscillates as γ is perturbed (red for $\gamma = 0.32$, green for $\gamma = 0.4$, and blue for $\gamma = 1/3$).

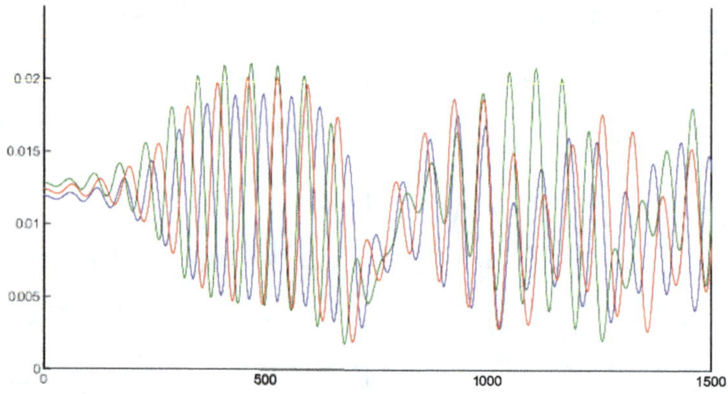

Fig. 5.10. Irregular growth rates with changes in γ.

5.6 A Two-Stage Cournot Game with R&D Spillover

Zhou *et al.* (2019) recently examined the dynamical behavior of a two-stage Cournot duopoly game with R&D spillover effect and product differentiation. They investigated the behavior of the model, by applying Jury criterion, central manifold theorem, norm form theory, as well as numerical simulation. They provided a detailed analysis of chaotic phenomena that occur within industrial competition.

The model deals with a market in which there are two technological firms, indexed by i ($i = 1, 2$). Each firm produces one product and two firms differentiated goods to supply the same market. The market demand function is

$$p_i\left(q_i, q_j\right) = a - q_i - bq_j,$$

where q_k is the output produced by firm k, p_i is the price of the product produced by firm i, a measures the market scale, and $b(\leq b \leq 1)$ denotes the degree of product differentiation. If $b = 1$, the two products are independent, and the duopoly market can be treated as two monopoly markets. If $0 < b < 1$, they are substitutes. If $b = 1$, they are identical. The two firms conduct R&D to improve production efficiency and reduce production costs. R&D activities are modeled as a two-stage game. In the first stage, the firms decide the levels of their R&D efforts. In the second stage, the firms choose the prices or quantity of products, and then they play a Bertrand or Cournot game.

There are spillover effects in association with R&D activities owing to, for example, externalities of production and R&D activities. We use x_i to stand for firm i's R&D efforts and consider its marginal cost function:

$$C_i(x_i, x_j) = c - x_i - \beta x_j,$$

where $c(a > c > 0)$ is the marginal cost without R&D effort and $\beta(\leq \beta \leq 1)$ measures the spillover effect between the two firms. The cost of firm's investment in R&D is given by $\gamma x_i^2/2$, where γ is the cost parameter of technical innovation.

With the previous descriptions, we have firms' profit functions:

$$\pi_i(q_i, q_j, x_i, x_j) = (p_i - C_i)\, q_i - \frac{\gamma x_i^2}{2}.$$

We first determine the quantities as functions of R&D efforts by solving the first-order conditions, $\frac{\partial \pi_i}{\partial q_i} = 0$, $i = 1, 2$. We substitute the optimal solution $q_i = q_i^*(x_i, x_j)$ into the profit function and can thus express the profits as functions of x_i and x_j, $\pi_i(x_i, x_j)$ By solving $\partial \pi_i(x_i, x_j)/\partial x_i = 0$, $i = 1, 2$. Nevertheless, in the model in this study, the story does not end at solving $\partial \pi_i/\partial x_i = 0$. It is assumed that firms may not have information, may be irrational, or may be myopic. Firms may adjust their strategies, for instance, according to the trial and error as proposed by Agliari *et al.* (2003). Based on the approach taken by Agliari *et al.*, the firms adjust their R&D strategies according to

$$x_i(t+1) = x_i(t) + \alpha_i \frac{\partial \pi_i(x_i, x_j)}{\partial x_i}, \quad i, j = 1, 2, \ i \neq j, \ \alpha_i > 0,$$

where α_i is the speed of adjustment of firm i which readjusts its R&D efforts at period $t + 1$ according to the marginal profit at period t. It can be shown that the above equations can be written as

$$x_1(t+1) = x_1(t) + \alpha_1 x_1(t)\left(\frac{U}{S}x_1(t) + \frac{T}{S}x_2(t) + \frac{R}{S}\right),$$

$$x_2(t+1) = x_2(t) + \alpha_2 x_2(t)\left(\frac{T}{S}x_1(t) + \frac{U}{S}x_2(t) + \frac{R}{S}\right),$$

where

$$R = 2(2 - b)(a - c)(2 - b\beta),$$

$$T = 2(2\beta - b)(2 - b\beta), \ S = \left(2 - b^2\right)^2,$$

$$U = 2(2 - b\beta)^2 - \gamma S.$$

This is a simple model. Its behavior is very complicated. We cited a few numerical simulation results by Zhou *et al.* The first case fixes the parameter values, except α_1 and α_2, as follows:

$$a = 61, \quad b = 0.85, \quad c = 51.5, \quad \beta = 0.75, \quad \gamma = 0.8.$$

Some behaviors of the system are displayed in Figure 5.11. It shows the bifurcation diagram and the largest Lyapunov exponent with α_2 as the bifurcation parameter, respectively, for $\alpha_1 = 0.1$ and $\alpha_1 = 0.45$ Figures 5.11(a) and 5.11(b) represent, respectively, the bifurcation diagram and the largest Lyapunov exponent at $\alpha_1 = 0.1$, while Figures 5.11(c) and 5.11(d) $\alpha_1 = 0.45$. If the largest Lyapunov exponent equals zero,

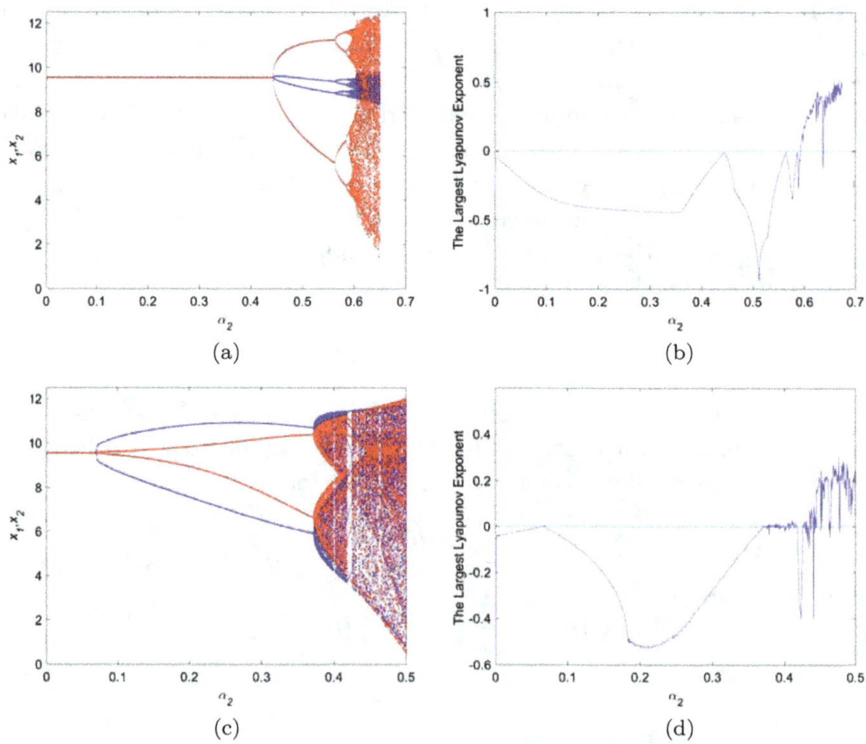

Fig. 5.11. The bifurcation diagram and the largest Lyapunov exponent.

the system is in quasi-period state. If the number is less than two, the system is in chaotic state. If the number is larger than two, then the system is in escaping state, which implies that firms will be forced out of market. Calculating various situations with both α_1 and α_2 as the bifurcation parameters, the authors plot the behavioral patterns in broader ranges of values of α_1 and α_2. At $\alpha_1 = 0.1$, a path of flip bifurcation (also called period-doubling bifurcation) occurs first. Further bifurcation in α_2 leads to chaos. At $\alpha_1 = 0.45$, a combination of the flip bifurcation and the Neimark–Sacker bifurcation is displayed in Figure 5.11(c). The market enters chaos after two values fluctuate.

Figure 5.12 illustrates changes in attractors with different values of α_2: (a) $\alpha_2 = 0.37$, (b) $\alpha_2 = 0.373$, (c) $\alpha_2 = 0.38$, (d) $\alpha_2 = 0.4$, (e) $\alpha_2 = 0.416$, (f) $\alpha_2 = 0.4182$, (g) $\alpha_2 = 0.436$, and (h) $\alpha_2 = 0.5$. Figure 5.12(a) shows that $\alpha_2 = 0.37$, the attractor is the period-2 focus with rough selvedges. Figures 5.12(b) and 5.12(c) display the case that as α_2 is increased, the period-2 focus forms two invariant cycles with rough selvedge by Nermark–Sacker bifurcation, and then the two invariant cycles enlarge in size and its rough selvedge vanishes. Figure 5.12(d) shows that a 14-piece attractor emerges. As α_2 is near 0.416, two invariant cycles again [Figure 5.12(e)]. In Figure 5.12(f), the trajectory becomes two periodic cycles of the period-4 with periodic point located along the invariant curve. Figures 5.12(g) and 5.12(h) display that the two invariant cycles are interwoven together as α_2 approaches 0.5. The system enters chaos when α_2 is further increased.

We now provide the bifurcation diagram with β as the bifurcation parameter when

$$a = 60.5, \quad b = 0.78, \quad c = 51.25, \quad \gamma = 0.775, \quad \alpha_2 = 0.775, \quad \alpha_2 = 0.774.$$

Figure 5.13 provides the bifurcation diagrams with differential conditions. Technology spillover coefficient causes structural changes in market. Figures 5.13(a) and 5.13(b) demonstrate, respectively, the bifurcation diagram with initial condition $(5, 7)$ and partial enlargement of Figure 5.13(a). Figures 5.13(c) and 5.13(d) represent, respectively, the bifurcation diagram with initial condition (4, 10) and partial enlargement of Figure 5.13(c). Figures 5.13(e) and 5.13(f) display, respectively, the bifurcation diagram with initial condition (4.82235, 4.853) and partial enlargement of Figure 5.13(e). There co-exist multiple attractors in the region.

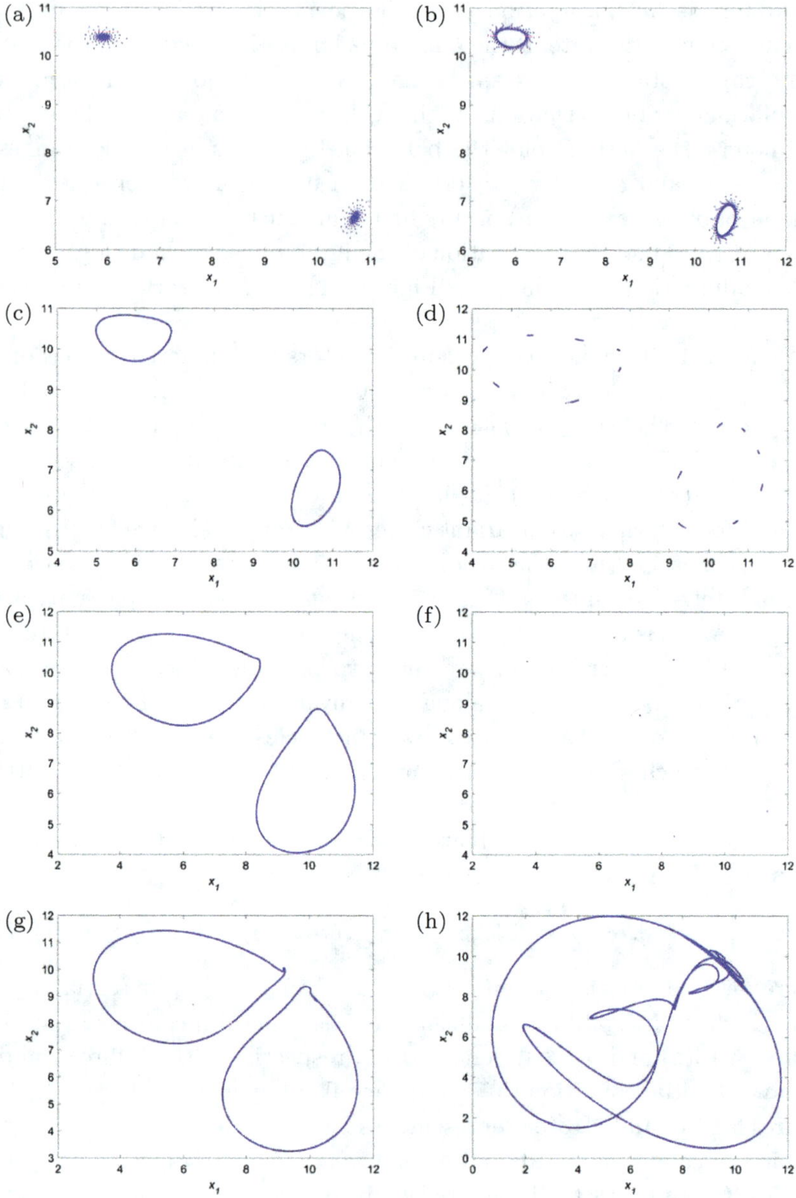

Fig. 5.12. Changes in attractors with different values of α_2.

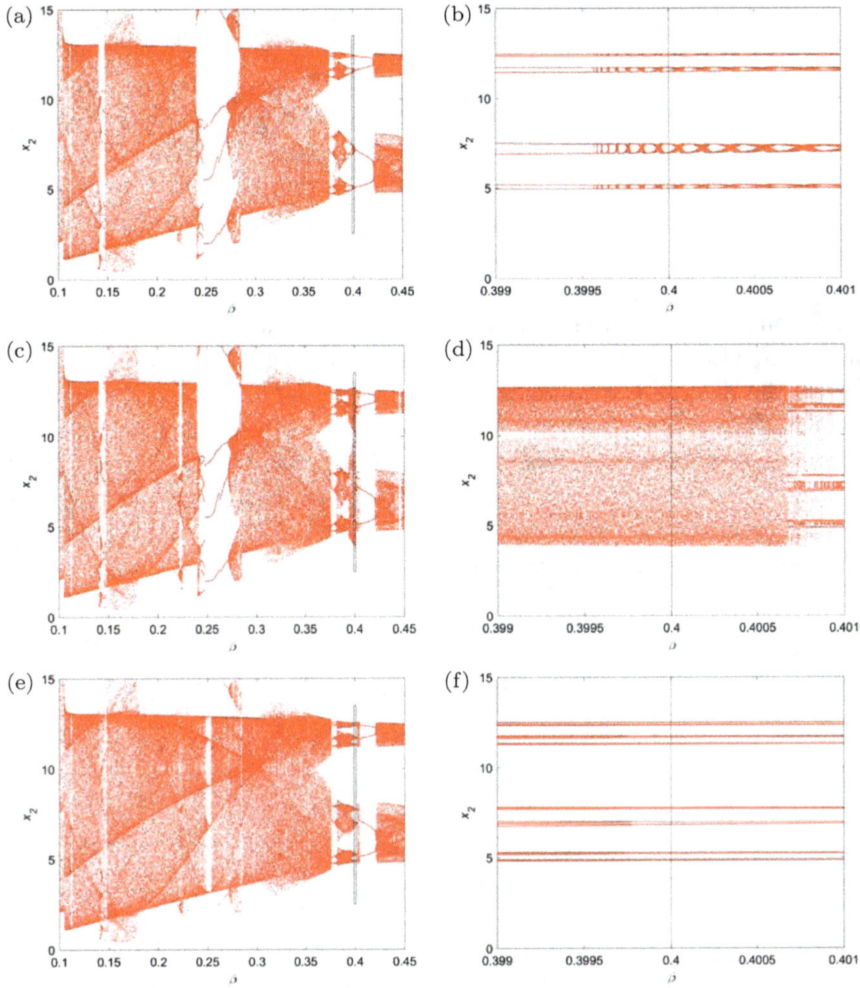

Fig. 5.13. The bifurcation diagram with β as the bifurcation parameter.

5.7 A Cobweb Model with Memory and Competing Technologies

This section introduces a model, studied by Agliari *et al.* (2018), based on the cobweb demand–supply framework with costly innovators and free imitators. Firms raise their productivity by either conducting R&D activities or making imitation. The current model especially examines stitching from innovation to imitation, and vice versa. Moreover, the selection between technologies is dependent on a performance measure which is related to the degree of memory. The study by Agliari *et al.* demonstrates, for instance, supercritical Neimark–Sacker bifurcation, flip bifurcation, ànd several multistability situations.

The model describes an industry with a large number of firms which produce the same product in a perfectly competitive market. All agents are endowed with rational expectations and have different cost structures for the technology they adopt. Each firm may adopt two strategies: either innovation or imitation. Innovation uses resources but reduces costs. Imitation adopts the currently available technology. Let $n_t(\leq n_t \leq 1)$ denote the relative fraction of innovators in period t. The relative fraction of imitators is $1 - n_t$. Let subscript index h denote the strategy of type that a firm chooses, $h = 1$ for innovation and $h = 2$ for imitation. The quality $S_h(p_t)$ supplied by a firm h is assumed to be dependent on the price and the cost structure. Let the total demand be denoted by $D(p_t)$ The demand and supply equilibrium is given by

$$D(p_t) = n_t S_{1,t}(p_t) + (1 - n_t) S_{2,t}(p_t).$$

The profits $\pi_{h,t}$ of a firm of type h in period t are

$$\pi_{h,t} = p_t q_{h,t} - c_h(q_{h,t}),$$

where $q_{h,t} \equiv S_{2,t}(p_t)$. The cost function is given by

$$c_h(q_{h,t}) = \frac{q_{h,t}^2}{s_h} + C_h,$$

where C_h is the fixed costs of the strategy. The parameter s_h is inversely proportional to the marginal cost of production and is interpreted as the productivity of innovation ($h = 1$) and imitation ($h = 2$), respectively. Maximizing the profit yields the supply function: $S_{h,t}(p_t) = s_h p_t$. The innovators' productivity is $s_1 = se^{bC}$ which implies that an innovator invests $C_1 = C > 0$ and gets productivity enhanced by e^{bC}. For an imitator, $s_2 = s$ and $C_2 = 0$.

It is assumed that firms will switch between the two strategies according to the following discrete choice model:

$$n_t = \frac{e^{\beta U_{t-1}^1}}{e^{\beta U_{t-1}^2} + e^{\beta U_{t-1}^1}} = \frac{1}{1 + e^{-\beta \Delta U_{t-1}}},$$

where U_{t-1}^h is a measurement of performance and $\Delta U_{t-1} \equiv U_{t-1}^1 - U_{t-1}^2$. The parameter β measures how sensitive firms are to select the best strategy. If $\beta = 0$, the number of agents choosing one strategy is equal to the number for the other. If $\beta = \infty$, all agents chose the strategy with the best past performance. If the role of memory in the performance is neglected, the measurement of the past performance is equal to the profit in the last period. This implies

$$U_t^1 = \pi_t^1 = \frac{s_1 p_t^2}{2} - C, \quad U_t^2 = \pi_t^2 = \frac{s_2 p_t^2}{2}, \quad \Delta U_t = \frac{s}{2}\left(e^{bC}\right) p_t^2 - C.$$

If the demand function is specified as $D(p_t) = a - dp_t$, then the demand and supply equilibrium is guaranteed by

$$p_t = \frac{a}{d + se^{bC} n_t + s(1 - n_t)} \equiv f(n_t).$$

So far, memory is not discussed yet. The main concern of the paper by Agliari *et al.* is about the role of memory in stabilizing market. They consider that agents consider profits from the most recent past. They suggest a simple case of two lags:

$$U_t^h = (1 - w)\pi_t^h + w\pi_{t-1}^h, \quad 1 \le w \le 0,$$

where w is the degree of memory. Accordingly, we have $\Delta U_t^h = (1 - w)\Delta\pi_t^h + w\Delta\pi_{t-1}^h$. With these conditions, it is straightforward to confirm that the map for the system is given by

$$n_{t+1} = \frac{1}{1 + e^{-\beta[(1-w)g(f(n_t)) + wg(f(m_t))]}},$$
$$m_{t+1} = n_t,$$

where m_t is a new variable and

$$g(f) \equiv \frac{s}{2}\left(e^{bC} - 1\right) f^2 - C.$$

We thus described the model. The behavior of the map is analyzed by Agliari *et al.* Intuitively, it is argued that nonlinear cycles may appear. As innovations lower the price, profits from innovations are too low to attract innovators and firms switch to imitation. As imitative behavior is continued, the price increases. The increased price would make innovation profitable again. Some firms switch to innovation. Dynamics are far more complicated than intuitive reasoning can illustrate. Figure 5.14 uses β and w as bifurcation parameters with the rest parameters specified as follows:

$$a = 4, \quad b = 1, \quad d = 1, \quad s = 2, \quad C = 1.$$

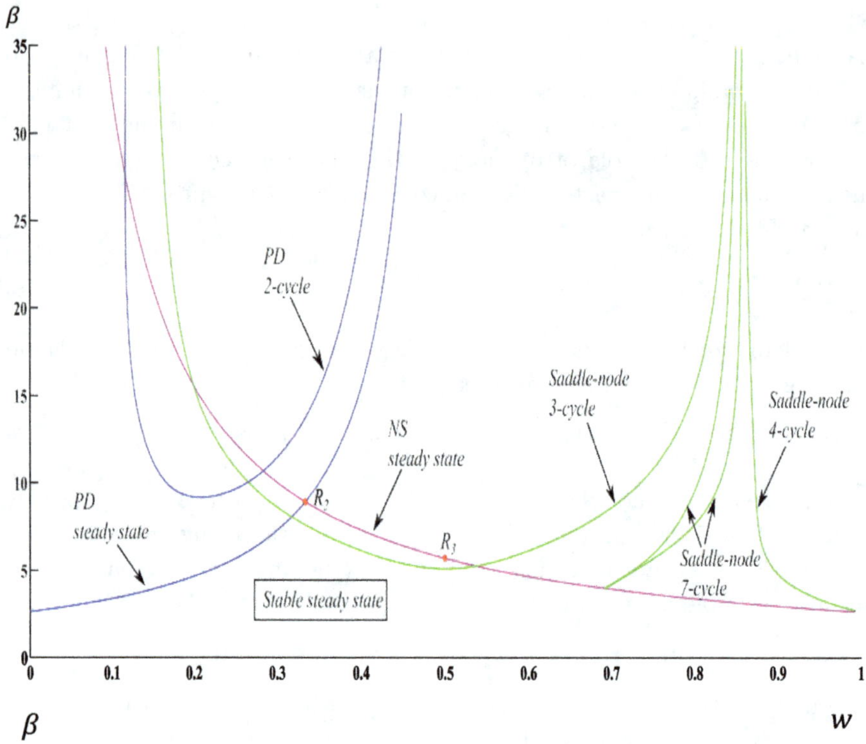

Fig. 5.14. Curves of period-doubling (PD) and Neimark–Sacker (NS).

The figure provides conditions for the emergence of period-doubling (blue curve), Neimark–Sacker (purple curve), the period-doubling of the 2-cycle (blue), and the saddle-node bifurcation curves (green).

Figure 5.15 provides the behavior of the system at $\beta = 9.8$ and, respectively, $w = 0.355$ and $w = 0.337432$. Figure 5.15(a) shows a stable 2-cycle F coexists with a stable 5-cycle G and a stable 3-cycle C. Figure 5.15(b) displays a case that may feature a fractal structure.

5.8 International Trade and Product Cycles in New Growth Theory

This section introduces a trade model with product cycles and growth cycles developed by Iwaisako and Tanaka (2017). The world consists of developed countries (the North, denoted by N) and developing countries (the South,

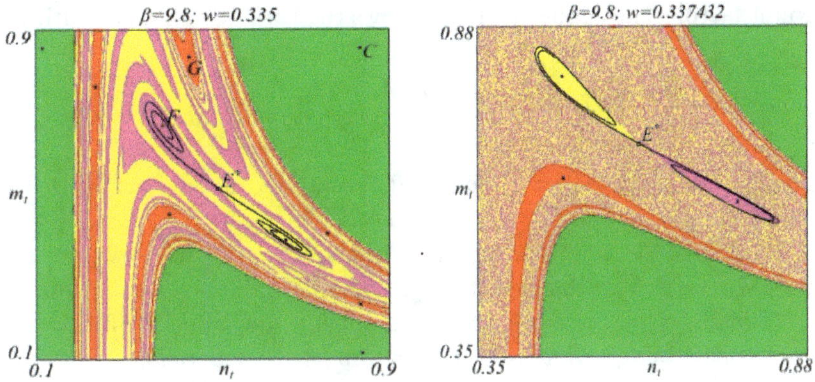

Fig. 5.15. Cycles and fractal structure.

denoted by S). Assuming that the North innovates, and the South imitates, they developed a two-period overlapping generations model on the basis of the ideas by Grossman and Helpman (1991a, 1991b) and demonstrated the existence of permanent cycles in innovation and imitation. A continuum of differentiated goods, indexed by n, is produced by the firms in either country where one unit of output requires one unit of labor input. Labor is internationally immobile. The variety of goods n expands owing to R&D activities which are conducted only by Northern firms. A Southern firm can produce a good by investing in imitating Northern goods. There is no form of barriers or tariffs in trade in commodities. Transportation costs are neglected. There is no financial flow between N and S.

We now describe the behavior of consumer $k \in \{N, S\}$ who lives for two periods, young and old, working in youth and retiring when old. In each period, L_k young individuals are born and each one supplies one unit of labor. An individual k maximizes utility subject to the budget constraint as follows:

$$\operatorname{Max} U_{k,t} = \log D^{y}_{k.t} + \beta \log D^{0}_{k.t+1}, \quad t = 0, 1, \ldots,$$

$$\text{s.t. } E^{y}_{k.t} + S_{k,t} = w_{k,t},$$

$$E^{o}_{k.t+1} = (1 + r_{k,t+1})\, S_{k,t},$$

where $E^{y}_{k.t}$ and $E^{y}_{k.t+1}$ are the expenditures of an individual k of generation t when young and old, respectively, $S_{k,t}$ is the savings in youth, $w_{k,t}$ is the wage, $r_{k,t+1}$ is the risk-free interest rate, and $\beta\,(0 < \beta < 1)$ is the discount factor. The subutility $D^h_{k.t}$ follows the Dixit–Stiglitz-type utility as

$$D^h_{k.t} = n_t^{v-\frac{1-\alpha}{\alpha}} \left\{ \int_0^{n_t} \left[d^h_{k.t}(i) \right]^{\alpha} di \right\}^{\frac{1}{\alpha}}, \quad 0 < \alpha < 1, \ \ i \in [0, n_t],$$

where $d^h_{k.t}(i)$ is the consumption of differentiated good i As in Benassy (1996), the parameter $\varepsilon = 1/(1-\alpha)$ is the elasticity of substitution between goods and v represents the degree of love of variety, which is the elasticity of utility with respect to the number of differentiated goods n Let $p(i)$ denote the price of good i Maximizing the subutility function D^h_k subject to the budget constraint $E^h_k = \int_0^n p(i)\, d^h_k(i)\, di$ yields

$$d^h_{k.t}(i) = \frac{p_t(i)^{-\varepsilon} E^h_k}{\int_0^{n_t} p_t(j)^{1-\varepsilon} dj}.$$

We also get

$$D^h_{k.t} = \frac{E^h_{k,t}}{P_{D,t}},$$

$$S_{k,t} = \frac{\beta}{1+\beta} w_{k,t},$$

$$x_t(i) = \frac{x_t(i)^{-\varepsilon}}{\int_0^{n_t} x_t(i)^{1-\varepsilon} di} E_t,$$

where $x_t(i)$ is the total demand for good i and E_t is the total expenditure in the world at time t:

$$P_{D,t} \equiv n_t^{-v+\frac{1}{\varepsilon-1}} \left\{ \int_0^{n_t} p_t(j)^{1-\varepsilon} dj \right\}^{\frac{1}{1-\varepsilon}},$$

$$x_t(i) \equiv \sum_{k=N,S} \left(d^y_{k.t}(i) + d^o_{k.t}(i) \right) L_k,$$

$$E_t \equiv \sum_{k=N,S} \left(E^y_{k.t} + E^0_{k.t} \right) L_k.$$

We now describe producer behavior. A Northern firm can charge a monopolistic price if its good is not imitated by the South. The price of goods produced in the North is $p_{N.t} = w_{N.t}/\alpha$. A Southern imitator can set its optimal price by $p_{S.t} = \min\{w_{S.t}/\alpha, w_{N.t}\}$. The investigation is limited to the case where Southern imitator can supply the good to both economies with the monopolistic price. The optimal profit of firm k is

$\pi_{k.t} = (1/\alpha - 1)\, w_{k.t} x_{k,t}$, where $x_{k,t}$ is the quantity of the good produced by firm k at time t

Before starting production, a Northern firm must carry out R&D to develop a new variety of good. A Northern entrepreneur covers the cost of R&D by issuing stocks in the Northern financial market. The issued stocks are purchased by the young generation in the North as part of savings. The development of a new good requires a_I/n_t, where a_I measures R&D productivity and n_t is interpreted as spillover from general knowledge accumulated by past innovation. The issued stocks are purchased by the young generation of the South as a part of savings. Imitation of a good requires $a_m/K_m\,(N_{S,t}, N_{N,t})$, units of labor input, where a_m measures imitation productivity, $N_{N,t}(= n_t - N_{S,t})$ are the number of goods that have been copied by period t and not copied until period t, respectively, and K_m denotes the knowledge stock available to the imitator to the South. Let $v_{N,t}$ stand for the ex-dividend stock value of the Northern firm before realization of the imitation activities of the South. The assumption of free entry into R&D leads to the following condition:

$$v_{N,t} \leq w_{N,t}\frac{a_I}{n_t}, \quad \text{with equality if } n_{t+1} - n_t > 0.$$

The shareholders of the imitator that copies a good at period t acquire $v_{S,t}$ which is the ex-dividend stock value in the South. The assumption of free entry into imitation activities leads to the following condition:

$$v_{S,t} \leq w_{S,t}\frac{a_m}{K_m}, \quad \text{with equality if } n_{S,t+1} - n_{S,t} > 0.$$

The no-arbitrage condition in the North is given by

$$1 + r_{N,t+1} = \left[1 - \frac{n_{s,t+1} - n_{s,t}}{(n_{t+1} - n_t) + n_{N,t}}\right]\frac{\pi_{N,t+1} + v_{N,t+1}}{1 + v_{N,t}},$$

where $(n_{s,t+1} - n_{s,t}) / ((n_{t+1} - n_t) + n_{N,t})$ is the probability that a Northern firm will lose its monopolistic position after period t The no-arbitrage condition in the South is given by

$$1 + r_{S,t+1} = \frac{\pi_{S,t+1} + v_{S,t+1}}{1 + v_{S,t}}.$$

The labor market-cleaning conditions for the two economies are

$$n_{N,t} x_{N,t} + l_{R,t} = L_N,$$

$$n_{S,t} x_{S,t} + l_{M,t} = L_S,$$

where $\ell_{R,t}$ and $\ell_{M,t}$ are respectively the quantities of labor engaging in R&D and imitation activities. The equilibrium conditions for the asset markets are

$$\frac{\beta}{1+\beta} w_{N,t} L_N = w_{N,t} \ell_{N,t} + n_{N,t} v_{N,t},$$

$$\frac{\beta}{1+\beta} w_{s,t} L_S = w_{S,t} \ell_{M,t} + n_{S,t} v_{S,t}.$$

The construction of the model is tedious. Iwaisako and Tanaka also conducted local and global analyses of the properties of the model. We illustrate their simulation example to illustrate the emergence of business cycles. They specify:

$$K_m = k\,(n_{s,t})^{\eta}\,(n_{N,t})^{1-\eta}, \quad 0 < \eta < 1, \;\; k = 1, \;\; \eta = 0.25,$$

$$L_N = 158.7, \;\; L_S = 782.4, \;\; P_{D,t} = 1, \;\; a_I = 35, \;\; v = 1.1, \;\; \beta = \alpha = 1/1.05.$$

Figure 5.16 plots the dynamics of output levels and TFPs of the two economies with different values of a_m.

The authors chose population sizes with regard to the ratio of populations of America and China in 2012. It might be better to choose Japan from the end of WWII to the present as an example because Japan has more reliable data. Figure 5.17 shows the rapid growth of imports from the South to the North and oscillations in R&D expenditures of the North.

5.9 Generalized Neoclassical General Equilibrium Theory with Uzawa Two-Sector, Uzawa–Lucas Two-Sector, and Onik–Uzawa Multi-Country Models

This section introduces the multi-country growth model with capital accumulation, human capital accumulation, economic structure, and international trade by Zhang (2020e). Each national economy consists of one tradable, one non-tradable, and one education sector. National economies are different in propensities to save, to obtain education, and to consume and in learning abilities. The model integrates the Solow growth model, the Uzawa two-sector growth model (Uzawa, 1961), the Uzawa–Lucas two-sector growth model, and the Oniki–Uzawa trade model (Oniki and Uzawa, 1965) within a comprehensive framework. Human capital accumulation is through education in the Uzawa–Lucas model (Uzawa, 1965; Lucas, 1988),

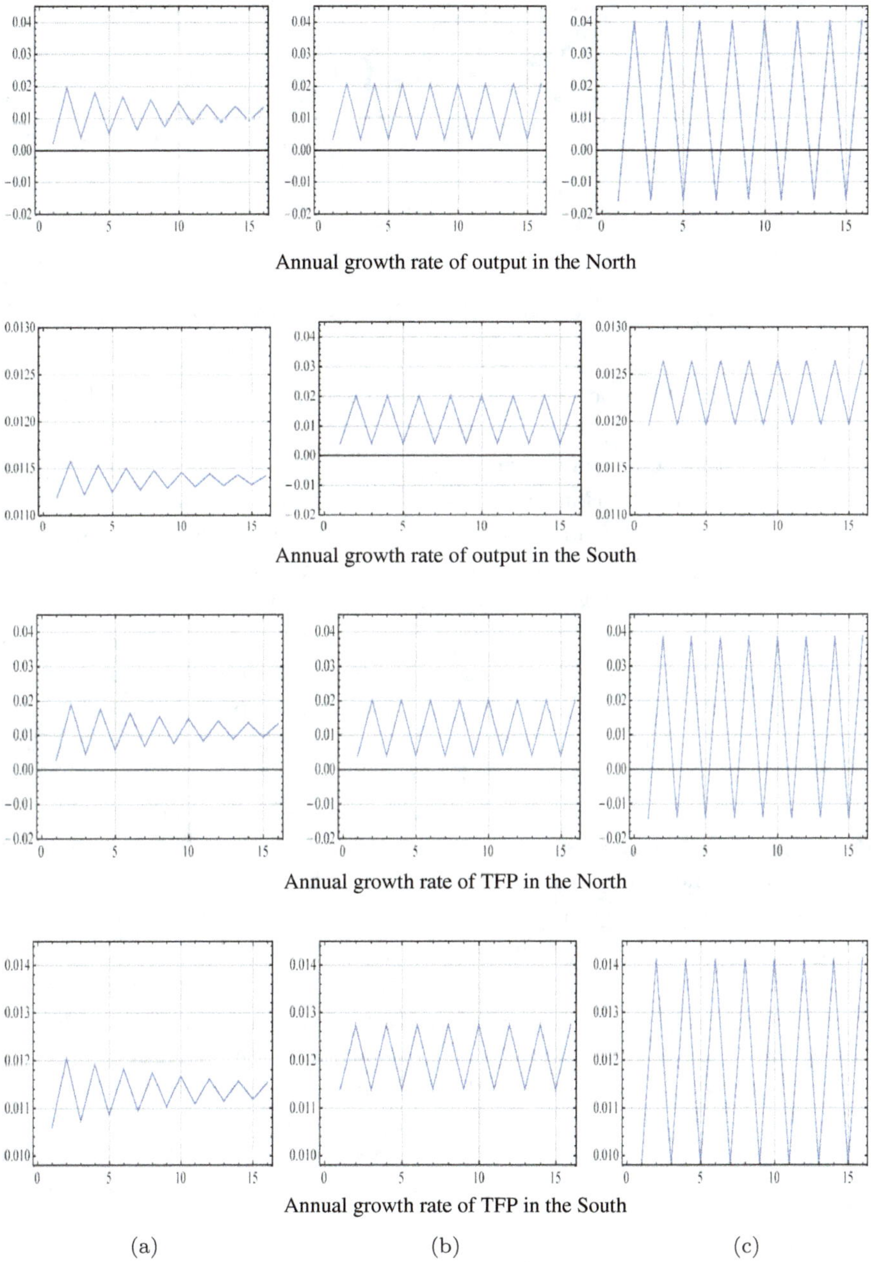

Fig. 5.16. Annual growth rates of output and TFP in North and South. (a) $a_m = 105$; (b) $a_m = 95.25$; (c) $a_m = 95$.

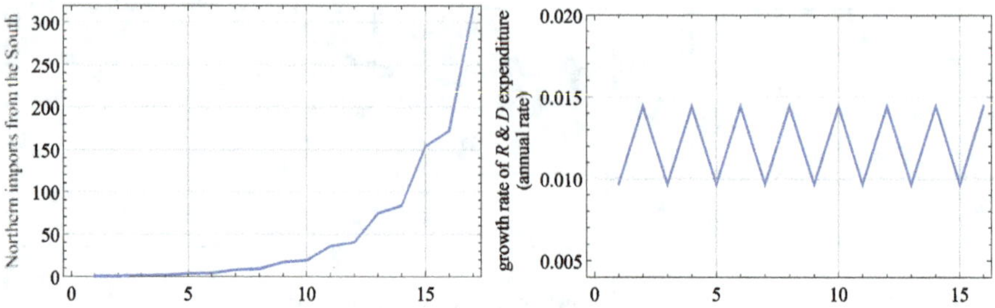

Fig. 5.17. Growth in trade and cycles in R&D expenditures with $a_m = 95.25$.

Arrow's learning by producing (Arrow, 1962), and Zhang's creative learning with leisure.

The economy consists of multiple countries, indexed by $j = 1, \ldots, J$ Country j has population $\hat{N}_j(t), j = 1, \ldots, J$ Each country has three sectors: one tradable good sector, one non-tradable goods sector, and one education sector. All the national economies can produce a homogenous tradable commodity (Ikeda and Ono, 1992). The commodity can be consumed and invested. Households own assets and distribute their incomes to consume, to receive education, and to save. Production sectors or firms use capital and labor. Exchanges take place in perfectly competitive markets. Production sectors sell their product to households or to other sectors, and households sell their labor and assets to production sectors. Factor markets work well; factors are inelastically supplied and the available factors are fully utilized at every moment. Savings is undertaken only by households, which implies that all earnings of firms are distributed in the form of payments to factors of production. Let price be measured in terms of the tradable good and the price of the good be unit. We denote wage and interest rates by $w_j(t)$ and $r_j(t)$, respectively, in the jth country. Capital depreciates at an exponential rate $\delta_{jk}(t)$ in country j Let $p_j(t)$ and $p_{js}(t)$ denote the price of education and the price of non-tradable goods in country j We use subscript indices i, s, and e to stand for the tradable good sector, non-tradable good sector, and education sector, respectively, in country j. We use $N_{jm}(t)$ and $K_{jm}(t)$ to stand for the labor force and capital stocks employed by sector m in country j Let $F_{jm}(t)$ stand for the output level of sector m in country j.

The aggregated labor force $N_j(t)$ of country j is given by

$$N_j(t) = H_j^{m_j(t)}(t)\, T_j(t) \bar{N}_j(t),$$

where $H_j(t)$ and $T_j(t)$ are respectively the level of human capital and work time in country j Here, $m_j(t)$ is a positive parameter measuring how household j effectively applies human capital at time t in country j.

We denote wage rate per unit qualified work time in country j and interest rates by $w_j(t)$ and $r_j(t)$ In the free trade system, the interest rate is identical throughout the world economy, i.e., $r(t) = r_j(t)$. We use $K(t)$ to stand for the capital stocks of the world economy. The total capital stock employed by country, $K_j(t)$, is allocated between the tradable, non-tradable, and education sectors. We use $\bar{K}_j(t)$ to stand for the wealth owned by country j. We use $N_{jq}(t)$ and $K_{jq}(t)$ to respectively stand for the labor force and capital stocks employed by sector q As full employment of labor and capital is assumed, we have

$$K_{ji}(t) + K_{js}(t) + K_{je}(t) = K_j(t), \quad N_{ji}(t) + N_{js}(t) + N_{je}(t) = N_j(t).$$

We rewrite the above relations as follows:

$$\begin{gathered} n_{ji}(t)\,k_{ji}(t) + n_{js}(t)\,k_{js}(t) + n_{je}(t)\,k_{je}(t) \\ = k_j(t),\, n_{ji}(t) + n_{js}(t) + n_{je}(t) = 1, \end{gathered}$$

in which

$$k_{jq}(t) \equiv \frac{K_{jq}(t)}{N_{jq}(t)}, \quad n_{jq}(t) \equiv \frac{N_{jq}(t)}{N_j(t)}, \quad k_j(t) \equiv \frac{K_j(t)}{N_j(t)}, \quad q = i, s, e.$$

We assume that the production of sector (j, q) is to combine qualified labor force $N_{jq}(t)$ and physical capital $K_{jq}(t)$. The production function $F_{jq}(t)$ is described by

$$\begin{gathered} F_{jq}(t) = A_{jq}(t)\,K_{jq}^{\alpha_{jq}(t)}(t)\,N_{jq}^{\alpha_j q(t)}(t), \\ \alpha_{jq}(t), \beta_{jq}(t) > 0, \quad \alpha_{jq}(t) + \beta_{jq}(t) = 1, \quad j = i, s, \end{gathered}$$

where $A_{jq}(t)$, $\alpha_{jq}(t)$, and $\beta_{jq}(t)$ are positive parameters. Let all the prices be measured in terms of the good. We use $p_{js}(t)$ to represent the price of services in country j Markets are competitive; thus labor and capital earn their marginal products, and firms earn zero profits. The marginal conditions are

$$\begin{gathered} r(t) + \delta_{jk}(t) = \alpha_{ji}(t)\,A_{ji}(t)\,k_{ji}^{-\beta_{ji}(t)}(t), \\ w_j(t) = \beta_{ji}(t)\,A_{ji}(t)\,k_{ji}^{\alpha_{ji}(t)}(t), \\ r(t) + \delta_{jk}(t) = \alpha_{js}(t)\,A_{js}(t)\,p_{js}(t)\,k_{js}^{-\beta_{js}(t)}(t), \\ w_j(t) = \beta_{js}(t)\,A_{js}(t)\,p_{js}(t)\,k_{js}^{\alpha_{js}(t)}(t), \end{gathered}$$

where $\delta_{jk}(t)$ is the depreciation rate of physical capital.

The education sector is characterized by perfect competition. Students are supposed to pay the education fee $p_j(t)$ per unit of time in the country. The education sector pays teachers and capital with the market rates. The cost of the education sector is given by $w_j(t) N_{je}(t) + (r(t) + \delta_{jk}(t)) K_{je}(t)$ The production function of the education sector is assumed to be a function of $K_{je}(t)$ and $N_{je}(t)$ as follows:

$$F_{je}(t) = A_{je}(t) K_{je}^{\alpha_{je}(t)}(t) N_{je}^{\alpha_{je}(t)}(t), \quad \alpha_{je}(t) \beta_{je}(t) > 0,$$
$$\times \alpha_{je}(t) + \beta_{je}(t) = 1,$$

where $A_{je}(t), \alpha_{je}(t)$, and $\beta_{je}(t)$ are positive parameters. The marginal conditions for the education sector are

$$r(t) + \delta_{jk}(t) = \alpha_{je}(t) A_{je}(t) p_{je}(t) k_{je}^{-\beta_{je}(t)}(t),$$
$$w_j(t) = \beta_{je}(t) A_{je}(t) p_{je}(t) k_{je}^{\alpha_{je}(t)}(t).$$

Let $\bar{k}_j(t)$ stand for the wealth of household j. Per household's current income from the interest payment $r(t) \bar{k}_j(t)$ and the wage payment $H_j^{m_j(t)}(t) T_j(t) w_j(t)$ is given by

$$y_j(t) = r(t) \bar{k}_j(t) + H_j^{m_j(t)}(t) T_j(t) w_j(t).$$

The per capita disposable income is then given by $\hat{y}_j(t) = y_j(t) + \bar{k}_j(t)$ Let $T_{je}(t)$ stand for the time spent on education. We assume that the total available time is distributed between education and work: $T_j(t) + T_{je}(t) = T_0$, where T_0 is the total available time. The consumer is faced with the following budget constraint:

$$c_j(t) + p_{js}(t) c_{js}(t) + s_j(t) + p_j(t) T_{je}(t) = \hat{y}_j(t).$$

We have

$$c_j(t) + p_{js}(t) c_{js}(t) + s_j(t) + \bar{p}_j(t) T_{je}(t) = \bar{y}_j(t), \tag{5.9.1}$$

where

$$\bar{p}_j(t) \equiv p_j(t) + \bar{w}_j(t), \ \bar{w}_j(t) \equiv H_j^{m_j(t)}(t) w_j(t),$$
$$\bar{y}_j(t) \equiv (1 + r(t)) \bar{k}_j(t) + T_0 \bar{w}_j(t). \tag{5.9.2}$$

Consumers decide on four variables, consumption levels of the two goods, level of savings, and education time. We assume that consumers' utility function is a function of the consumption level of tradable good $c_j(t)$, the consumption level of non-tradable good $c_{js}(t)$, the education time $T_{je}(t)$, and the level of savings $s_j(t)$ as follows:

$$U_j(t) = c_j^{\xi_{j0}(t)}(t)\, c_{js}^{\gamma_{j0}(t)}(t)\, s_j^{\lambda_{j0}(t)}(t)\, T_{je}^{\eta_{j0}(t)}(t),$$

$$\gamma_{j0}(t), \quad \xi_{0j}(t), \quad \lambda_{j0}(t), \quad \eta_{j0}(t) > 0,$$

where $\xi_{0j}(t)$ is called the propensity to consume tradable good, $\gamma_{j0}(t)$ is the propensity to consume non-tradable good, $\eta_{j0}(t)$ is the propensity to own wealth, and $\lambda_{j0}(t)$ is the propensity to receive education. Maximizing $U_j(t)$ subject to the budget constraint yields

$$c_j(t) = \xi_j(t)\,\bar{y}_j(t), \quad p_{js}(t)\,c_{js}(t) = \gamma_j(t)\,\bar{y}_j(t),$$
$$s_j(t) = \lambda_j(t)\,\bar{y}_j(t), \quad \bar{p}_j(t)\,T_{je}(t) = \eta_j(t)\,\bar{y}_j(t),$$

where

$$\xi_j(t) \equiv \xi_{0j}(t)\,\rho_j(t), \quad \gamma_j(t) \equiv \gamma_{j0}(t)\,\rho_j(t),$$
$$\lambda_j(t) \equiv \lambda_{j0}(t)\,\rho_j(t), \quad \eta_j(t) \equiv \eta_{j0}(t)\,\rho_j(t),$$
$$\rho_j(t) \equiv \frac{1}{\xi_{0j}(t) + \gamma_{j0}(t) + \lambda_{j0}(t) + \eta_{j0}(t)}.$$

According to the definitions of $s_j(t)$, the wealth accumulation of the representative household in country j is given by

$$\dot{\bar{k}}_j(t) = s_j(t) - \bar{k}_j(t) - \frac{\dot{N}_j(t)}{N_j(t)}\bar{k}_j(t).$$

Human capital accumulates according to

$$\dot{H}_j(t) = \frac{\upsilon_{je}(t)\,F_{je}^{a_{je}(t)}(t)\left(H_j^{m_j(t)}(t)\,T_{je}(t)\,\bar{N}_j(t)\right)^{b_{je}(t)}}{H_j^{\pi_{je}(t)}(t)\,\bar{N}_j(t)}$$
$$+ \frac{\upsilon_{ji}(t)\,F_{ji}^{a_{ji}(t)}(t)}{H_j^{\pi_{ji}(t)}(t)\,\bar{N}_j(t)} + \frac{\upsilon_{jh}(t)\,c_j^{a_{jh}(t)}(t)}{H_j^{\pi_{jh}(t)}(t)}$$
$$+ \frac{\upsilon_{js}(t)\,c_{js}^{a_{js}(t)}(t)}{H_j^{\pi_{js}(t)}(t)} - \delta_{jh}(t)\,H_j(t),$$

where $\delta_{jh}(t)$ is the depreciation rate of human capital, $\upsilon_{je}(t), \upsilon_{ji}(t)$, $\upsilon_{jh}(t), a_{je}(t), b_{je}(t), a_{ji}(t)$, and $b_{ji}(t)$ are non-negative time-dependent parameters. The signs of the parameters $\pi_{je}(t), \pi_{ji}(t)$, and $\pi_{jh}(t)$ are not specified as they may be either negative or positive. The equation is a synthesis and generalization of Arrow's, Uzawa's, and Zhang's ideas about human capital accumulation. The term

$$\frac{\upsilon_{je}(t) F_{je}^{a_{je}(t)}(t) \left(H_j^{m_j(t)}(t) T_{je}(t) \bar{N}_j(t)\right)^{b_{je}(t)}}{H_j^{\pi_{je}(t)}(t) \bar{N}_j(t)}$$

is the contribution to human capital improvement through education. The term implies that human capital rises in the level of education service F_{je} and in the (qualified) total study time $H_j^{m_j} T_{je} \bar{N}_j$. The term $H_j^{\pi_{je}}$ indicates that it may be more difficult (in the case of π_{je} being large) or easier (in the case of π_{je} being small) to accumulate more human capital. There are many factors which may affect education quality. For instance, there are studies on the relationship between class size and student achievement. The term $\upsilon_{ji} F_{ji}^{a_{ji}} / H_j^{\pi_{ji}}$ implies learning by producing effects in human capital accumulation.

For the education sector, the demand and supply balances in each country: $T_{je}(t) \bar{N}_j(t) = F_{je}(t)$. The demand for non-tradable good equals the supply $c_{js}(t) \bar{N}_j(t) = F_{js}(t)$. The total capital stocks in international markets employed by the production sectors are equal to the total wealth owned by all the countries:

$$K(t) \equiv \sum_{j=1}^{J} K_j(t) = \sum_{j=1}^{J} \bar{N}_j(t) \bar{N}_j(t).$$

The world production is equal to the world consumption and world net savings:

$$C(t) + S(t) - K(t) + \sum_{j=1}^{J} \delta_{kj}(t) K_j(t) = K(t),$$

where

$$C(t) \equiv \sum_{j=1}^{J} c_j(t) \bar{N}_j(t), \quad S(t) \equiv \sum_{j=1}^{J} s_j(t) \bar{N}_j(t), \quad F(t)$$
$$\equiv \sum_{j=1}^{J} F_{ji}(t).$$

5.10 International Trade

The trade balances of the economies are given by

$$E_j(t) = \left(\bar{K}_j(t) - K_j(t)\right) r(t).$$

When $E_j(t)$ is positive (negative), we say that country j is in trade surplus (deficit). When $E_j(t)$ is zero, country j trade is in balance.

We built the model with trade, economic growth, and physical and human capital accumulation in the world economy in which the domestic markets of each country are perfectly competitive, international product and capital markets are freely mobile, and labor is internationally immobile. The model synthesizes the main ideas in economic growth theory and trade theory in a comprehensive framework. The model is general in the sense that some well-known models in economics can be considered as its special cases, in terms of economic structures. To carry out numerical simulation, we specify

$$\begin{aligned}
&N_1 = 5, && N_2 = 10, && N_3 = 20, && T_0 = 1,\\
&m_1 = 0.9, && m_2 = 0.85, && m_3 = 0.75, &&\\
&A_{1i} = 1.3, && A_{1s} = 1.2, && A_{1e} = 1.1, &&\\
&\alpha_{1i} = 0.32, && \alpha_{1s} = 0.35, && \alpha_{1e} = 0.45, &&\\
&A_{2i} = 1.25, && A_{2s} = 1.1, && A_{2e} = 1, &&\\
&\alpha_{2i} = 0.32, && \alpha_{2s} = 0.36, && \alpha_{2e} = 0.45, &&\\
&A_{3i} = 1.2, && A_{3s} = 1, && A_{3e} = 0.9, &&\\
&\alpha_{3i} = 0.32, && \alpha_{3s} = 0.37, && \alpha_{3e} = 0.45, &&\\
&\delta_{1k} = 0.06, && \delta_{2k} = 0.05, && \delta_{3k} = 0.05. &&
\end{aligned}$$

The total factor productivities are different between three economies. Country 1's total factor productivity is the highest and Country 3's total factor productivity is the lowest. We call Countries 1, 2, and 3 respectively as highly developed, developed, and lowly developed economies (HDE, DE, and LDE). The output elasticities with respect to labor and capital also vary between countries. We specify the values of the parameters, α_j, in the Cobb–Douglas productions approximately equal to 0.3. The depreciation rate of physical capital is specified near 0.05. We specify the household preferences of the three economies as

$$\gamma_{10} = 0.06, \quad \eta_{10} = 0.07, \quad \xi_{10} = 0.1, \quad \lambda_{10} = 0.73, \quad \gamma_{20} = 0.06,$$
$$\eta_{20} = 0.06, \quad \xi_{20} = 0.1, \quad \lambda_{20} = 0.07, \quad \gamma_{30} = 0.06, \quad \eta_{30} = 0.05,$$
$$\xi_{30} = 0.1, \quad \lambda_{30} = 0.68.$$

The HDE's propensity to save is 0.73, the DE's propensity to save is 0.7, and the LDE's propensity to save is 0.6. We specify the human capital accumulation as follows:

$$\upsilon_{1e} = 1.2, \quad \upsilon_{1i} = 3, \quad \upsilon_{1h} = 1.2, \quad \upsilon_{1s} = 1.2, \quad a_{1e} = 0.3, \quad b_{1e} = 0.5,$$
$$a_{1i} = 0.4, \quad a_{1h} = 0.1, \quad a_{1s} = 0.3, \quad \pi_{1e} = 0.1, \quad \pi_{1i} = 0.7, \quad \pi_{1h} = 0.1,$$
$$\pi_{1s} = 0.1, \quad \delta_{1h} = 0.05, \quad \upsilon_{2e} = 1.1, \quad \upsilon_{2i} = 2.7, \quad \upsilon_{2h} = 1, \quad \upsilon_{2s} = 1,$$
$$a_{2e} = 0.3, \quad b_{2e} = 0.5, \quad a_{2i} = 0.4, \quad a_{2h} = 0.1, \quad a_{2s} = 0.3, \quad \pi_{2e} = 0.1,$$
$$\pi_{2i} = 0.7, \quad \pi_{2h} = 0.1, \quad \pi_{2s} = 0.1, \quad \delta_{2h} = 0.05, \quad \upsilon_{3e} = 1, \quad \upsilon_{3i} = 2.5,$$
$$\upsilon_{3h} = 1, \quad \upsilon_{3s} = 1, \quad a_{3e} = 0.3, \quad b_{3e} = 0.5, \quad a_{3i} = 0.4, \quad a_{3h} = 0.1,$$
$$a_{3s} = 0.3, \quad \pi_{3e} = 0.1, \quad \pi_{3i} = 0.7, \quad \pi_{3h} = 0.1, \quad \pi_{3s} = 0.1, \quad \delta_{3h} = 0.05.$$

The human capital depreciation rates of the three economies are equal. The HDE's human capital accumulation efficiency due to education υ_{1e} is the highest, the DE's is next, and the LDE's is the lowest. The HDE is most effective in accumulating human capital, the DE is next, and the LDE is least effective. As we already provided the procedure to follow the motion of each variable in the system, it is straightforward to plot the motion with computer. We specify the initial conditions as follows:

$$k_{1i}(0) = 7.4, \quad \bar{k}_2(0) = 230, \quad \bar{k}_3(0) = 139, \quad H_1(0) = 92,$$
$$H_2(0) = 84, \quad H_3(0) = 67.$$

The motion of the system is given in Figure 5.18. In the figure, the GDP per capita and the global GDP are defined as follows:

$$g_j \equiv \frac{F_{ji} + p_{js}F_{js} + p_{je}F_{je}}{\bar{N}_j}, \quad Y \equiv \sum_j (F_{ji} + p_{js}F_{js} + p_{je}F_{je}).$$

The HDE's GDP per capita and human capital are enhanced over time, while the other two countries' GDP per capita and human capital are lowered. The HDE's total labor force and capital stocks employed are augmented and the other two economies' total labor forces and capital

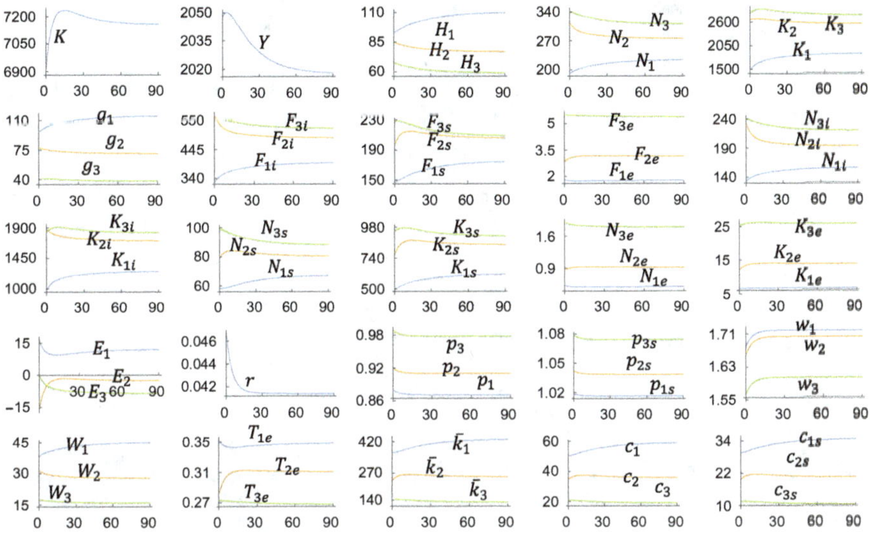

Fig. 5.18. The motion of the global economy.

stocks employed are lowered. The prices of education and non-tradable goods fall slightly in the three economies. The rate of interest falls and the wage rates are increased. The HDE's wage income per capita is increased, and the other two economies' wage incomes per capita are reduced. The labor and capital are redistributed between the three sectors in each economy over time. The system approaches an equilibrium point in the long term.

This implies that the world economy is stable. This implies that we can effectively conduct comparative dynamic analysis. First, we study the effects of the HDE's technological change in the tradable sector on the global economy. It has been argued that productivity differences explain much of the variation in incomes across countries, and technology plays a key role in determining productivity. We see what will happen to the global economy when the total factor productivity of the HDE's tradable sector experiences the following fluctuations: $A_{1i}(t) = 1.3 + 0.1\sin(t)$. The simulation result is plotted in Figure 5.19. It is remarked that the variable value in curve in the figure stands for the variable value after the parameter change. This is the same for the rest figures in this section. As the system contains many variables and these variables are connected to each other in nonlinear relations, it is difficult to verbally explain these interactions

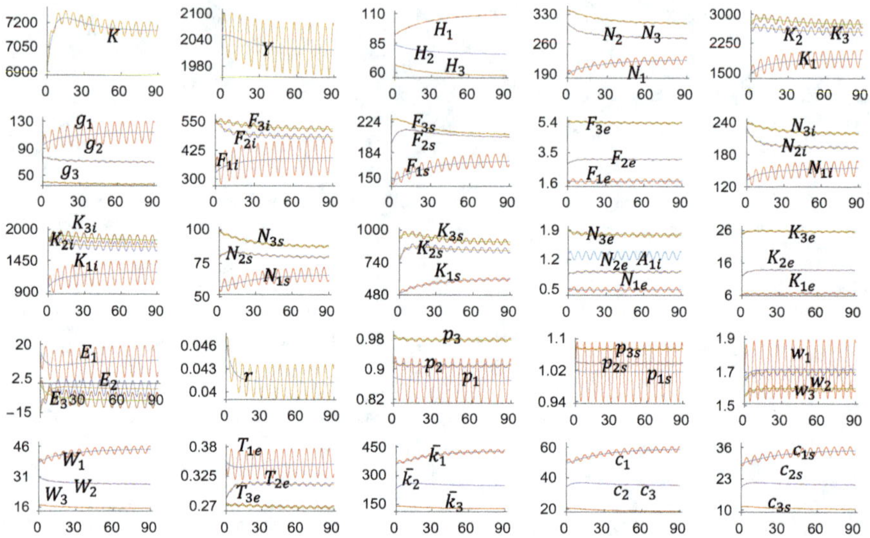

Fig. 5.19. Fluctuations in the total factor productivity of the HDE's tradable sector.

over time. As the total factor productivity is fluctuated, the output levels of the three economies' tradable sectors are oscillatory. The output of the HDE's non-tradable sector is oscillatory and the output levels of the other two economies' non-tradable sectors are reduced initially and are slightly affected in the long term. The human capital levels are slightly affected. The FDE's education fee and education time fluctuate, while the other economies' education fees and education times are slightly affected. The trades and rate of interest oscillate. The wealth levels and consumptions do not fluctuate in any economy.

We now study the effects of the following fluctuations in the HDE's propensity to receive education $\eta_{10}(t) = 0.07 + 0.01 \sin(t)$. The simulation result is plotted in Figure 5.20. As the representative household's preference to receive education fluctuates, they cause oscillations in the global wealth and global product. The trade patterns are affected periodically.

We now allow the LDE's propensity to save to experience the following perturbations: $\lambda_{10}(t) = 0.73{+}0.02 \sin(t)$. The simulation results are plotted in Figure 5.21. We observe that fluctuations in the propensity to save cause weak perturbations in the world economy. A reason is that the effects of savings and dissavings balance each other over time.

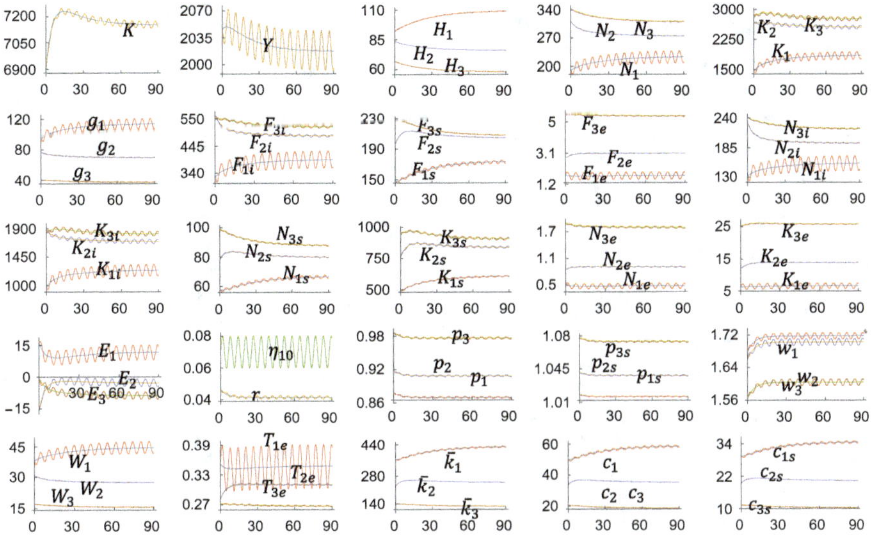

Fig. 5.20. Fluctuations in the HDE's propensity to receive education.

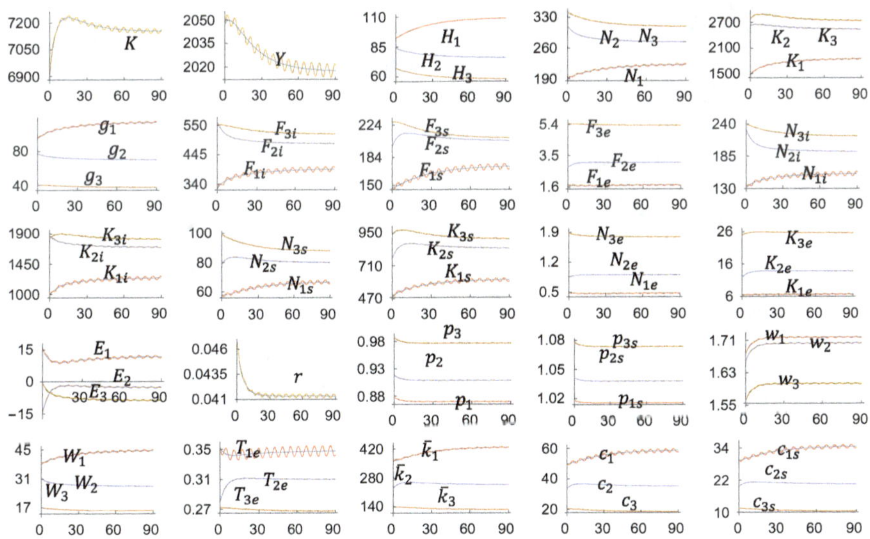

Fig. 5.21. Fluctuations in the LDE's propensity to save.

Chapter 6

Economic Complexity with Environment and Resources

Environment is now becoming a key concern of mankind. Russell Means pointed out a source of the concerns: "All European tradition, Marxists included, has conspired to defy the natural order of all things. Mother Earth has been abused, the powers have been abused, and this cannot go on forever. No theory can alter that simple fact. Mother Earth will retaliate, the whole environment will retaliate, and the abusers will be eliminated." The 2021 Nobel Prize in physics was unexpectedly awarded to American-Japanese Syukuro Manabe and Klaus Hasselmann for their works which laid the foundation of our knowledge of the Earth's climate and how humanity affects it. The Royal Swedish Academy of Sciences made the choice because they made "groundbreaking contributions to our understanding of complex physical systems" and they built "the physical modeling of Earth's climate, qualifying variability, and reliably predicting global warming." Environment and resources are important factors in economic growth and development. As more economies and people are accessing modern lifestyles, capacities of polluting the environment and utilizing resources of mankind have been increasingly unbearable for the Earth. There is much truth in what E.O. Wilson said: "If all mankind were to disappear, the world regenerate back to the rich state of equilibrium that existed ten thousand years ago. If insects were to vanish, the environment would collapse into chaos." Complexity theory tells us that man can theoretically make any arguments on such a complicated issue. Without man, there is even no concept of equilibrium. The concept of equilibrium is an imagined state of movement.

Modern economic theory is obviously misleading even from its founding father, Adam Smith. The reader of this book immediately sees some visionary mistakes by Edmund Phelps — 2006 Nobel Prize winner in economics for deepening "our understanding of the relation between short-run and long-run effects of macroeconomic policy" — "At the simplest level, economics can better show us the consequences of our actions. Less simple are cases in which we don't have the knowledge to predict the full consequences. Global warming and climate change are examples." America has insisted on the validity of Newtonian approach. Paul Samuelson rightly pointed out: "I think that it's more important for an economist to be wise and sophisticated in scientific method than it is for a physicist because with controlled laboratory experiments possible, they practically guide you; you couldn't go astray. Whereas in economics, by dogma and misunderstanding, you can go very sadly astray." It is always easier to say than to do. The well-recognized economist with his Nobel Prize and best-sold textbook had played a significant role in leading American economics into the trap of searching for a stable single equilibrium point over almost half a century. If the world is genuinely chaotic, the only way to establish order is to have a fixed point in one's imagination, called faith. Faith in order enables people to play around with a sense of meaning as well as belonging. This chapter studies economic complexity with environment and resources. Section 6.1 represents the economic growth model with an endogenous environment by Liuzzi and Venturi (2021). It explains the existence of pollution-induced poverty traps. Section 6.2 studies the model by Antoci *et al.* (2011) who apply global analysis techniques to economic growth development with natural resources. Section 6.3 presents the model of economic growth and environmental resources within an overlapping generations framework proposed by Antoci (2016). Section 6.4 introduces the model by Bosi and Desmarchelier (2018), which is built by integrating the Levins model and the Solow–Ramsey model with pollution externality. Section 6.5 studies the Cournot game model built by Fanti (2015). The model deals with the impact of public environmental policies in a Cournot duopoly game with heterogeneous expectations and limited rationality. Section 6.6 introduces the model of environmental dynamics and development.

6.1 An Economic Growth Model with Pollution-Induced Poverty Traps

This section introduces an economic growth model with an endogenous environment proposed by Liuzzi and Venturi (2021). Production produces pollution and pollution reduces productivity. Technology is related to production. Pollution is treated as a negative production externality. They applied an S-shaped aggregate production function proposed by Skida (1978) to take account of the impact of pollution on production. A similar approach is taken by Brecher *et al.* (2014) and La Torre (2015). The model is composed of the following differential equations:

$$\dot{k}(t) = \frac{sf(k(t))(1-u)^{\varepsilon}}{1+bp(t)} - \delta_k k(t),$$

$$\dot{p}(t) = \theta(1-u)f(k(t)) - \delta_p p(t),$$

in which $k(t)$ is the capital, $f(k)$ is the production, $p(t)$ is a measurement of undesired by-product of economic activity, s is the savings rate, δ_k is the depreciation rate of capital, and b is a positive parameter. The term $1/(1+bp(t))$ is interpreted as the damage function, which implies that the higher the pollution, the lower the productivity. The government applies tax rate τ on output and uses the revenue for abatement activities which reduce a share u of emissions. We have $1-u$ as unabated emissions. A relation between τ and $(1-u)$ is assumed as follows: $1-u=(1-\tau)^{\varepsilon}$ with $\varepsilon \geq 1$. The term $\theta(1-u)f$ represents the amount of unabated emissions and stands for natural purification rate. The economy's production function is specified on an S-shape:

$$f(k(t)) = \frac{\alpha_1 k^q}{1+\alpha_2 k^q}, \quad \alpha_1, \alpha_2 > 0, \quad q > 1,$$

where α_1, α_2, and q are parameters. Figure 6.1 illustrates the properties of the specified functions.

The rest of this section specifies $\varepsilon = 1$, $q = 2$, and $\alpha_1 = \alpha_2 = \alpha$. When $b = 0$, the capital accumulation has three equilibrium points, 0, k_{ip} and k^*, with k_{ip} being unstable and the rest two stable. When the parameters are taken on the following values,

$$\delta_k = 0.05, \quad \delta_p = 0.04, \quad b = 1, \quad \alpha = 1, \quad \theta = 1.$$

We illustrate the behavior of the system with a few combinations of s and u as in Figure 6.2. In the figure, the light gray area stands for the basin of attraction of the origin, while the dark gray area for the basin of attraction of the sustainable equilibrium. The two full circles represent the two non-zero equilibrium points. The dashed line stands for $\dot{k} = 0$, while the solid line for $\dot{p} = 0$. If the savings rate is increased (with the environment policy invariant), the sustainable basin is enlarged; if the environment policy is strengthened (with the savings rate constant), the sustainable basin is reduced.

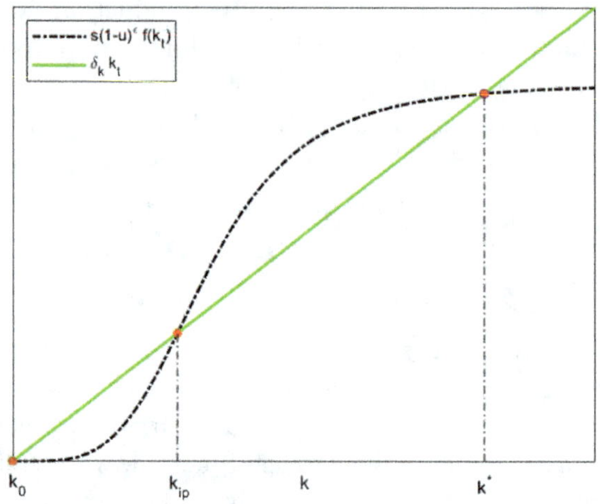

Fig. 6.1. The S-shaped production function.

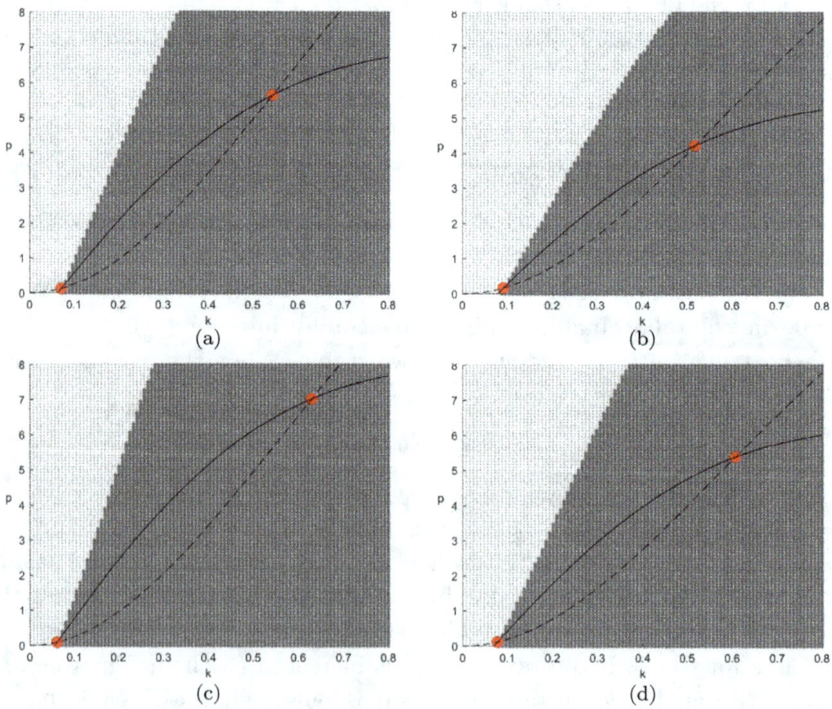

Fig. 6.2. A few combinations of savings and environment policy. (a) Phase Diagram (k, p) with $s = 0.8$, $u = 0.01$. (b) Phase Diagram (k, p) with $s = 0.8$, $u = 0.2$. (c) Phase Diagram (k, p) with $s = 0.9$, $u = 0.01$. (d) Phase Diagram (k, p) with $s = 0.9$, $u = 0.02$.

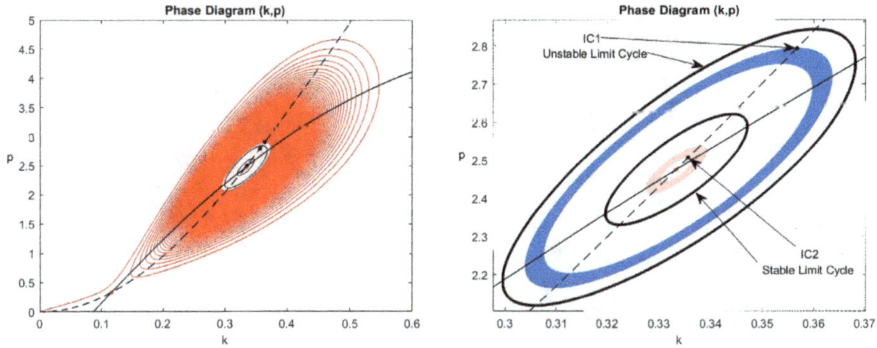

Fig. 6.3. The Hopf bifurcation at $s = \hat{s}$.

In the rest of this section, we further fix $u = 0.01$ and allow the savings rate to vary. At $s = \hat{s} = 0.585$, the system at the equilibrium has a pair of pure imaginary eigenvalues, a condition for searching Hopf bifurcation. It was demonstrated that at $s = 0.59$ (which is larger than the bifurcation value), the sustainable equilibrium point is stable, but its basin is a closed region inside an unstable limit cycle. The phase plane is reshaped in comparison to Figure 6.2 (with $s = 0.8$). The dynamic system exhibits a stable limit cycle as a consequence of a Hopf bifurcation at $s = \hat{s}$ as plotted in Figure 6.3. The left plot shows a red trajectory initiated from the point just outside the unstable limit cycle. The trajectory finally ends at the origin. The right plot is focused on the movement around the cycles. The initial point IC1 starts the trajectory in light blue that finally spirals to the stable cycle in a solid back curve. Another point IC2 within the Hopf cycle also starts a trajectory which finally achieves on the cycle.

The savings rate is reduced from its bifurcation value, for instance, to $s = 0.58$. The left plot in Figure 6.4 shows that the phase plane is dominated by the attraction force of the origin, called the pollution-induced poverty trap engine. The right plot depicts the behavior near IC2 as in Figure 6.3.

6.2 Poverty Trap with Natural Resources in a Solow–Ramsey-Based Model

The Ramsey growth model introduces microeconomic foundation for household behavior to the Solow model. The multi-sector Ramsey model

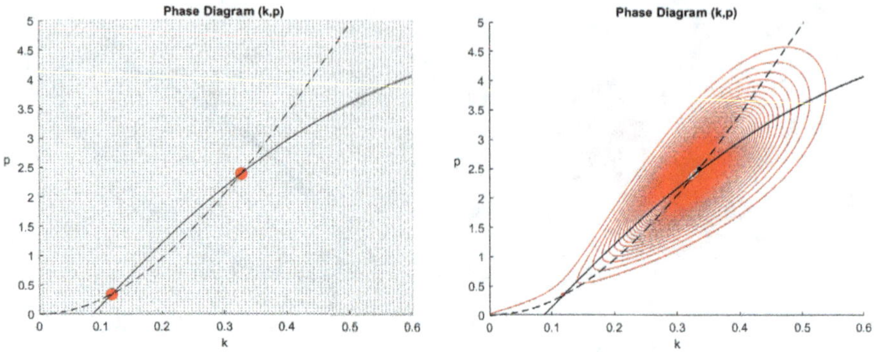

Fig. 6.4. A way for the system to collapse at $s = 0.58$.

manifests Hopf bifurcation and aperiodic behavior as shown, for instance, by Zhang (1988b, 1989b). This section introduces a model by Antoci *et al.* (2011) who apply global analysis techniques to economic growth development with natural resources within the Ramsey growth modeling framework (e.g., Wirl, 1995, 1997). The authors emphasize global analysis by quoting Matsuyama (1991): "Knowing the local dynamics is not enough, because, for example, demonstrating the uniqueness of the perfect foresight path in a neighborhood of a stationary state does not necessarily rule out the existence of other perfect foresight paths in the large."

The representative agent produces the output $Y(t)$ with the labor force $L(t)\,(0 \leq L(t) \leq 1)$, the physical capital $K(t)$, and the stock $E(t)$ of an open-access renewable natural resource. The production process is described by

$$Y(t) = K^{\alpha}(t)L^{\beta}(t)E^{\gamma}(t), \quad \alpha\beta\gamma > 0,\ \alpha + \beta < 1.$$

The representative agent chooses the consumption $C(t)$ and leisure $1 - L(t)$ to maximize the happiness. The consumer problem is formed as follows:

$$\int_{0}^{\infty} \frac{[C(1-L)^{\epsilon}]^{1-\eta}}{1-\eta} e^{-\theta t} dt$$

subject to

$$\dot{K} = Y - C,$$

$$\dot{E} = E(\bar{E} - E) - \delta Y,$$

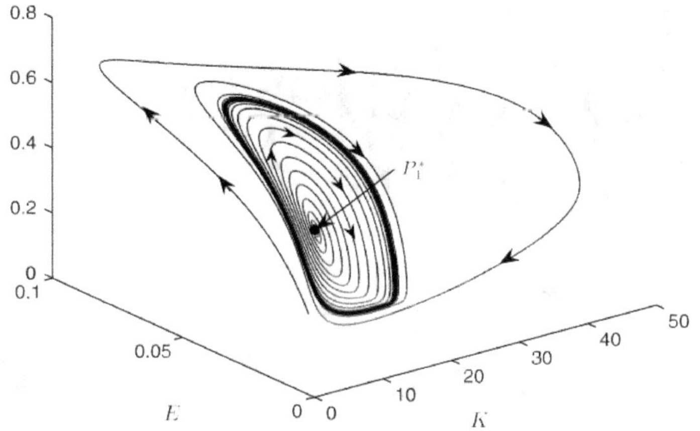

Fig. 6.5. An attracting limit cycle around P_1^*.

where θ is the discount rate. The instantaneous utility function is additively non-separable and is concave in the two variables, which is guaranteed by $\eta > \epsilon/(1+\epsilon)$. The parameter η denotes the inverse of the intertemporal elasticity of substitution in consumption. The parameter $\bar{E}$ is the carrying capacity of the natural resource and δY implies that the negative impact is proportionally related to the output.

Antoci *et al.* analyzed the general properties of the model. This section shows some behavior of the model. First, we specify

$$\alpha = 0.1, \quad \beta = 0.8, \quad \gamma = 0.58, \quad \epsilon = 1, \quad \delta = 0.05,$$
$$\eta = 1.5, \quad \theta = 0.001, \quad \bar{E} = 0.21.$$

The local motion is illustrated in Figure 6.5, which shows a locally attracting limit cycle around a stationary point P_1^* via Hopf bifurcation. For every initial K_0 and E_0 close to the projection of the plane (K, E) there is a continuum of L_0 such that the trajectory from (K_0, E_0, L_0) approaches the cycle.

We now introduce another case with the following parameters:

$$\alpha = \theta = 0.19, \quad \beta = \gamma = 0.8, \quad \epsilon = 0.2, \quad \delta = 8.42228, \quad \eta = \frac{4}{9}, \quad \bar{E} = 7.06$$

As displayed in Figure 6.6, there are two limit cycles. There are two stationary points P_1^*, which is named as a poverty trap, and P_2^*. At P_1^*, there are one negative and two positive real-part complex eigenvalues, while at P_2^*, three positive real-part eigenvalues. It is numerically identified that

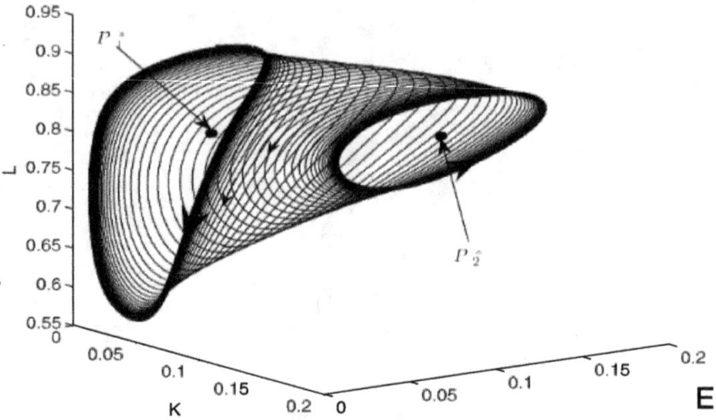

Fig. 6.6. Two attracting limit cycles around P_1^* and P_2^*.

the limit cycle around P_1^* is an attracting one, while the one around P_2^* is a non-attracting one.

6.3 Growth and Resources in an Overlapping Generations Model

The previous section introduced the growth model with renewable resources in a Solow–Ramsey-based framework by Antoci (2011). This section deals with economic growth and environmental resources within an overlapping generations framework proposed by Antoci (2016). Individuals choose leisure and consumption of goods to maximize lifetime utility. There is a free access to the environmental resource. The production activity deteriorates the environmental resource. The economy produces a single product whose price is unity. Let K_t and l_t represent the stock of capital. The economy is comprised of a continuum of identical agents, and any individual's impact on environment is negligible. An agent lives for two periods: youth and old age. Each generation's population is 1. Each young individual chooses how to allocate his time endowment (set to equal 2) between work and leisure $l_t(0 < l_t < 2)$ with the wage rate w_t and leisure activities $2 - l_t$. Young individuals do not consume the good which they produce and hence their savings $s_t = w_t$, which is invested to form capital $K_{t+1} = s_t$ (under the assumption that capital completely depreciates in one period). The interest rate is R_{t+1} The old man consumes

$$C_{t+1} = R_{t+1}s_t = R_{t+1}l_tw_t.$$

Individuals consume leisure time when young and goods when old. Their happiness is also affected by the environment. Their lifetime utility is given by

$$U_t = \frac{(2 - l_t)^{1-\gamma}}{1-\gamma} + \frac{(C_{t+1}E_{t+1}^{\tau})^{1-\sigma}}{1-\sigma}, \quad \gamma,\ \sigma > 0, \gamma \neq 1,\ \sigma \neq 1.$$

The parameters $\gamma, \sigma > 0$ imply the constant elasticity of utility with respect to consumption and leisure. If $0 < \sigma < 1\,(\sigma > 1)$, the increase in U_t due to an increase in C is positively related to the environment (and vice versa). The parameter $\tau \geq 0$ implies that good environment enhances welfare. The production technology is specified as

$$Y_t = AK_t^{\alpha} l_t^{1-\alpha}, \quad 0 < \alpha < 1.$$

The environmental quality evolves according to

$$E_{t+1} = \frac{\bar{E}}{1 + Y_t^{\rho}}, \quad \rho > 0$$

where $\bar{E}$ is the maximum value of environmental quality. We thus described the model. The agents maximize profits, and the agents maximize utility subject to the constraints. The motion of the economy is described by a two-dimensional map:

$$K_{t+1} = V(K_t, l_t) \equiv \beta A K_t^{\alpha} l_t^{\beta},$$

$$l_{t+1} = Z(K_t, l_t) \equiv K_t^{-\frac{\alpha^2}{\beta}} \left[\frac{l_t^{\alpha\beta(1-\sigma)}}{(2 - l_t)^{\gamma}}\right]^{\frac{1}{\beta(1-\sigma)}} \left[\frac{(1 + (AK_t^{\alpha} l_t^{\beta})^{\rho})^{\tau}}{\alpha\beta^{\alpha} A^{1+\alpha} \bar{E}^{\tau}}\right]^{\frac{1}{\beta}},$$

where $\beta \equiv 1 - \alpha$. The map is said to be globally indeterminate if there is coexistence of attractors and/or saddles. Figure 6.7 illustrates global indeterminacy when we have the following parameters:

$$A = 1.25, \quad \bar{E} = 12.2, \quad \alpha = 0.2, \quad \gamma = 1.1, \quad \sigma = 3, \quad \tau = 1.1.$$

Varying ρ, we observe different behaviors. If $\rho < 0.873$, the map has a unique fixed saddle point. Figure 6.7(a) illustrates the case of $\rho = 0.2$. Near $\rho = 0.873$, a flip bifurcation occurs. The map has a unique fixed point. Figure 6.7(b) illustrates the case of $\rho = 1$. In the figure, the gray area represents the basin of attraction of the fixed point (K_1^*, l_1^*). The white area is the region of unfeasible trajectories.

As ρ is further increased near $\rho = 3.08$, the map has two attracting fixed points, (K_1^*, l_1^*) and (K_3^*, l_3^*), and one saddle point, (K_2^*, l_2^*), as plotted in Figure 6.8(a). The basins of attraction are separated by the stable manifold of the saddle point (K_2^*, l_2^*). The point with low capital and less work hours

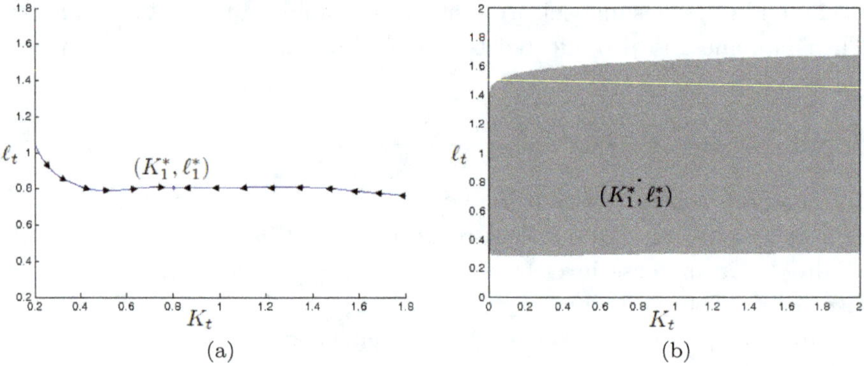

Fig. 6.7. Existence of a unique fixed point.

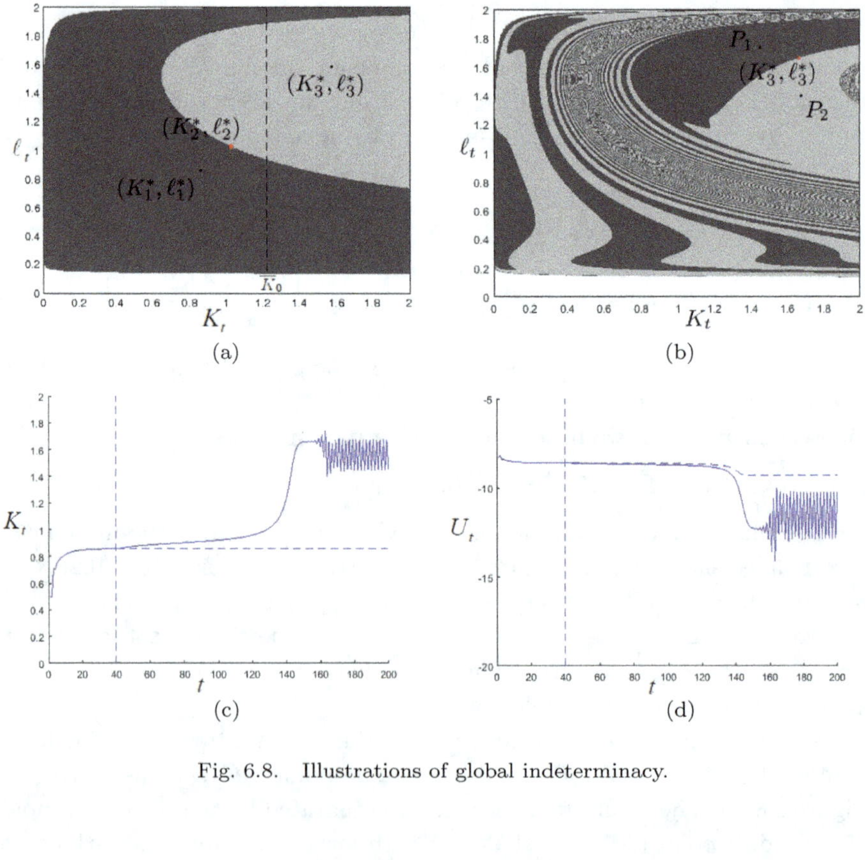

Fig. 6.8. Illustrations of global indeterminacy.

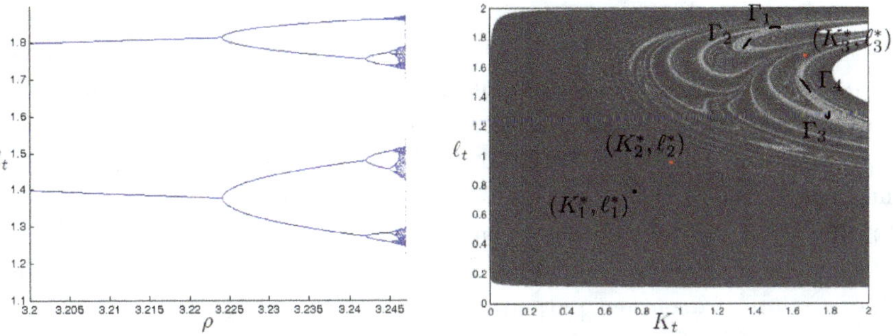

(a) (b)

Fig. 6.9. Bifurcation diagram and indeterminacy.

is a happy state, while the other states are not so happy as (K_1^*, l_1^*). This is confirmed by $U = -8.57$ at (K_1^*, l_1^*), $U = -8.88$ at (K_2^*, l_2^*), and $U = -11.29$ at (K_3^*, l_3^*). This depends on how the agent evaluates leisure and environment. In this situation, there are some initial points at which the economy might move towards any of the three points. The dashed vertical line shows that it is possible to reach any of the three fixed points by opportunely selecting an initial state. As ρ is further increased, (K_1^*, l_1^*) moves near to (K_2^*, l_2^*) and (K_3^*, l_3^*) loses its stability and a supercritical flip bifurcation occurs. Figure 6.8(b) displays what happens to the economy at $\rho = 3.28$. The basins of attraction of P_1 and P_2 are separated by the stable manifold of (K_3^*, l_3^*). Figures 6.8(c) and 6.8(d), in which the dashed lines represent the economy before the exogenous change, show how a change in ρ affects paths of capital and utility.

Figure 6.9(a) displays the bifurcation diagram with ρ from $\rho = 3.2$ to $\rho = 3.245$ as the bifurcation parameter. Figure 6.9(b) shows the basins of attraction when the fixed point coexists with a four-piece chaotic attractor when $\rho = 3.2465$. The dark gray area depicts the basin of attraction of the fixed point (K_1^*, l_1^*). The light gray area displays the "chaotic" region in which the attractions are tangled. This exemplifies the concept of global indeterminacy (multistability).

6.4 Business and Environmental Cycles in a Solow–Ramsey-Based Model

This section introduces a model by Bosi and Desmarchelier (2018), which is built by integrating the Levins model and the Solow–Ramsey model with pollution externality. The concept of metapopulation, which was introduced in ecology in 1969 by Levins (Levins, 1969), implies a spatially fragmented population of the same species. The model by Bosi and Desmarchelier is a synthesis of ideas in economics and ecology. It addresses issues related to coupled evolution between economy and biodiversity as modeled by Lafuite and Loreau (2017). The consumption is influenced by environmental quality. Wildlife habitat is a part of environmental quality. A drop in wildlife entails a lower consumption. Wildlife is assimilated to s single metapopulation. The fraction of occupied patches (a measure of environmental quality) is assumed to affect the marginal utility of consumption. The study uses green tax on production to finance depollution.

The economy consists of households, firms, and the government. Households work, consume, and enjoy the nature. Production is carried out by firms. There is pollution in association with production. The government taxes the firms to improve the environment. Consider that space is represented by a partition of patches occupied or unoccupied by the metapopulation. We use P to denote the fraction of patches occupied at a given time. Let us denote P as the aggregate stock of pollution. The change of $q(t)$ is modeled as

$$\dot{q} = \varphi(P)q(1-q) - \beta(P)q,$$

where φ represents the migration rate and β is the extinction rate. The term φq means the migration pressure on the unoccupied patches $(1-q)$ The pollution positively affects the extinction rate and negatively affects the migration rate, that is, $\varphi' < 0$ and $\beta' > 0$. The functions are specified as follows: $\beta = A_\beta P^{\varepsilon_\beta}$ and $\varphi = A_\varphi P^{\varepsilon_\varphi}$. The colonization rate is defined as the difference between the migration and extinction rate: $s \equiv \varphi - \beta$. The pollution elasticities of migration and extinction and the pollution impact on colonization are given by

$$\varepsilon_\varphi \equiv \frac{P\varphi'}{\varphi}, \quad \varepsilon_\beta \equiv \frac{P\beta'}{\beta}, \quad d \equiv \varepsilon_\varphi - \varepsilon_\beta.$$

The per capita output given by the neoclassical technology is denoted by $f(k) = Ak^\alpha$, where $k = K/L, K$ being the total capital stock and L the labor force. Let r and w denote the real interest rate and wage rate, respectively. The marginal conditions for profit maximization are

$$r = (1-\tau)f', \, w = (1-\tau)(f - kf'),$$

where τ is the tax rate.

We use $c(t)$ and $h(t)$ to denote the consumption level of and wealth of the representative household. The household maximizes the utility subject to the budget constraint:

$$\text{Max} \int_0^\infty \frac{(cq^\eta)^{1-\varepsilon}}{1-\varepsilon} e^{-\theta t} dt$$

subject to $c + \dot{h} \leq w + (r - \delta)h$,
where θ is the rate of time preference, δ is the depreciation rate of physical capital, η is the propensity to wildlife, and $1/\varepsilon$ is the elasticity of intertemporal substitution of the composite good (cq^η).

The government uses its tax revenue to finance the depollution expenditures η:

$$M = \tau f N.$$

The pollution accumulation follows a linear question:

$$\dot{P} = -aP + bY - \gamma M, \; ab\gamma \geq 0,$$

where a, b, and γ are, respectively, the natural rate of pollution absorption, the rate of population accumulation owing to economic production, and the pollution abatement efficiency. We thus described the model.

Bosi and Desmarchelier chose parameter values for numerical simulation. First, the parameters, $A = 1$, $A_\beta = 1$, $\varepsilon_\beta = 1$, $A_\varphi = 1$,and $\varepsilon_\varphi = -1$ are normalized. Some other parameters are specified as

$$\alpha = 0.33, \quad \theta = 0.01, \quad \delta = 0.025, \quad \tau = 0.002, \quad a = 0.003,$$
$$b = 0.0015, \quad \gamma = 0.3.$$

Applying the Hopf bifurcation theorem, they demonstrate the existence of unstable limit cycles as in Figure 6.10.

6.5 The Role of Environment in Dynamics of Cournot Game

Cournot game is a basic model in industrial economics. The model has a simple structure and is intuitively easy to understand. It has been a popular model for illustrating the complexity of economic behavior. Its different versions and generalizations appear in the literature of nonlinear economics (e.g., Okuguchi, 1976; Medio, 1992; Bischi *et al.*, 2010; Puu, 2018). This section introduces a Cournot game model suggested by Fanti (2015). The model deals with the impact of public environmental policies in a Cournot

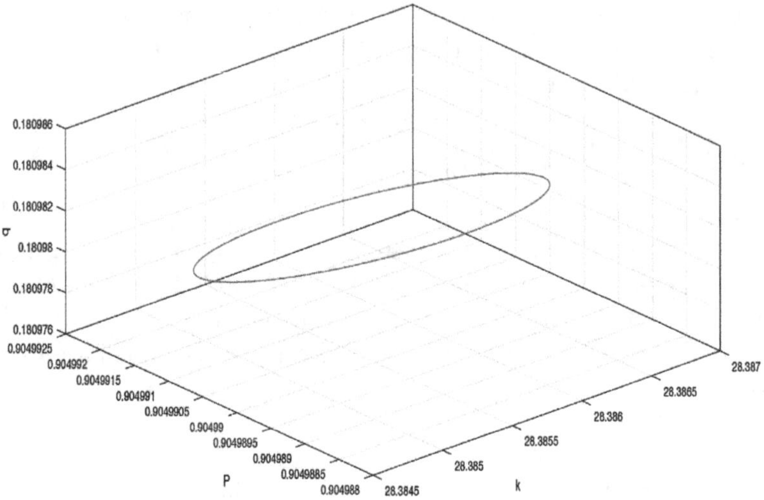

Fig. 6.10. Existence of limit cycles with endogenous environment.

duopoly game with heterogeneous expectations and limited rationality. It is the first study to integrate a dynamic Cournot game with both irrationality and environmental policies. It demonstrates that an increase in upper limits to emissions may destabilize markets.

The system consists of two private firms, producing a homogeneous product with the same polluting technology. Each unit of the product produced causes one unit of pollutant. A public agent maintains environmental quality by setting up and applying environmental policy. The firms abate pollution emissions to comply with the government policy. The abatement cost of firm $i, i = 1, 2$, is supposed to take on the following form:

$$CA_i = k\frac{(q_i - e)^2}{2}, \quad k > 0, \ q_i, \ e \geq 0,$$

where q_i is the output level, e is the environmental standard determined by the government, and $q_i - e$ is the emission abated by firm i. Both firms have zero marginal cost of production. The demand function for the homogeneous product is $p = a - (q_1 + q_2)$. The profit of firm i is $\pi_i = pq_i - CA_i$. The dynamics of bounded rational firm i is given by

$$q_{i,t+1} = q_{i,t} + \alpha q_{i,t}\frac{\partial \pi_i}{\partial q_{i,t}}.$$

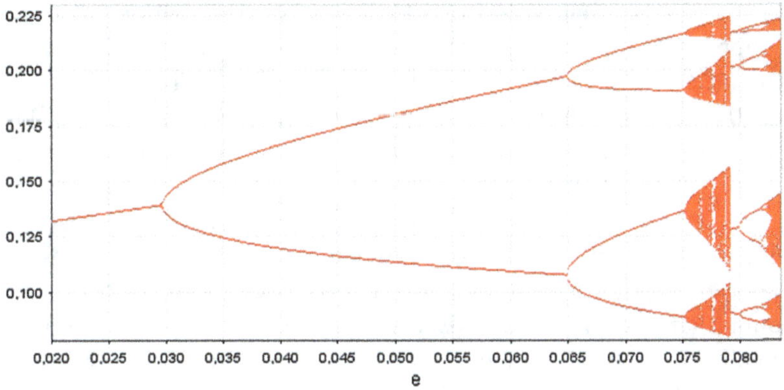

Fig. 6.11. Bifurcation diagram for the environmental policy.

It is straightforward to show that the map of the economy is given by

$$q_{1,t+1} = q_{1,t} + \alpha q_{1,t}(a - (2+k)q_{1,t} - q_{2,t} + ek),$$

$$q_{2,t+1} = q_{2,t} + \alpha q_{2,t}(a - (2+k)q_{2,t} - q_{1,t} + ek).$$

The map has a unique equilibrium at which the two firms produce the same level of output. Figure 6.11 provides the bifurcation diagram with the environmental policy e as the bifurcation parameter when parameters are taken on the following values: $\alpha = 1.2$, $a = 1.4$, and $k = 9$.

6.6 Environmental Dynamics and Development in a Multi-Regional Economy

Regional agglomeration and environmental changes are the main features of contemporary economies. Moreover, economies experience business cycles during development processes. It is a greatly challenging task for economists to develop genuine dynamic models which exhibit business cycles, economic growth, and spatial agglomeration on microeconomic foundation. Kuznets (1966) discussed spatial unequal economic development over space long time ago. He examined interdependence between spatial agglomeration and industrialization. Myrdal (1957) and Hirschman (1958) earlier argued for dynamic interactions between industrial growth and the geographical concentration of industry. There are numerous studies on various aspects of spatial economic developments (e.g., Fujita *et al.*, 1999; Forslid and Ottaviano, 2003). Different from earlier literature on spatial agglomeration,

Zhang extended neoclassical growth theory to multi-regional economies. This approach is different from the so-called new economic geography (e.g., Krugman, 1993). In the literature of the new economic geography, Tabuchi (2014: 50) reviews: "The scopes of the theoretical studies published thus far have been limited to two regions in order for researchers to reach meaningful analytical results. The two-region NEG models tend to demonstrate that spatial distribution is dispersed in the early period (high trade costs or low manufacturing share) and agglomerated in one of the two regions in the late period (low trade costs or high manufacturing share). However, it is no doubt that the two-region NEG models are too simple to describe the spatial distribution of economic activities in real-world economies. Since there are only two regions, their geographical locations are necessarily symmetric, and thus diverse spatial distributions cannot occur." Dynamic interdependence between economic growth and environmental changes is extensively studied (e.g., Ploude, 1972; Gassebner *et al.*, 2011; Glaeser *et al.*, 2001; Walenta, 2018). This section introduces the multi-regional dynamic model, proposed by Zhang (2019), with wealth and pollutant accumulation. The model treats regional amenities as endogenous variables dependent on the region's population and level of pollutants. Regional differences in productivities and amenities are important for modeling regional agglomeration. The government decides environmental tax rates on production, consumption, wealth, income from wealth, and housing.

The economy is composed of J regions, indexed by $j = 1, \ldots, J$. Each region has one production sector and one environment sector. The production sector is the same as in the Solow growth model. The system produces one (durable) good. Assets are owned by households. Capital and labor are inputs of the production sector. Productivities of the production sector are fully utilized. Savings is undertaken only by households. Commodities are traded without any barriers. We neglect transport costs. We measure prices in terms of the commodity and the price of the commodity is unity. We represent wage and interest rates by $w_j(t)$ and $r_j(t)$, respectively, in the jth region. The interest rate is equal across regions, i.e., $r(t) = r_j(t)$. We consider that the national population $N(t)$ is homogenous. Workers are free to choose their workplace and residential location. Workers work and reside in the same region. Each region has land $L_j(t)$ which is used only for residential purposes. Regions have different productivities and living conditions. We use subscripts, i, e, to denote the production and environment sectors, respectively. Let $F_{qj}(t)$ stand for the output levels of q's sector in region j at time $t, q = i, e$. Each region has one environmental sector. The role of the regional government is to collect different taxes on producers and consumers to financially support the sector. The tax income is used up for employing labor and capital to purify the environment. The production functions are specified as follows:

$$F_{ij}(t) = A_{ij}(t)\Gamma_{ij}(E_j(t))K_{ij}^{\alpha_{ji}(t)}(t)N_{ij}^{\beta_{ij}(t)}(t),$$
$$A_{ij}(t),\ \alpha_{ij}(t),\ \beta_{ij}(t) > 0, \alpha_{ij}(t) + \beta_{ij}(t) = 1,$$

where $A_{ij}(t), \alpha_{ij}(t)$, and $\beta_{ij}(t)$ are positive parameters. Here, $\Gamma_{ij}(E_j(t))$ is a function of the environmental quality measured by the level of pollution, $E_j(t)$, in region j It is assumed that the productivity of the capital goods sector is non-positively related to the pollution level. Let δ_{kj} stand for the depreciation rate of physical capital in region j We use $\tau_{ij}(t)$ to stand for the tax rate on the capital goods sector. The marginal conditions of the production sector are

$$r(t) + \delta_{kj}(t) = \frac{\alpha_{ij}(t)\bar{\tau}_{ij}(t)F_{ij}(t)}{K_{ij}(t)}, \quad w_j(t) = \frac{\beta_{ij}(t)\bar{\tau}_{ij}(t)F_{ij}(t)}{N_{ij}(t)},$$

where $\bar{\tau}_{ij}(t) \equiv 1 - \tau_{ij}(t), 0 < \tau_{ij}(t) < 1$.

We specify the dynamics of the stock of pollutants as follows:

$$\dot{E}_j(t) = \theta_{ij}(t)F_{ij}(t) + \theta_{cj}(t)C_j(t) - F_{ej}(t) - \bar{\theta}_j(t)E_j(t) + \Omega_j((E_q(t))),$$

in which $\theta_{ij}(t), \theta_{cj}(t)$, and $\bar{\theta}_j(t)$ are positive parameters and

$$F_{ej}(t) = A_{ej}(t)\Gamma_{ej}(E_j(t))K_{ej}^{\tilde{\alpha}_{ej}(t)}(t)N_{ej}^{\tilde{\beta}_{ej}}(t)$$
$$A_{ej}(t),\ \tilde{\alpha}_{ej}(t)\tilde{\beta}_{ej}(t) > 0,$$

where $A_{ej}(t), \alpha_{ej}(t)$, and $\beta_{ej}(t)$ are positive parameters and $\Gamma_{ej}(E_j)(\geq 0)$ is a function of $E_j(t)$. The term $\theta_{ij}(t)F_{ij}(t)$ means that pollutants that are emitted during production processes are linearly positively proportional to the output level. The parameter, $\theta_{ij}(t)$, means that in consuming one unit of the good, the quantity $\theta_{ij}(t)$ is left as waste. The creation of pollutants by consumers is given as $\theta_{cj}(t)C_j(t)$. The parameter $\bar{\theta}_j(t)$ is called the rate of natural purification.

We take account of the effects of transboundary pollution by $\Omega_j((E_q(t)))$, where Ω_j is a function of pollutants of all the regions.

All the income from land is evenly redistributed among the population. Region j's land is $L_j(t)$ and the land rent is $R_j(t)$. The land revenue $\bar{r}(t)$

per worker is as follows:

$$\bar{r}(t) = \frac{1}{N} \sum_{j=1}^{J} L_j(t) R_j(t).$$

Let $\bar{k}_j(t)$ stand for per capita wealth of region j. We have $\bar{k}_j(t) = \bar{K}_j(t)/N_j(t)$, where $K(t)$ is the total wealth held by region j We use $\tau_{kj}(t)$ and $\tau_{wj}(t)$ to stand for the tax rates on the wealth income and wage income in region j, respectively. Per capita current income from the land ownership, the interest payment $r(t)\bar{k}_j(t)$, and the wage payment $w_j(t)$ is

$$y_j(t) = \bar{r}(t) + \bar{\tau}_{kj}(t) r(t) \bar{k}_j(t) + \bar{\tau}_{wj}(t) w_j(t),$$

where $\bar{\tau}_{kj}(t) \equiv 1 - \tau_{kj}(t)$ and $\bar{\tau}_{wj}(t) \equiv 1 - \tau_{wj}(t)$. The per capita disposable income is the sum of the current disposable income and the value of wealth: $\hat{y}_j(t) = \bar{k}_j(t) + y_j(t)$. The disposable income is used for savings and consumption. At each point in time, a consumer would distribute the total available budget between housing $l_j(t)$, savings $s_j(t)$, and consumption $c_j(t)$ The budget constraint is given by

$$(1 + \tau_{Rj}(t)) R_j(t) l_j(t) + (1 + \tau_{cj}(t)) p_j(t) c_j(t) + s_j(t) = \hat{y}_j(t),$$

where $\tau_{Rj}(t)$ is the tax rate on housing and $\tau_{cj}(t)$ is the tax rate on consumption.

Utility level $U_j(t)$ is dependent on the consumption levels of lot size, commodity, and savings. The utility level of the typical consumer in region j is represented by

$$U_j(t) = \theta_j(t) l_j^{\eta_0(t)}(t) c_j^{\xi_0(t)} s_j^{\lambda_0(t)}(t),$$
$$\eta_0(t), \xi_0(t), \lambda_0(t) > 0,$$

in which $\eta_0(t), \xi_0(t)$, and $\lambda_0(t)$ are the elasticities of utility with regard to lot size, commodity, and savings. We call $\eta_0(t), \xi_0(t)$, and $\lambda_0(t)$ propensities to consume lot size, and goods, and to hold wealth, respectively. In the utility function, $\theta_j(t)$ is region j's amenity level (e.g., Diamond and Tolley, 1981; and Saracoglu and Roe, 2019). We specify $\theta_j(t)$ as follows:

$$\theta_j(t) = \bar{\theta}_j(t) E_j^{\omega(t)}(t) N_j^{d(t)}(t), \quad j = 1, \ldots, J,$$

where $\bar{\theta}_j(t)\,(> 0), \omega(\leq 0)$, and $d(t)$ are parameters and $N_j(t)$ is region j's population. We don't specify signs of $d(t)$ as population may have either positive or negative effects on regional attractiveness. Maximizing $U_j(t)$ subject to the budget yields

$$l_j(t)R_j(t) = \eta_j(t)\hat{y}_j(t), c_j(t) = \xi_j(t)\hat{y}_j(t), s_j(t) = \lambda_j(t)\,\hat{y}_j(t),$$

where

$$\eta_j(t) \equiv \frac{\eta_0(t)\rho(t)}{1+\tau_{Rj}(t)}, \quad \xi_j(t) \equiv \frac{\xi_0(t)\rho(t)}{1+\tau_{cj}(t)}, \quad \lambda(t) \equiv \lambda_0(t)\rho(t),$$

$$\rho(t) \equiv \frac{1}{\eta_0(t)+\xi_0(t)+\lambda_0(t)}.$$

The wealth accumulation of the representative household in region j is

$$\dot{\bar{k}}_j(t) = s_j(t) - \bar{k}_j(t).$$

We assume that households are freely mobile between the regions. The utility levels of homogenous population between regions are assumed to be equal at any point in time. That is,

$$U_j(t) = U_q(t), \;\; j, \quad q = 1, \ldots, J.$$

Each region's governmental tax income consists of the tax incomes on the production sector, consumption, wage income, and wealth income as follows:

$$\begin{aligned} Y_{ej}(t) = \tau_{ij}(t)F_{ij}(t) &+ \tau_{Rj}(t)l_j(t)R_j(t)N_j(t) \\ &+ \tau_{cj}(t)c_j(t)N_j(t) + \tau_{wj}(t)w_j(t)N_j(t) \\ &+ \tau_{kj}(t)r(t)\bar{k}_j(t)N_j(t). \end{aligned}$$

The government's income is used up only for the environmental purpose. The government budget is as follows:

$$(r(t)+\delta_k(t))k_{ej}(t) + w_j(t)N_{ej}(t) = Y_{ej}(t).$$

The government employs labour and capital stocks for purifying the environment in such a way that the purification rate is maximized under the given budget constraint. The government's optimal problem is thus formed by maximizing the efficiency of the environment sector:

$$\max_{\{K_{ej}(t), N_{ej}(t)\}} F_{ej}(t) \quad \text{s.t. the budget.}$$

The optimal solution is

$$(r(t)+\delta_k(t))K_{ej}(t)=\alpha_{ej}(t)Y_{ej}(t), w_j(t)N_{ej}(t)=\beta_{ej}(t)Y_{ej}(t),$$

where

$$\alpha_{ej}(t)\equiv\frac{\tilde{\alpha}_{ej}(t)}{\tilde{\alpha}_{ej}(t)+\tilde{\beta}_{ej}(t)},\quad \beta_{ej}(t)\equiv\frac{\tilde{\beta}_{ej}(t)}{\tilde{\alpha}_{ej}(t)+\tilde{\beta}_{ej}(t)}.$$

Each region's capital stocks $K_j(t)$ are fully employed: $K_{ij}(t)+K_{ej}(t)=K_j(t)$. The total capital stock $K(t)$ employed by the production sectors is equal to the total wealth owned by the households of all the regions:

$$K(t)=\sum_{j=1}^{J}K_j(t)=\sum_{j=1}^{J}\bar{k}_j(t)N_j(t).$$

The assumption that labor force and land are fully employed is represented by

$$N_{ij}(t)+N_{ej}(t)=N_j(t),\sum_{j=1}^{J}N_j(t)=N(t).$$

Land resource is utilized fully:

$$l_j(t)N_j(t)=L_j(t),\quad j=1,\ldots,J.$$

We have thus built the model. We simulate the case that the economy is composed of three regions. We specify the functions dependent on environmental quality as follows:

$$\Gamma_{mj}(E_j(t),t)=E_j^{-b_{mj(t)}}(t),\Gamma_j(E_j(t),t)=E_j^{-b_j(t)}(t),$$
$$j=1,2,3,\quad m=i,e.$$

We require $b_{ji},b_{js},b_j\geq 0$ and $b_{je}\leq 0$. We specify transboundary pollution functions as

$$\Omega_q\left((E_q(t)),t\right)=\sum_{j,j\neq q}^{J}\theta_{jq}(t)E_j(t).$$

The transboundary pollution functions imply that any region is also polluted by the other two regions and the speed is linearly related to the pollutant levels of other regions. We first examine the case that all the parameters are constant. We specify the parameters as follows:

$$N = 20, \quad \lambda_0 = 0.75, \quad \xi_0 = 0.1, \quad \eta_0 = 0.1, \quad d = -0.05, \quad \omega = -0.08,$$

$$\tau_{ij} = \tau_{cj}, \quad \theta_{jq} = 0.01, \quad j \neq q, j, q = 1, 2, 3,$$

$$\begin{pmatrix} L_1 \\ L_2 \\ L_2 \end{pmatrix} = \begin{pmatrix} 3 \\ 4 \\ 3 \end{pmatrix}, \begin{pmatrix} A_{i1} \\ A_{12} \\ A_{12} \end{pmatrix} = \begin{pmatrix} 1.2 \\ 1 \\ 0.8 \end{pmatrix}, \begin{pmatrix} A_{21} \\ A_{i2} \\ A_{i2} \end{pmatrix} = \begin{pmatrix} 1.1 \\ 1 \\ 0.9 \end{pmatrix}, \begin{pmatrix} \alpha_{11} \\ \alpha_{i2} \\ \alpha_{12} \end{pmatrix} = \begin{pmatrix} 0.31 \\ 0.31 \\ 0.31 \end{pmatrix}$$

$$\begin{pmatrix} b_{21} \\ b_{iz} \\ b_{33} \end{pmatrix} = \begin{pmatrix} b_{e1} \\ b_{e2} \\ b_{es} \end{pmatrix} = \begin{pmatrix} 0.01 \\ 0.08 \\ 0.01 \end{pmatrix}, \begin{pmatrix} g_1 \\ \overline{\sigma_2} \\ \overline{\sigma_1} \end{pmatrix} = \begin{pmatrix} 0.08 \\ 0.1 \\ 0.11 \end{pmatrix}$$

$$\begin{pmatrix} \tau_{k1} \\ \tau_{k2} \\ \tau_{k3} \end{pmatrix} = \begin{pmatrix} \tau_{w1} \\ \tau_{w2} \\ \tau_{w3} \end{pmatrix} = \begin{pmatrix} 0.005 \\ 0.0006 \\ 0.007 \end{pmatrix}, \begin{pmatrix} \tilde{a}_{ej} \\ \tilde{\beta}_{ej} \\ \tau_{ij} \end{pmatrix} = \begin{pmatrix} 0.4 \\ 0.2 \\ 0.005 \end{pmatrix},$$

$$\begin{pmatrix} b_j \\ \theta_{1j} \\ g_{ci} \end{pmatrix} = \begin{pmatrix} 0.01 \\ 0.08 \\ 0.03 \end{pmatrix}, \begin{pmatrix} d_{k1} \\ s_{ky} \\ d_{iv} \end{pmatrix} = \begin{pmatrix} 0.05 \\ 0.04 \\ 0.04 \end{pmatrix}.$$

We choose initial conditions:

$$z_1(0) = 0.038, \quad \bar{r}(0) = 1.42, \quad \bar{k}_1(0) = 12.7, \quad \bar{k}_2(0) = 11,$$

$$\bar{k}_3(0) = 9.7, \quad E_1(0) = 8.3, \quad E_2(0) = 9.8, \quad E_3(0) = 6.4.$$

The motion of the variables is plotted in Figure 6.12.

From the plot, we see that the system becomes stationary over time. We identified an equilibrium point. It is straightforward to calculate the eigenvalues as follows:

$$\{-0.18 \pm 0.02l, -0.2, -0.15, -0.1, -0.07, -0.005, 0\}$$

The real parts of the seven eigenvalues are negative and one is zero. The unique equilibrium is locally stable. This implies the validity of conducting comparative dynamic analysis. We now identify business cycles by allowing various exogenous periodic shocks. We use $x_j(t)$ to stand for the change rate of the variable, $x_j(t)$, in percentage due to changes in a parameter value. In the rest of this section, we use the variable with the same meaning. We now study the effects of the following periodic oscillations in the national population: $N(t) = 20 + 0.2\sin(t)$. The simulation results are plotted in Figure 6.13. The change rates in the regional populations are regionally oscillatory. The per household consumption and wealth

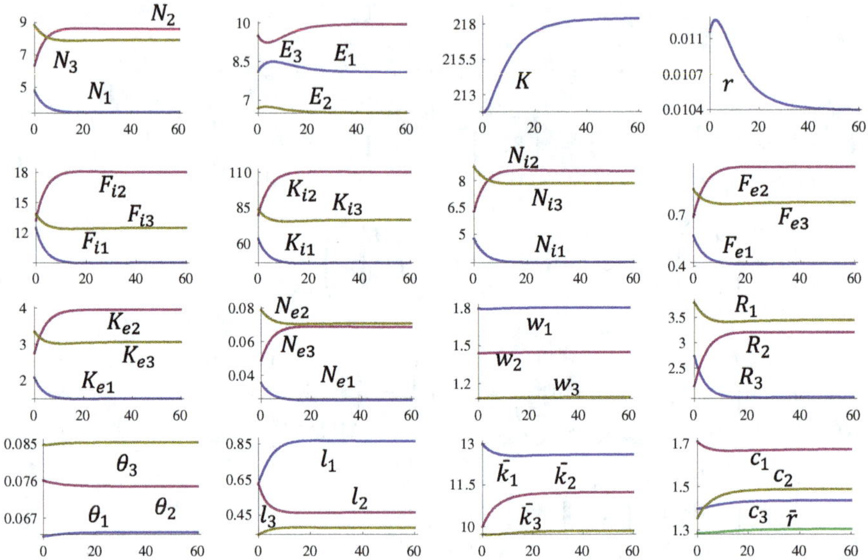

Fig. 6.12. The motion of the national and regional economies.

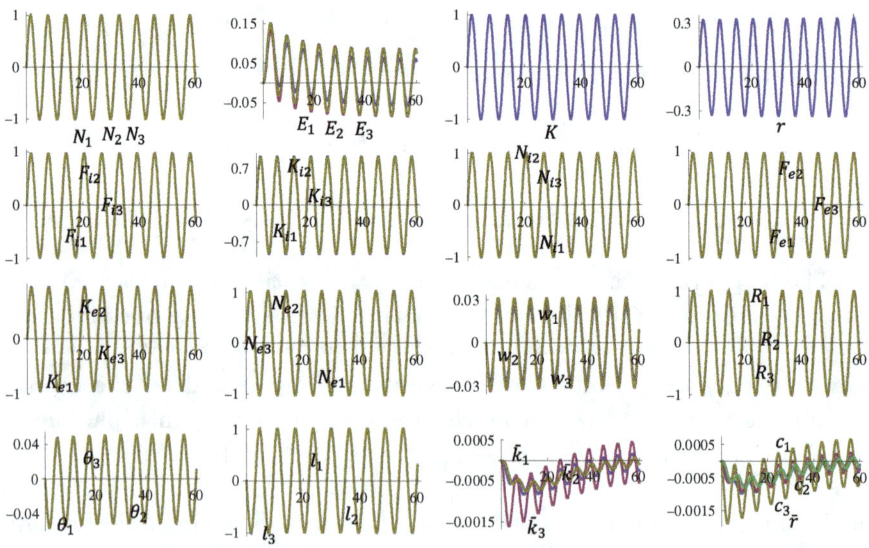

Fig. 6.13. Periodic oscillations in the population.

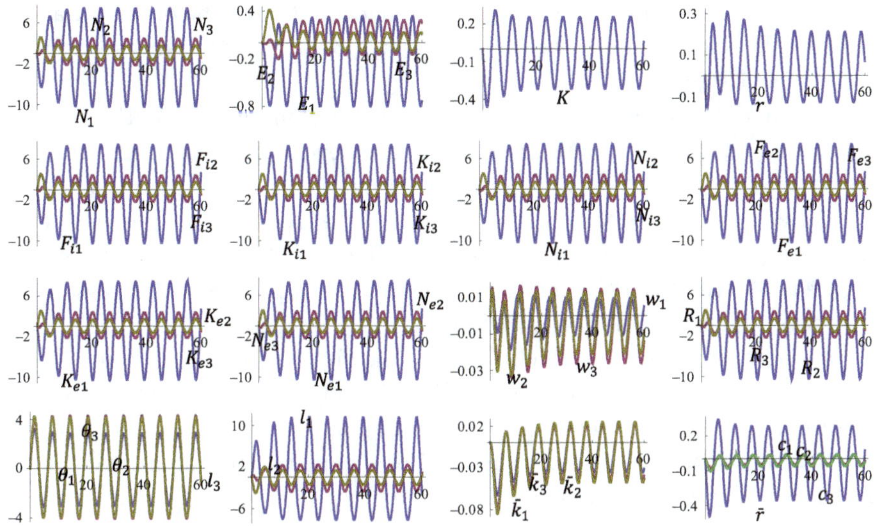

Fig. 6.14. The impact of population on amenity being periodically perturbed.

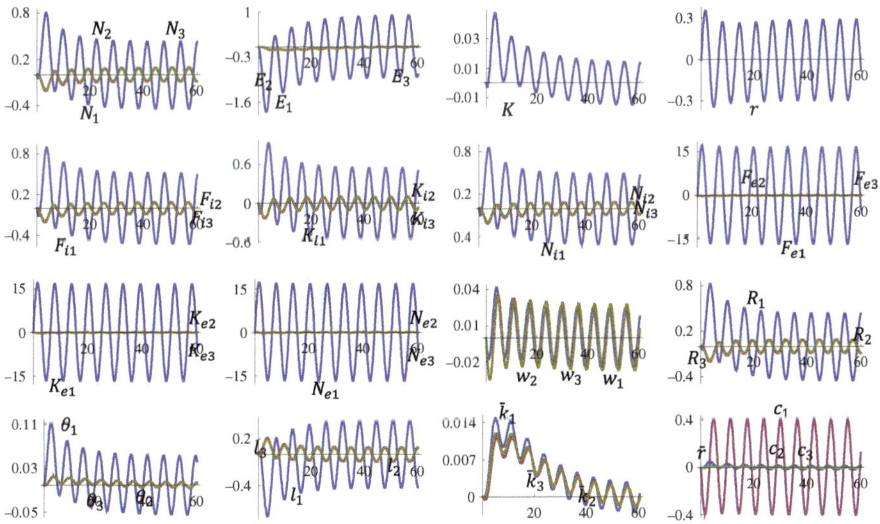

Fig. 6.15. Region 1's tax rate on consumption is periodically changed.

levels across the regions are slightly affected, even though the other variables change greatly in amplitude. The national economy experiences business cycles over time.

The population may affect amenity in different ways. In this study, we consider that the population has a negative impact on the amenity. We assume parameter d equal across regions. We now examine the effects when the negative impact of the population is periodically perturbed as follows: $d(t) = -0.05 + 0.02\sin(t)$. The simulation results are plotted in Figure 6.14. Although the regional variables change periodically, region 1's macro variables vary largely in amplitude.

We now examine the effects of the following change in region 1's tax rate: $\tau_{c1}(t) = 0.005 + 0.004\sin(t)$. The simulation results are plotted in Figure 6.15. Region 1 spends more resources on purifying the environment. The two input factors and output level of region 1's sectors are increased. The level of pollutants is reduced and the region's amenity is enhanced. As pollutants are reduced in region 1, the productivity of the region is improved. The better environment attracts more people to live in region 1. The lot size falls in region 1 and the land rent rises. As shown in the figure, a rise in the tax rate brings positive effects on all aspects of regional and national economies.

Chapter 7

Complexity of Economies and Evolution of Economics

Rasch (1991) recalled what Warren Weaver argued in 1948: "As Warren Weaver put it in his famous article of 1948, *Science and Complexity*, seventeenth-, eighteenth-, and nineteenth-century science succeeded in solving problems of simplicity, while the science of the first half of the twentieth century learned, by means of statistical analysis and probability theory, to deal with problems of disorganized complexity. It was his contention, then, that the task of the latter half of the twentieth century was to develop means of investigating the dynamics of organized complexity, complexity not characterized by random behavior and therefore not explicable by the rules of probability. By and large, Weaver's call for a research program into organized complexity has been heeded, especially in those domains where traditional, simple-system science had made little headway — the various biologics, economics, and political and social theories." This book demonstrates different economic mechanisms which give rise to business cycles and economic chaos. There are many studies on the subject (see also, for instance, Zhang, 1991; Lorenz, 1993; Flaschel *et al.*, 1997; Chiarella and Flaschel, 2000; Shone, 2002; Gandolfo, 2005; Puu, 2018). Chaos theory enables us to re-examine past wisdom and conclusions of traditional sciences from some new perspectives. It also teaches many mechanisms and phenomena which cannot be found in traditional sciences. It shows what George Shaw observed long time ago: "If all the economists were laid end to end, they'd never reach a conclusion." If there was no finite conclusion, it would be strange to get one, except faith. It is fortune for modern world that economists have no blind (or Newtonian) faith like Adam Smith or Karl Marx. What Benjamin Franklin said "In this world nothing can be said to be certain, except death and taxes" is still applicable. This book shows the reasons for uncertainties which he might have little idea about. Nobel Prize Winner Robert Solow asked an obvious question: "Why does a public discussion of economic policy so often show the abysmal ignorance of the participants?" He got the prize because he effectively neglected policy in his key model and theoretically showed the sustainability of unlimited economic growth without any politics. Albert Einstein complained about the complexity of daily life: "The hardest thing in the world to understand is the income tax." Perhaps anything human might be hard for the genius to fully comprehend. "Chaos was the law of nature; Order was the dream of man," Henry Adams believed. Chaos theory reveals chaos out of order. "Music creates order of chaos: for rhythm imposes unanimity upon the divergent, melody imposes continuity upon the disjointed, and harmony imposes compatibility upon the incongruous," Yehudi Menunin described. "Chaos in the midst of chaos isn't funny, but chaos in the midst of order is," Steve Martin reveals the mystery of humor. "Painting calmed the chaos that shook my soul" is another way to appreciate the role of painting by Niki de St. Phalle. Chaos, like order, exists everywhere. The yin and yang coexist within a single unity. Beauty lies in the eyes of the beholder. Everything has beauty.

"The curious task of economics is to demonstrate to men how little they really know about what they imagine they can design," Friedrich August von Hayek had criticized economic planning and supported free markets without any additional conditions. He deeply penetrated the invalidity of socialism in the last century but had little idea about chaos and instabilities in capitalist systems. His intellectual focus is on principles for failures of socialism and his heart was to sing songs of beautifying capitalism. This kind of intellectual is the leading figure of fashion academic world but has little to do with truth or life as a whole, like a young heart who sings beautiful songs of love and passionately hunts after lovers. Let's be or do things according to our age. Each stage of life has its ways of pleasure and survival. This is true for society as well. Paul Samuelson commented on unpredictability in financial markets: "What we know about the global financial crisis is that we don't know very much." It is applicable to almost every aspect of life, depending on what time scale of life one valuates. This book shows that some economic models which are extensions and generalizations of the models within the frameworks of early mathematical models under market mechanisms exhibit chaos, disorder, poverty traps, and catastrophe. Unpredictability is not limited to any ideology; it is the character of human life — an organic complexity under constantly changing environment.

Mankind has still poor understanding about complex problems, daily occurring around and within us. Mainstreams of modern theoretical economics have developed with the isolation of gender, sexual orientation, climate change, environment, knowledge, human capital, governance, human gaming, as well as international relations. Man is still in the middle of the process of finding out the complexity in man's decision-making. Issues such as global environment and gun control (in America) are well addressed in a politically correct manner. But complicated and often politically sensitive complex problems such as positive or negative population growth, meanings and sustainability of democracy, and long-term implications of gender markets are not deeply and comprehensively studied, at least from perspectives of complexity theory. Leibniz (1646–1716) proposed a theory to deal with complex problems, even though modern concepts and methods, such as bifurcations, chaos, and catastrophes, were not yet created in modern sense. With regard to justice, Leibniz had the idea to create a system of universal justice or Universal Jurisprudence, based on knowledge in separate fields of linguistics, management, ethics, politics, economics, and sociology (e.g., Riley, 1996; Andrés-Gallego, 2015). For Leibniz, justice is not only a system of written rules but also the application of wisdom. In complexity theory, justice is made with a complex system and written rules may not give a solution to justice.

Studies of complex systems often involve interdisciplinary approach which combines two or more academic disciplines. Even in understanding one person as an organic whole, we need psychology, economics, and sociology, not to say medical and biological knowledge. A society, like Japan, cannot be effectively explained by a single discipline. Even the evolution of its political system can hardly be comprehended by concentrating only on its political dynamics. It requires a united science and comprehensive knowledge which synthesizes various ideas in separated academic fields to explore daily apparently "simple" phenomena, such as gender relations, national relations, issues of human rights, and global trade patterns. Even a few decades ago, interdisciplinary research was only emphasized, but a few fruitful scientific results had been achieved owing to low capacity of computing. No nation could know its economy, for instance, in detail in contemporary standard because it is only a few decades ago that nations have high capacity of analyzing large data. Rapidly increasing computing capacity enables scholars to mathematically deal with complex problems from interdisciplinary studies. Ortega y Gasset (1932) described: "Previously, men could be divided simply into the learned and the ignorant, those more or less the one, and those more or the less the other. But your specialist cannot be brought in under either of these two categories. He is not learned, for he is formally ignorant of all that does not enter into his specialist; but neither is he ignorant, because he is a 'scientist' and 'knows' very well his own tiny portion of the universe. We shall have to say that he is a learned ignoramus, which is a very serious matter, as it implies that he is a person who is ignorant, not in the fashion of the ignorant man, but with all the petulance of one who is learned in his own special line."

Kitto (1957: 173–174) pointed out: "The modern mind divides, specifies, thinks in categories: the Greek instinct was the opposite, to take the widest view, to see things as an organic whole.... The Olympic games were designated to test the arete of the whole man, not a merely specified skill.... The great event was the pentathlon, if you won this, you were a man. Needless to say, the Marathon race was never heard of until modern times: the Greeks would have regarded it as a monstrosity." Interdisciplinary approach is necessary when traditional disciplines are unable to deal with important problems. For instance, traditional Malthusian theory is not effective in explaining decreasing populations in developed economies. It has become empirically clear that accumulated wealth and education of, especially, women play key roles in lowing birth rates and enriching life and human capital. If one synthesizes the traditional approaches of population growth and endogenous economic growth theory, a new theory of population and growth appears. If one further takes account of approaches in gender studies and psychology into the population growth theory, one can more effectively explain why population grows in some regions and declines in other regions. This kind of research was not so fruitful or academically productive because there was neither computer nor proper data to explore these complex problems.

Neurath (1983: 172–173) showed practical reasons for the coexistence of schools: "Our actual situation is as if we were on board a ship on an open sea and were required to change various parts of the ship during the voyage. We cannot find an absolute immutable basis for science; and our various discussions can only determine whether scientific statements are accepted by a more or less determinate number of scientists and other men. New ideas may be compared with those historically accepted by the sciences, but not with an unalterable standard of truth." In *Word and Object*, Quine (1960) talked about the construction of a boat which is already at sea: "We are like sailors who on the open sea must reconstruct their ship but are never able to start afresh from the bottom. Where a beam is taken away a new one must at once be put there, and for this the rest of the ship is used as support. In this way, by using the old beams and driftwood the ship can be shaped entirely anew, but only by gradual reconstruction." Nagel (1961: 336) argued for the ideal of building "a comprehensive theory which will integrate all domains of natural science in terms of a common set of principles." This book makes some further contribution to building a general economic theory with a common set of economic principles as in Zhang (2020a).

Bibliography

Agliari, A., Bischi, L., and Gardini, L. (2003). Some methods for the global analysis of dynamic game represented by iterated noninvertible maps, eds., Puu, T. and Sushko, J., *Oligopoly Dynamics: Models and Tools* (Springer-Verlag, Berlin) pp. 31–83.

Agliari, A., Naimzada, A., and Pecoraa, N. (2018). Bifurcation structures of a cobweb model with memory and competing technologies, *Communications in Nonlinear Science and Numerical Simulation*, 58, pp. 78–91.

Agliari, A., Naimzada, A., and Pecora, N. (2018a). Boom-bust dynamics in a stock market participation model with heterogeneous traders, *Journal of Economics & Control*, 91, pp. 458–68.

Agnew, T.T. (1978). Optimal exploitation of an employing a nonlinear harvesting function, *Ecological Modelling*, 6, pp. 47–57.

Andrés-Gallego, J. (2015). Are humanism and mixed methods related? Leibniz's universal (Chinese) dream, *Journal of Methods Research*, 29(2), pp. 118–32.

Antoci, A., Galeotti, M., and Russu, P. (2011). Poverty trap and global indeterminacy in a growth model with open-access, *Natural Resources. Journal of Economic Theory*, 146, pp. 569–91.

Antoci, A., Gori, L., and Sodini, M. (2016). Nonlinear dynamics and global indeterminacy in an overlapping generations model with environmental resources, *Communications in Nonlinear Science and Numerical Simulation*, 38, pp. 59–71.

Arrow, K.J. (1962). The economic implications of learning by doing, *Review of Economic Studies*, 29, pp. 155–73.

Arrow, K.J. and Debreu, G. (1954). Existence of an equilibrium for a competitive economy, *Econometrica*, 22(3), pp. 265–90.

Arrow, K.J. and Hahn, F.H. (1971). *General Competitive Analysis* (Holden-Day, Inc., San Francisco), pp. 217.

Asada, T. (2012). Modeling financial instability, *European Journal of Economics and Economic Policies*, 9, pp. 215–32.

Asada, T. (2014). Mathematical modeling of financial instability and macroeconomic stabilization policies, eds., Dieci, R., He, X.Z., and Hommes, C., *Non-linear Economic Dynamics and Financial Modeling, Essays in Honor of Carl Chiarella* (Switzerland Springer) pp. 41–63.

Asada, T., Demetrian, M., and Zimka, R. (2019). On dynamics in a Keynesian model of monetary and fiscal stabilization policy mix with twin debt accumulation, *Metroeconomica*, 70, pp. 365–83.

Axelrod, R. and Cohen, M.D. (2001). *Harnessing Complexity* (Basic Books, New York).

Barro, R.J. and Becker, G. (1989). Fertility choice in a model of economic growth, *Econometrica*, 57, pp. 481–501.

Becker, G.S., Murphy, K.M., and Tamura, R. (1990). Human capital, fertility and economic growth, *Journal of Economic Economy*, 98, pp. 12–37.

Bella, G. (2017). Homoclinic bifurcation and the Belyakov degeneracy in a variant of the Romer model of endogenous growth, *Chaos, Solitons and Fractals: Nonlinear Science and Nonequilibrium and Complex Phenomena*, 104, pp. 452–60.

Bella, G. and Mattana, P. (2018). Bistability of equilibria and the 2-tori dynamics in an endogenous growth model undergoing the Cust-Hopf singularity, *Nonlinear Analysis: Real World Applications*, 39, pp. 185–201.

Bella, G., Mattana, P., and Venturi, B. (2017). Shilnikov chaos in the Lucas model of endogenous growth, *Journal of Economic Theory*, 172, pp. 451–77.

Bellomo, N., Nigris, S.D., Knopoff, D., Morini, M., and Terna, P. (2020). SWARMS dynamics approach to behavioral economy: Theoretical tools and price sequences, *Networks and Heterogeneous Media*, 15(3), pp. 353–68.

Benassy, J.P. (1996). Taste for variety and opium production patterns in monopolistic competition, *Economics Letters*, 52, pp. 41–47.

Benhabib, J. and Farmer, R. (1994). Indeterminacy and increasing returns, *Journal of Economic Theory*, 63, pp. 19–46.

Benhabib, J. and Perli, R. (1994). Uniqueness and indeterminacy on the dynamics of endogenous growth, *Journal of Economic Theory*, 63, pp. 113–42.

Benhabib, J., Schmitt-Grohe, S., and Uribe, M. (2001). The perils of Taylor rules, *Journal of Economic Theory*, 96, pp. 40–69.

Benhabib, J., Evans, G.W., and Honkapohja, S. (2014). liquidity traps and expectation dynamics: Fiscal stimulus or fiscal austerity, *Journal of Economic Dynamics & Control*, 45, pp. 220–38.

Bernanke, B. and Gertler, M. (1989). Agency costs, net worth, and business fluctuations, *American Economic Review*, 79, pp. 14–31.

Bischi, G.I., Chiarella, C., Kopel, M., and Szidaroszky, F. (2010). *Nonlinear Oligopolies: Stability and Bifurcations* (Springer, Berlin).

Boppart, T. and Krusell, P. (2020). Labor supply in the past, present, and future: A balanced-growth perspective, *Journal of Political Economy*, 128, pp. 118–57.

Barro, R.J. and Becker, G.S. (1989). Fertility choice in a model of economic growth, *Econometrica*, 57, pp. 481–501.

Bosi, S. and Desmarchelier, D. (2018). An economic model of metapopulation dynamics, *Ecological Modelling*, 387, pp. 196–204.

Bosi, S. and Seegmuller, T. (2012). Mortality differential and growth: What do we learn from the Barro-Becker model? *Mathematical Population Studies*, 19, pp. 27–50.

Brock, W.A. and Hommes, C.H. (1998). Heterogeneous beliefs and routes to chaos in a simple asset pricing model, *Journal of Economic Dynamics and Control*, 22(8), pp. 1235–74.

Burmeister, E. and Dobell, A.R. (1970). *Mathematical Theories of Economic Growth* (Collier Macmillan Publishers, London).

Chakrabarti, R. (1999). Endogenous fertility and growth in a model with old age support, *Economic Theory*, 13, pp. 393–416.

Chen, B.S. and Chen, J.J. (2012). Bifurcation and chaotic behavior of a discrete singular biological economic system, *Applied Mathematics and Computation*, 219, pp. 2371–86.

Chen, W. (2008). Dynamics and control of a financial system with time-delayed feedbacks, *Chaos, Solitons and Fractals: Nonlinear Science and Nonequilibrium and Complex Phenomena*, 37, pp. 1198–1207.

Chiarella, C. (1992). The dynamics of speculative behavior, *Annals of Operations Research*, 37(1), pp. 101–23.

Chiarella, C. and Flaschel, P. (2000). *The Dynamics of Keynesian Monetary Growth: Macro Foundations* (Cambridge University Press, Cambridge).

Cilliers, P. (1998). *Complexity and Postmodernism: Understanding Complex Systems* (Routledge, London).

Clark, C.W. (1976). *Mathematical Bioeconomics: The Optimal Management of Renewable Resources* (Wiley, New York).

Clark, C.W. (1985). *Bioeconomic Modelling and Fisheries Management* (Wiley, New York).

Day, R.H. and Huang, W. (1990). Bulls, bears and market sheep, *Journal of Economic Behavior & Organization*, 14(3), pp. 299–29.

Deng, L.C. and Khan, M.A. (2018). On growing through cycles: Matsuyama's M-map and Li-Yorke chaos, *Journal of Mathematical Economics*, 74, pp. 46–55.

Diamond, D.B. and Tolley, G.S. eds. (1981). *The Economics of Urban Amenities* (Academic Press, New York).

Ding, Y.T., Jiang, W.H., and Wang, H.B. (2012). Hopf pitchfork bifurcation and periodic phenomena in nonlinear financial system with delay, *Chaos, Solitons and Fractals: Nonlinear Science and Nonequilibrium and Complex Phenomena*, 45, pp. 1048–57.

Dixit, A. and Stiglitz, J.E. (1977). Monopolistic competition and optimum product diversity, *American Economic Review*, 67(3), pp. 297–308.

Engels, F. (1981). *The Origin of the Family, Private Property and State* (International Publishers, New York).

Fanti, L. (2015). Environmental standards and Cournot duopoly: A stability analysis, *Environmental Resource Economics*, 61, pp. 577–93.

Flaschel, P., Franke, R., and Semmler, W. (1997). *Dynamic Macroeconomics* (The MIT Press, Mass., Cambridge).

Forslid, R. and Ottaviano, G.I.P. (2003). Trade and location: Two analytically solvable models, *Journal of Economic Geography*, 3, pp. 229–40.

Fujita, M., Krugman, P., and Venables, A. (1999). *The Spatial Economy* (The MIT Press, Mass., Cambridge).

Gandolfo, G. (2005). *Economic Dynamics* (Springer, Berlin).

Galor, O. and Weil, D.N. (1996). The gender gap, fertility, and growth, *American Economic Review*, 86, pp. 374–87.

Galor, O. and Weil, D. (1999). From Malthusian stagnation to modern growth, *American Economic Review*, 89, pp. 150–54.

Gassebner, M., Lamlay, M.J., and Sturmz, J.E. (2011). Determinants of pollution: What do we really know? *Oxford Economic Papers*, 63, pp. 568–95.

Glaeser, E.L. and Maré, D.C. (2001). Cities and skills, *Journal of Labor Economics*, 19, pp. 316–42.

Greenwood, J. (2019). *Evolving Households: The Imprint of Technology on Life* (The MIT Press, Mass., Cambridge).

Grossman, G.M. and Helpman, E. (1991a). Endogenous product cycles, *Economic Journal*, 101, pp. 1214–29.

Grossman, G.M. and Helpman, E. (1991b). *Innovation and Growth in the Global Economy* (The MIT Press, Mass., Cambridge).

Goodwin, R. (1967). A growth cycle, ed., Feinstein, C.H., *Socialism, Capitalism and Economic Growth, Essays Presented to Maurice Dobb* (Cambridge University Press, Cambridge) pp. 54–58.

Gu, K., Niculescu, S., and Chen, J. (2005). On stability crossing curves for general systems with two delays. *Journal of Mathematical Analysis and Applications*, 311, pp. 231–52.

Guerrini, L., Matsumoto, A., and Szidarovszky, F. (2017). Neoclassical growth model with two fixed delays, *Metroeconomica*, 70, pp. 423–41.

Guevara, G.C. and Escot, L. (2021). Monetary policy rules: An approach based on the theory of chaos control, *Results in Control and Optimization*, 4, pp. 1–16.

Gupta, R.P., Banerjee, M., and Chandra, P. (2014). Period doubling cascades of preypredator model with nonlinear harvesting and control of over exploitation through taxation, *Communications in Nonlinear Science and Numerical Simulation*, 19, pp. 2382–405.

Haavelmo, T. (1954). *A Study in the Theory of Economic Evolution* (North-Holland, Amsterdam).

Haken, H. (1977). *Synergetics: An Introduction* (Springer-Verlag, Berlin).

Haken, H. (1981). *Light: Waves, Photons, and Atoms* (North Holland, Amsterdam).

Haken, H. (1983). *The Science of Structure: Synergetics* (Reinhold, Van Nostrand).

Hadeler, K.P. and Ruan, S.G. (2007). Interaction of diffusion and delay, *Discrete and Continuous Dynamical Systems*, 8(1), pp. 95–105.

Handa, J. (2009). *Monetary Economics* (Routledge, London).

Henderson, D.W. and McKibbin, W. (1993). A comparison of some basic monetary policy regimes for open economies: Implications of different degrees of instrument adjustment and wage persistence, *Carnegie-Rochester Conference Series on Public Policy*, 39, pp. 221–318.

Hirschman, A.O. (1958). *The Strategy of Economic Development* (Yale University Press, New Haven, CT).

Hock, H. and Weil, D.N. (2012). On the dynamics of the age structure, dependency, and consumption, *Journal of Population Economics*, 25, pp. 1019–43.

Hommes, C.H. (1991). *Chaotic Dynamics in Economic Models: Some Simple Case-Studies* (Wolters-Noordhoff, Groningen).

Ikeda, S. and Ono, Y. (1992). Macroeconomic dynamics in a multi-country economy — A dynamic optimization approach, *International Economic Review*, 33, pp. 629–44.

Iong K.K. and Irmen, A. (2021). The supply of hours worked and fluctuations between growth regime, *Journal of Economic Theory*, 194, pp. 1–35.

Iwaisako, T. and Tanaka, H. (2017). Product cycles and growth cycles, *Journal of International Economics*, 105, pp. 22–40.

Jones, C.I. (1995). R&D-based models of economic growth, *Journal of Political Economy*, 103, pp. 759–84.

Kalecki, M. (1935). A macrodynamic theory of business cycles, *Econometrica*, 3, pp. 327–44.

Kalecki, M. (1971). *Selected Essays on the Dynamics of the Capitalist Economy* (Cambridge University Press, Cambridge).

Kindleberger, C.P. (1996). *Manias, Panics, and Crashes: A History of Financial Crises*, 3rd ed. (John Wiley & Sons, Inc., New York).

King, R.G. and Rebelo, S.T. (1993). Transitional dynamics and economic growth in the neoclassical model, *American Economic Review*, 83, 908–31.

Kirk, D. (1996). Demographic transition theory, *Population Studies*, 50, pp. 361–87.

Kitto, H.D.F. (1957). *The Greeks* (Penguin, Middlesex).

Krugman, P.R. (1979). A model of innovation, technology transfer, and the world distribution of income, *Journal of Political Economy*, 87(2), pp. 253–66.

Krugman, P.R. (1993). On the number and location of cities, *European Economic Review*, 37, pp. 293–98.

Kuang, Y. (1993). *Delay Differential Equations with Applications in Population* (Academic Press, Boston).

Kuznets, S. (1966). *Modern Economic Growth, Rate Structure, and Spread* (Yale University Press, New Haven).

Kydland, F.E. and Prescott, E. (1982). Time to build and aggregate fluctuations, *Econometrica*, 50, pp. 1345–70.

La Torre, D., Liuzzi, D., and Marsiglio, S. (2015). Pollution diffusion and statement activities across space and over time, *Mathematical Social Sciences*, 78, pp. 48–63.

Lafuite, A.S. and Loreau, M. (2017). Time-delayed biodiversity feedbacks and the sustainability of social-ecological systems, *Ecological Modelling*, 351, pp. 96–108.

Levins, R. (1969). Some demographic and generic consequences of environmental heterogeneity for biological control, *Bulletin of the Entomological Society of America*, 15, pp. 237–40.

Li, T.Y. and Yorke, Y. (1975). Period three implies chaos, *American Mathematical Monthly*, 82, pp. 985–92.

Liu, X.D., Cai, W.L., Lu, J.J., and Wang, Y.Y. (2015). Stability and Hopf bifurcation for a business cycle model with expectation and delay, *Communications in Nonlinear Science and Numerical Simulation*, 25, pp. 149–61.

Liuzzi, D. and Venturi, B. (2021). Pollution-induced poverty traps via Hopf bifurcation in a minimal integrated economic model, *Communications in Nonlinear Science and Numerical Simulation*, 93, pp. 1–15.

Lorenz, E.N. (1963). Deterministic nonperiodic flow, *Journal of the Atmospheric Sciences*, 20, pp. 130–41.

Lorenz, H.W. (1993). *Nonlinear Dynamic Economics and Chaotic Motion* (Springer-Verlag, Berlin).

Lucas, R.E. (1988). On the mechanics of economic development, *Journal of Monetary Economics*, 22, pp. 3–42.

Lux, T. (1998). The socio-economic dynamics of speculative markets: Interacting agents, chaos, and the fat tails of return distributions, *Journal of Economic Behavior & Organization*, 33(2), pp. 143–65.

Ma, J.H. and Chen, Y.S. (2001a). Study for the bifurcation topological structure and the global complicated character of a kind of non-linear finance system (I), *Applied Mathematics and Mechanics*, 22, pp. 1240–51.

Ma, J.H. and Chen, Y.S. (2001b). Study for the bifurcation topological structure and the global complicated character of a kind of non-linear finance system (II), *Applied Mathematics and Mechanics*, 22, pp. 1375–82.

Ma, J.H., Ren, W.B., and Zhan X.L. (2017). Complexity dynamics and Hopf bifurcation analysis based on the first Lyapunov coefficient about 3D IS-LM macroeconomics systems, *Communications in Nonlinear Science and Numerical Simulation*, 45, pp. 129–39.

Maiti, A., Jana, M.M., and Samata, G.P. (2007). Deterministic and stochastic analysis of a ratio-dependent predator system with delay, *Nonlinear Analysis: Modelling and Control*, 12(3), pp. 383–98.

Matsuyama, K. (1991). Increasing returns, industrialization, and indeterminacy of equilibrium, *Quarterly Journal of Economics*, 106, pp. 617–50.

Matsuyama, K. (1999). Growing through cycle, *Econometrica*, 67, 335–47.

Matsuyama, K. (2013). The God, the bad, and the ugly: An inquiry into the causes and nature of credit cycles, *Theoretical Economics*, 8, pp. 623–51.

Matsuyama, K., Sushko, I., and Gardini, L. (2016). Revisiting the model of credit cycles with good and bad projects, *Journal of Economic Theory*, 163, pp. 526–56.

Medio, A. (1992). *Chaotic Dynamics: Theory and Applications to Economics* (Cambridge University Press, Cambridge).

Mendoza, E.G. and Terrones, M.E. (2008). An anatomy of credit booms: Evidence from macro aggregates and micro data, *NBER Working Paper*, 14049.

Meng, Q.L. and Yip, C.Y. (2004). Investment, interest rate rules, and equilibrium determinacy, *Economic Theory*, 23, pp. 863–78.

Mirowski, P. (1990). From Mandelbrot to chaos in economic theory, *Southern Economic Journal*, 57(2), pp. 289–307.

Murray, J.D. (2003). *Mathematical Biology*, 3rd ed. (Springer, New York).

Myrdal, G. (1957). *Economic Theory and Underdeveloped Regions* (Duckworth, London).

Nagatani, K. (1970). A note on Professor Tobin's "money and economic growth," *Econometrica*, 38(1), pp. 171–75.

Nagel, E. (1961). The *Structure of Science: Problems in the Logic of Scientific Explanation* (Harcourt, Brace, and World, New York).

Neugart, M. (2004). Complicated dynamics in a flow model of the labor market, *Journal of Economic Behavior & Organization*, 53, pp. 193–213.

Neurath, O. (1983). *Philosophical Papers, 1913–1946* (Reidel, Dordrecht).

Okuguchi, K. (1976). *Expectations and Stability in Oligopoly Models*, Lecture Notes in Economics and Mathematical Systems, vol. 138 (Springer, Berlin).

Oniki, H. and Uzawa, H. (1965). Patterns of trade and investment in a dynamic model of international trade, *Review of Economic Studies*, 32, pp. 15–38.

Onozaki, T., Sieg, G., and Yokoo, M. (2000). Complex dynamics in a cobweb model with adaptive production adjustment, *Journal of Economic Behavior & Organization*, 41, pp. 101–15.

Ortega y Gasset, J. (1932). *The Revolt of the Masses* (New American Library, New York).

Patinkin, D. (1965). *Money, Interest, and Prices: An Integration of Monetary and Value Theory*, 2nd ed. (Harper & Row, New York).

Plouder, G.C. (1972). A model of waste accumulation and disposal, *Canadian Journal of Economics*, 5, pp. 119–25.

Puu, T. (1996). Complex dynamics with three oligopolists, *Chaos, Solitons and Fractals: Nonlinear Science and Nonequilibrium and Complex Phenomena*, 7, pp. 2075–81.

Puu, T. (2018). *Disequilibrium Economics: Oligopoly, and Macroeconomics. Trade* (Springer, Berlin).

Quine, W.V.O. (2013; 1960). *Word and Object*, new ed. (The MIT Press, Mass., Cambridge).

Rao, F., Castillo-Chavez, C., and Kang, K. (2018). Dynamics of a diffusion reaction preypredator model with delay in prey: Effects of delay and spatial components, *Journal of Mathematical Analysis and Applications*, 461, pp. 1177–214.

Rao, R. (2019). Global stability of a Markovian jumping chaotic financial system with partially unknown transition rates under impulsive control involved in the positive interest rate, *Mathematics, MDPI*, 7(7), pp. 1–15.

Rasch, W. (1991). Theories of complexity, complexities of theory: Habermas, Luhmann, and the study of social systems, *German Studies Review*, 41(1), pp. 65–83.

Raut, L.K. and Srinivasan, T.N. (1994). Dynamics of endogenous growth, *Economic Theory*, 4, pp. 777–90.

Riley, P. (1996). *Leibniz' Universal Jurisprudence: Justice as the Charity of the Wise* (Harvard University Press, Mass., Cambridge).

Romer, P.M. (1990). Endogenous technological change, *Journal of Political Economy*, 98, pp. S71–S103.

Ros, J. (2000). *Development Theory and the Economics of Growth* (The University of Michigan Press, Ann Arbor).

Ruiz-Herrera, A. (2017). Carry-over effects: Population abundance, ecological shifts, and the (dis-)appearance of oscillations, *Ecological Modelling*, 349, pp. 26–32.

Samuelson, P. (1970). Classical and neoclassical monetary theory, ed., Clower, R., *Monetary Theory* (Penguin, Baltimore).

Saracoglu, D.S. and Roe, T.L. (2019). Regional cost-of-living differentials, rural-urban migration, and the contribution to economic growth, *Paper in Regional Science*, 98(2), pp. 973–94.

Sasaki, H. (2013). Cyclical growth in a Goodwin-Kalecki-Marx model. *Journal of Economics*, 108: pp. 145–71.

Schmitt, N. and Westerhof, F. (2022). Speculative housing markets and rent control: Insights from nonlinear economic dynamics, *Journal of Economic Interaction and Coordination*, 17, pp. 141–63.

Schmitt-Grohe, S, and Uribe, M. (2009). Liquidity traps with global Taylor rules, *International Journal of Economic Theory*, 5, pp. 85–106.

Shone, R. (2002). *Economic Dynamics — Phase Diagrams and Their Economic Application* (Cambridge University Press, Cambridge).

Sidrauski, M. (1967). Inflation and economic growth, *Journal of Political Economy*, 75, pp. 789–810.

Slobodyan, S. (2007). Indeterminacy and stability in a modified Romer model, *Journal of Macroeconomics*, 29, pp. 169–77.

Solow, R. (1956). A contribution to the theory of growth, *Quarterly Journal of Economics*, 70, pp. 65–94.

Solow, R. (1999). Neoclassical growth theory, eds., Taylor, J.B., and Woodford, M., *Handbook of Macroeconomics*, vol. 1A (Elsevier, Amsterdam) pp. 637–67.

Sparrow, C. (1982). *The Lorenz Equations, Bifurcations, Chaos, and Strange Attractors* (Springer, Berlin).

Stutzer, M. (1980). Chaotic dynamics and bifurcation in a macro economics, *Journal of Economic Dynamics and Control*, 2, pp. 253–73.

Su, Y., Wei, J.J., and Shi, J.P. (2009). Hopf bifurcations in a reaction-diffusion population model with delay effect, *Journal of Differential Equations*, 247(4), pp. 1156–84.

Swan, T.W. (1956). Economic growth and capital accumulation, *Economic Record*, XXXII, pp. 334–61.

Syzdlowski, M. and Krawiec, A. (2004). A note on Kaleckian lags in the Solow model, *Review of Political Economy*, 16, pp. 501–6.

Tabuchi, T. (2014). Historical trends of agglomeration to the capital region and new economic geography, *Regional Science and Urban Economics*, 44, pp. 50–59.

Taylor, J.B. (1993). Discretion versus policy rules in practice, *Carnegie-Rochester Conference Series on Public Policy*, 39, pp. 195–214.

Tobin, J. (1965). Money and economic growth, *Econometrica*, 33, pp. 671–84.

Toffler, A. (1984). The foreword, eds., Prigogine I. and Stengers, I., *Order out of Chaos* (Bantam Doubleday Dell, New York).

Turner, J.R. and Baker, R. (2020). Just doing the do: A case study testing creativity and innovative processes as complex systems, *New Horizons in Adult Education and Human Resource Development*, 32(2), pp. 40–61.

Uzawa, H. (1961). On a two-sector model of economic growth, *Review of Economic Studies*, XXIX, pp. 47–70.

Uzawa, H. (1965). Optimal technical change in an aggregative model of economic growth, *International Economic Review*, 6, pp. 18–31.

Walras, L. (1874). *Elements of Pure Economics*, translated from the French by W. Jaffé, 1954 (Allen and Unwin, London).

Walenta, J. (2018). The limits to private-sector climate change action — The geographies of corporate climate governance, *Economic Geography*, 94(5), pp. 461–84.

Ward, M. (1995). Butterflies and bifurcations: Can chaos theory contribute to our understanding of family systems? *Journal of Marriage and Family*, 57(3), pp. 629–89.

Wirl, F. (1995). The cyclical exploitation of renewable resource stocks may be optimal, *Journal of Environmental Economics and Management*, 29, pp. 252–61.

Wirl, F. (1997). Stability and limit cycles in one-dimensional dynamic optimizations of competitive agents with a market externality, *Journal of Evolutionary Economics*, 7, pp. 73–89.

Yang, X.N., Yu, P., Yue, X., and Xue, W. (2019). Nonlinear dynamics of a duopoly Stackelberg game with marginal costs. *Nonlinear Analysis: Real World Applications*, 39, pp. 185–191.

Zak, P. (1999). Kaleckian lags in general equilibrium, *Review of Political Economy*, 11, pp. 321–30.

Zhang, W.B. (1988a). Urbanizing processes with moving boundaries, *Geographical Analysis*, 20, pp. 328–39.

Zhang, W.B. (1988b). Hopf bifurcations in multisector models of optimal economic growth, *Economics Letters*, 26, pp. 329–34.

Zhang, W.B. (1989a). Coexistence and separation of two residential groups — An interactional spatial dynamic approach, *Geographical Analysis*, 21, pp. 91–102.

Zhang, W.B. (1989b). Existence of aperiodic time-dependent solutions in optimal growth economy with three sectors, *International Journal of Systems Science*, 20, pp. 1943–53.

Zhang, W.B. (1990). The complexity of nonlinear dynamic economic systems — The Kaldorian model with government policy of bond finance, *Journal of Mathematical Sociology*, 15(4), pp. 259–69.

Zhang, W.B. (1991). *Synergetic Economics* (Springer-Verlag, Heidelberg).

Zhang, W.B. (2005). *Differential Equations, Bifurcations, and Chaos in Economics* (World Scientific, Singapore).

Zhang, W.B. (2006a). *Growth with Income and Wealth Distribution* (Macmillan, London).

Zhang, W.B. (2006b). *Discrete Dynamical Systems, Bifurcations and Chaos in Economics* (Elsevier, Amsterdam).

Zhang, W.B. (2008). *International Trade Theory: Capital, Knowledge, Economic Structure, Money and Prices over Time and Space* (Springer, Berlin).

Zhang, W.B. (2009). *Monetary Growth Theory: Money, Interest, Prices, Capital, Knowledge, and Economic Structure over Time and Space* (Routledge, London).

Zhang, W.B. (2017). Government debt and education subsidies by synthesizing the Uzawa-Lucas two-sector model and Diamond growth-debt model, *Journal of Interdisciplinary Economic Research*, 2017(June), pp. 22–33.

Zhang, W.B. (2019). Growth, environment and business cycles in a multi-regional economy, *Green Finance*, 1(2), pp. 205–20.

Zhang, W.B. (2020a). *The General Economic Theory: An Integrative Approach* (Springer International Publishing, Switzerland).

Zhang, W.B. (2020b). The Taylor rule and business cycles in the Solow-Tobin model, *Asian Journal of Economics and Business*, 1(2), 95–109.

Zhang, W.B. (2020c). Business cycles in a dynamic general equilibrium model with monopolistic and perfect competition, *Bingol University Journal of Economics and Administrative Sciences*, 4(1), pp. 11–33.

Zhang, W.B. (2020d). Population, wealth, and business cycles with job discrimination, *Sumerianz Journal of Social Science*, 3(3), pp. 23–32.

Zhang, W.B. (2020e). Global development, trade, human capital, and business cycles, *Oradea Journal of Business and Economics*, V(Special Issue), pp. 9–29.

Zhang, W.B. (2021a). *The Butterfly Effect in China's Economic Growth — From Socialist Penury towards Marx's Progressive Capitalism* (Macmillan, London).

Zhang, W.B. (2021b). *The America the Great and Its Self-Destruction: Viewing the Superpower Through the Lenses of Ancient Confucianism and Chaos Theory* (Algora Publisher, New York).

Zhang, W.B. (2021c). Monetary growth with the Solow, Tobin, IS-LM, and Dixit-Stiglitz models synthesized, *Indian Journal of Commerce and Management Studies*, XII(2), pp. 23–37.

Zhao, L.W., Du, J.G., and Wang Q.W. (2019). Nonlinear analysis and chaos control of the complex dynamics of multi-market Cournot game with bounded rationality, *Mathematics and Computer in Simulation*, 162, pp. 45–57.

Zhou, J., Zhou, W., Chub, T., Changa, Y.X., and Huang, M.J. (2019). Bifurcation, intermittent chaos and multi-stability in a two-stage Cournot game with r&d spillover and product differentiation, *Applied Mathematics and Communications*, 341, pp. 358–378.

Zuo, W. and Wei, J. (2011). Stability and Hopf bifurcation in a diffusive predator-prey system with delay effect, *Nonlinear Analysis: Real World Applications*, 12(4), pp. 1998–2011.

Index

Series on Advances in Mathematics for Applied Sciences

Series on Advances in Mathematics for Applied Sciences

Aims and Scope

This Series reports on new developments in mathematical research relating to methods, qualitative and numerical analysis, mathematical modeling in the applied and the technological sciences. Contributions rlated to constitutive theories, fluid dynamics, kinetic and transport theories, solid mechanics, system theory and mathematical methods for the applications are welcomed.

This Series includes books, lecture notes, proceedings, collections of research papers. Monograph collections on specialized topics of current interest are particularly encouraged. Both the proceedings and monograph collections will generally be edited by a Guest editor.

High quality, novelty of the content and potential for the applications to modern problems in applied science will be the guidelines for the selection of the content of this series.

Instructions for Authors

Submission of proposals should be addressed to the editors-in-charge or to any member of the editorial board. In the latter, the authors should also notify the proposal to one of the editors-in-charge. Acceptance of books and lecture notes will generally be based on the description of the general content and scope of the book or lecture notes as well as on sample of the parts judged to be more significantly by the authors.

Acceptance of proceedings will be based on relevance of the topics and of the lecturers contributing to the volume.

Acceptance of monograph collections will be based on relevance of the subject and of the authors contributing to the volume.

Authors are urged, in order to avoid re-typing, not to begin the final preparation of the text until they received the publisher's guidelines. They will receive from World Scientific the instructions for preparing camera-ready manuscript.

Series on Advances in Mathematics for Applied Sciences

ISSN: 1793-0901

Published:*

Vol. 77 Continuum Thermodynamics
by K. Wilmanski

Vol. 78 Advanced Mathematical and Computational Tools in Metrology and Testing
eds. F. Pavese et al.

Vol. 79 From Genetics to Mathematics
eds. M. Lachowicz and J. Miękisz

Vol. 80 Inelasticity of Materials: An Engineering Approach and a Practical Guide
by A. R. Srinivasa and S. M. Srinivasan

Vol. 81 Stability Criteria for Fluid Flows
by A. Georgescu and L. Palese

Vol. 82 Applied and Industrial Mathematics in Italy III
eds. E. De Bernardis, R. Spigler and V. Valente

Vol. 83 Linear Inverse Problems: The Maximum Entropy Connection
by H. Gzyl and Y. Velásquez

Vol. 84 Advanced Mathematical and Computational Tools in Metrology and Texting IX
eds. F. Pavese et al.

Vol. 85 Continuum Thermodynamics
Part II: Applications and Examples
by B. Albers and K. Wilmanski

Vol. 86 Advanced Mathematical and Computational Tools in Metrology and Testing X
eds. F. Pavese et al.

Vol. 87 Mathematical Methods for the Natural and Engineering Sciences (2nd Edition)
by R. E. Mickens

Vol. 88 Road Vehicle Dynamics: Fundamentals of Modeling and Simulation
by G. Genta and A. Genta

Vol. 89 Advanced Mathematical and Computational Tools in Metrology and Testing XI
eds. A. B. Forbes et al.

Vol. 90 Advanced Mathematical and Computational Tools in Metrology and Testing XII
eds. F. Pavese et al.

Vol. 91 Fractal Analysis: Basic Concepts and Applications
by C. Cattani, A. B. Mabrouk and S. Arfaoui

Vol. 92 Chaos, Complexity, and Nonlinear Economic Theory
by Wei-Bin Zhang

*To view the complete list of the published volumes in the series, please visit:
https://www.worldscientific.com/series/samas

www.ingramcontent.com/pod-product-compliance
Lightning Source LLC
LaVergne TN
LVHW010335220926
848484LV00004BB/904
9789811267413